D1212330

North American Economic Integration

North American Economic Integration

Theory and Practice

Norris C. Clement
San Diego State University, USA

Gustavo del Castillo Vera
Colegio de la Frontera Norte, Mexico

James Gerber
San Diego State University, USA

William A. Kerr, Alan J. MacFadyen, Stanford Shedd
University of Calgary, Canada

Eduardo Zepeda
Universidad Autonoma de Coahuila, Mexico

Diana Alarcón
Inter-American Development Bank, USA

Edward Elgar
Cheltenham, UK • Northampton, MA, USA

© Norris C. Clement, Gustavo del Castillo Vera, James Gerber, William A. Kerr, Alan J. MacFadyen, Stanford Shedd, Eduardo Zepeda and Diana Alarcón, 1999.

All rights reserved. No part of this publication may be reproduced, stored in a retrieval system or transmitted in any form or by any means, electronic, mechanical or photocopying, recording, or otherwise without the prior permission of the publisher.

Published by
Edward Elgar Publishing Limited
Glensanda House
Montpellier Parade
Cheltenham
Glos GL50 1UA
UK

Edward Elgar Publishing, Inc.
136 West Street
Suite 202
Northampton
Massachusetts 01060
USA

A catalogue record for this book
is available from the British Library

Library of Congress Cataloguing in Publication Data
North American economic integration : theory and practice / Norris C.
Clement ... [et al.].
Includes bibliographical references and index.
1. Free trade—North America. 2. North America—Economic
integration. I. Clement, Norris C.
HF1746.N6687 1999
337.1'7—dc21 99-22084
CIP

ISBN 1 84064 102 9

Printed and bound in Great Britain by Biddles Ltd, Guildford and King's Lynn

Contents

Figures

Tables

Notes on Authors

Dr Norris C. Clement is currently Professor of Economics and the Director of International Programs at the Institute for Regional Studies of the Californias at San Diego State University. He is co-author of *Economia: Enfoque America Latina*, McGraw-Hill International, an economics text used widely in Latin America and co-book editor of the *Journal of Borderland Studies.* His current interests include: globalization-regionalization issues and the development of international border regions.

Dr Gustavo del Castillo Vera is presently the coordinator of the Political Economy Working Group at the Colegio de la Frontera Norte. He has researched on North American trade policies over the last 25 years, and was an early proponent of a North American free trade region in the early 1980s. He is presently working questions on the significance of economic security within an integrating North American region.

Dr James Gerber is Associate Professor of Economics at San Diego State University and Economic Research Fellow at San Diego Dialogue at the University of California, San Diego. He is the author of *International Economics*, Addison Wesley Longman and has published several articles on NAFTA. He has been a visiting lecturer at universities in both Canada and Mexico.

Dr William A. Kerr has been at the University of Calgary since 1980 and Professor of Economics since 1989. His research interests include international trade and international commercial policy. He has done work on issues pertaining to non-tariff barriers under the NAFTA and CUSFTA, the liberalization of transPacific trade and trade disputes between Canada and the European Union. He has coauthored four books and over 150 academic publications. Recent titles include *The Economics of International Business*, Chapman and Hall, 1995 (with N. Perdikis), 'Trade as an Agency of Social Policy–NAFTA's Schizophrenic Role in Agriculture' in S.J. Randall and H.W. Konrad (eds), *NAFTA in Transition*, The University of Calgary Press (with James Gerber) and 'Can Trade Measures Induce Compliance in TRIPS?', *Journal of the Asia-Pacific Economy*, (with R. Yampoin) (forthcoming).

Dr Alan J. MacFadyen is Associate Professor of Economics at the University of Calgary. He was educated at McGill University (BA Honors Economics) and Pennsylvania University (PhD). His research interests are in the areas of energy economics, including the international crude oil industry and economic psychology. His publications include *Modelling Exploration Success in Alberta Oil Plays*, Canadian Energy Institute, 1983 (with K.D. Fouts) and *Economic Psychology: Intersections in Theory and Applications*, North-Holland Publishing Company, 1987 (jointly edited with H.W. MacFadyen). He is currently completing an economic history of the Alberta petroleum industry (with G.D. Watkins).

Dr Stanford Shedd is a consulting economist. He taught for thirty years at Southern Illinois University, Carbondale and the University of Calgary. His research has been in the areas of social policy and Canadian content regulations. Recent publications include *Economic Issues: A Canadian Perspective* (with C. Michael Fellows and Greg Flanagan), McGraw-Hill, 1997 and 'Family and Social Services, the Alberta Deficit Elimination Program, and Social Welfare', in *A Government Reinvented*, C.J. Bruce, R.D. Kneebone and K.J. McKenzie (eds), Oxford University Press, 1997.

Eduardo Zepeda has a PhD in Economics, University of California, Riverside. He is currently Professor of Economics at the Center for Socioeconomic Studies, Universidad Autonoma de Coahuila, Mexico.

His research has dealt with regional development and economic issues associated with NAFTA and the US-Mexico border. Currently he is doing research in development and labor markets in Mexico, both at the regional and national level. Among his publications are the book *Manufacturing and Services in the Mexican Northern Border* (1995).

Diana Alarcón has a PhD in Economics, University of California, Riverside. She is currently an economist at the Inter-American Institute for Social Development, Inter-American Development Bank. Her research has dealt with poverty and income distribution with emphasis on the Mexican case, as well as labor markets and development in Mexico. She has published the book *Changes in the Distribution of Income in Mexico and Trade Liberalization* (1994).

Preface

Many books and academic articles have been published on North American economic integration in the last decade. In fact, this vast outpouring of literature has produced what the economist Peter Kresl referred to, only partly in jest, as one of the most dramatically expanding industries in North America, the 'Free Trade Debate Industry'. Nevertheless, until the publication of this book there was, to our knowledge, no single volume providing a balanced and accessible introduction to this complex and controversial subject.

The project that led to the writing and subsequent publication of this book brought together economists from three North American universities: San Diego State University, El Colegio de la Frontera Norte and the University of Calgary. This endeavor, and the book itself, grew out of a larger project entitled 'North American Integration', funded by the United States Information Agency's University Affiliations Program. Subsequently, other organizations contributed the modest amounts necessary for the authors to convene a series of workshops and bring the book to fruition.

While there is considerable diversity among the authors in terms of background, training and beliefs regarding the virtues of international economic integration, all share the view that North American economic integration has been under way for several decades. That is, North American economic integration did not start with the implementation of the North American Free Trade Agreement (NAFTA) in January 1994, nor would it have stopped had the agreement not been signed. Therefore, we regard NAFTA not as a milestone dramatically altering an historical process, but rather as a tool that may serve to better manage the ongoing phenomenon of North American integration in an efficient and equitable manner.

The authors' overall objective has been to produce a book that will help the reader understand the agreement itself, the context in which it was forged, the various debates that preceded its approval in the three countries and how it is changing the North American economy. The organization, level and style of the book make it accessible to readers from any discipline who have a basic understanding of the principles of economics, and it will provide the tools necessary to undertake more advanced reading on the subject. Thus, it can be read by the interested lay person or be utilized in a wide variety of undergraduate and graduate courses in business, economics, international relations and the emerging field of North American studies.

We recommend it as a core text, to be supplemented with additional reading if desired, for special courses such as 'North American Economic Relations' now being taught at San Diego State University (in San Diego, California, USA) and at the Institute of Economics and Business Administration at Lajos Kossuth University in Debrecen, Hungary. Alternatively, it can be used as a supplementary text in both graduate and undergraduate courses in business, international relations and economics, such as the 'International Economics' course at the University of Calgary or 'International Trade' at El Colegio de la Frontera Norte.

This book focuses on the integration experience of the United States, Canada and Mexico. Each chapter is written as a separate module, so that it may be updated and revised as necessary. As more countries are invited to join NAFTA, or as NAFTA evolves into something quite different, the book will be expanded to include chapters on the new NAFTA countries and/or the shape of the new agreements which will be authored by specialists from the new member countries and/or on the subsequent negotiations.

A major strength of this book is that it was developed by a multinational team of economists and advisers from other, related, disciplines. This team approach, we believe, has produced a balanced perspective on each country, on NAFTA itself and the controversies it engendered, both within and between countries.

The book complements another volume, soon to be published, entitled *North American Federalism*, which focuses on the political dimension of North American integration and is authored by political scientists from the same three universities that are represented here.

We wish to express our thanks to the organizations that provided financial support for this effort, including the United States Information Agency; the Center for International Business Education and Research and the Center for Latin American Studies, both at San Diego State University; and the Canadian Studies Grant Program of the Canadian government. We are also grateful to Francisco Botrán, a graduate student in Latin American Studies and International Business at San Diego State University, who worked for several months gathering data for the project coordinators, preparing graphics and assisting with other administrative tasks and Rhonda McCubbin, a University of Calgary student, who assisted in preparing the glossary. We also wish to acknowledge the input of two colleagues who read drafts of the chapters, participated in a three-day workshop and provided valuable comments on the book's direction: Tony Cherin, Professor of Finance, and Paul Ganster, Director of the Institute for Regional Studies of the Californias at San Diego State University. We would also like to thank Herb Emery of the University of Calgary for his advice on the economic history of Canada. Finally, we wish to thank those who worked so diligently to make this an integrate book: Sandra del Castillo of the Center for US-Mexican Studies at the University of California, San Diego, who edited the first complete manuscript and helped to mold them into an integrated volume; Stanford Shedd and William Kerr of the University of Calgary who prepared the final version of the manuscript for the publisher; Gregory Flanagan of Saint Mary's College (Alberta) who provided technical assistance in preparing the final camera ready manuscript and Judi Pearce for some final touches.

Norris Clement and Gustavo del Castillo Vera (project managers)

January, 1999

PART I

Introduction

On a global basis, international trade and commercial relations are expanding at much more rapid rates than national economies are growing. As a result, international commerce is expected to be one of the major engines of economic betterment in the new millennium. The technological advances underlying the process of globalization–primary electronic transfers of information at low cost and improvements in transportation–are taking place without significant government involvement. Governments, however, have been active in enhancing the role of trade in their economic development through the negotiation of trade agreements which reduce trade barriers and other impediments to international commercial relations. The aim of these agreements is to foster the deepening of economic integration among countries while at the same time safeguarding national sovereignty. Achieving the right balance between these two contradictory objectives is a great challenge.

The North American Free Trade Agreement (NAFTA) reached by Canada, Mexico and the United States is one of the most important trade agreements ever negotiated. This is because it allows for the integration of the extremely large North American market, it has provisions which go far beyond the removal of trade barriers, it brings together both developing and developed economies in a regional trade organization and it may provide a model for a larger trade organization spanning the Western Hemisphere.

This book brings together the views and experience of authors from the three NAFTA partners. It represents a unique insight into the forces which shaped NAFTA and which will shape the future course of economic integration in North America. The book provides the essential background to the NAFTA negotiations, an evaluation of the Agreement's strengths and weaknesses, an assessment of its operation to date and a discussion of the future prospects for the process of North American economic integration. The discussion of NAFTA is put within the general backdrop of globalization and considers the possibilities for its extension to other countries in the Americas.

1. NAFTA in the Global Context

Readers of this book are conscious of a trend toward increasing internationalization the of economic life as imported goods flood national markets and foreign corporations become more noticeable. People involved in business have also become aware of the growing importance of international economic organizations such as the World Trade Organization (WTO) and the International Monetary Fund (IMF) which have been created to coordinate the global economy. The North American Free Trade Agreement (NAFTA) which came into being in 1994 has achieved considerable notoriety throughout the three-country region that bears its name in just a few years.

This book tells the story of how the ongoing economic integration of Canada, the US and Mexico in the post-World War II era led these countries, in recent years, to negotiate formal treaties– first the Canadian-United States Free Trade Agreement (CUSFTA) and subsequently the North American Free Trade Agreement (NAFTA)–that today provide a framework for facilitating and managing the expanding trade and investment flows that virtually gush over their borders.

The main actors in our story are: the US, a technologically advanced, prosperous and economically diversified country with a large population; Canada, a prosperous, resource- and technology-based country with a small population; and Mexico, a developing country with a medium-sized but rapidly growing population. Together these countries comprise about 7 percent (370 million) of the world's population (approximately 5.5 billion). The setting for our story is the global economy of the post-World War II period (1945–present) which was characterized by: rising prosperity for many nations, persistent poverty for others; rapidly expanding international trade and investment flows; explosive population growth; and a deteriorating global environment.

We believe that the story of how these countries came to 'free trade' is an interesting one and that understanding it will give the reader valuable insights into how the region's economy functions. The major shortcoming of the story is that the ending has not yet been written: it will take another 10–20 years before that chapter can be written. Nevertheless, not knowing how the story ends contributes suspense and provides the basis for serious debate between those who believe that the ending will be a happy one (that is , more jobs, higher incomes and an improved environment) and those who believe that it will be disastrous (that is, a rising gap between 'haves and have-nots', rising job insecurity for most working people and a rapidly deteriorating environment).

NAFTA's ROCKY ROAD

Implementation of (NAFTA) began on January 1, 1994. Scarcely eleven months later, on December 9, 34 heads of state met for three days at the Economic Summit of the Americas in Miami to begin the creation of a Free Trade Area of the Americas (FTAA), to be implemented by the year 2005. At that same summit, Canada, the United States and Mexico announced that negotiations with Chile would soon begin to provide for that country's accession to NAFTA. This was to be the first step toward a hemispheric free trade agreement. Thus, for a brief time, it appeared that the 'gospel of free trade' had finally been accepted throughout the entire Western Hemisphere.

A few days later, however, on December 20, Mexico's newly-elected government announced that, in response to a growing trade deficit (that is, imports greater than exports), dwindling international currency reserves and a pressing need to refinance part of its short-term foreign debt, the government of Ernesto Zedillo would allow the peso to depreciate relative to the US dollar, the currency of its principal trading partner. Almost immediately, Mexican and foreign investors panicked, selling stocks and exchanging pesos for dollars. During the latter half of 1994, the Mexican government had financed the growing gap between imports and exports with inflows of investment capital, much of it attracted by the rapidly rising stock market. However, the economic situation deteriorated, investors lost confidence in the economy and simply cashed out of the stock market and Mexican pesos. This crisis was aggravated by a series of political events that also lowered investor confidence.

Over the next few months the Mexican stock market, which had experienced a strong boom in recent years, lost a good portion of its gains, the peso fell to approximately half its previous value, inflation skyrocketed and economic output and employment took their deepest plunge in 50 years. The country found itself in a deep recession, the deepest since 1981, when a previous 'liquidity crisis' had forced the Mexican government to declare a moratorium on debt service payments which, in turn, triggered a generalized debt crisis throughout the entire developing economies. There is a debate regarding the source of macroeconomic instability in Mexico. On the one hand are those who feel that deficiencies in the structure of the 'real economy' are to blame, while others blame financial and macroeconomic mismanagement (see Chapter 6).

In 1994 the crisis in Mexico again spread to other countries of Latin America, especially Argentina and Brazil, as the so-called 'tequila effect' stimulated investors to reassess the risk involved in Latin America's 'emerging markets' and reduce their short-term investments in those countries. Even the US and Canadian dollars and some European currencies weakened in this environment, especially after it was announced that a support package of some US$50 billion had been assembled, involving the US Federal Reserve (Currency Stabilization Fund), the Canadian Central Bank (Bank of Canada), the IMF, the Bank of International Settlements and a small number of advanced industrial countries (see Chapters 2 and 3 for details relating to these institutions).

The irony of the situation is that throughout the late 1980s and early 1990s Mexico was held up as one of the 'bright stars' of developing countries by the International Monetary Fund and other proponents of market-oriented structural reforms. In response to its infamous 1981 debt crisis, Mexico had implemented an ambitious market-oriented plan to restructure its heretofore protected, state-oriented economy. In very general terms, Mexico had pursued a policy of import-substitution (ISI) which required protection of its manufacturing sector through tariffs and quotas and government action in terms of subsidies and, in some cases, government ownership and operation of enterprises in key industrial sectors (for example, oil and gas). (See Chapters 3 and 6 for a more detailed discussion.) This plan included liberalizing international trade and investment (Mexico joined the General Agreement on Tariffs and Trade (GATT) in 1986); privatizing government enterprises; cutting government expenditures and subsidies in order to balance the budget; and decentralizing governmental functions.

Despite the record high rates of inflation, deteriorating terms of trade and falling real wages that characterized much of the 1980s, by 1993 Mexico was able to reduce inflation to the single-digit range, achieve modest economic growth and attain balance-of-payments stability in the context of a relatively stable peso. Additionally, private capital was returning, mainly financing the country's rising imports but also providing badly needed investment in plant and equipment. All of this was accomplished while servicing and restructuring the external debt, which rose from about US$86 billion in 1982 to $119 billion in 1993.

Meanwhile, in 1994, a conservative Republican majority took control of both houses of Congress in the US for the first time in several decades. While the Republican congressional leadership historically has supported free trade initiatives such as the Uruguay Round of negotiations of GATT and NAFTA itself, many conservative members of Congress strongly opposed NAFTA when it was debated and finally approved in November 1993. They, and many liberal Democrats who fear massive job displacements from US multinationals exporting jobs to low-wage Mexico, strongly oppose expanding that agreement and the recently negotiated WTO, because they will diminish US leverage in international trade disputes. (The Uruguay Round refers to a series of negotiatons between 1986 and 1994 that substantially expanded the 'rules of the game' for international trade under GATT. Additionally, a new institution, the World Trade Organization (WTO) was created which provided expanded powers to settle international trade disputes.

For more details, see the discussion of the GATT and the WTO in Chapter 2.)

The December 1994 Mexican peso crisis provided NAFTA opponents in the United States with an example of how closer relations with 'unstable Latin American countries' can negatively impact on the US economy. During the NAFTA debates the United States enjoyed a trade surplus (that is, exports greater than imports) with Mexico, which helped compensate for its large trade deficit with Japan and other Asian countries. From this perspective, closer trade relations with Mexico looked very attractive; but that perception changed quickly following Mexico's crisis–when the US surplus turned into a deficit–and suddenly NAFTA appeared to many US observers as simply a bad deal. However, focusing on the events of the December 1994 crisis provides a distorted view of NAFTA in its entirety.

Canadians, too, have had their problems with NAFTA. Confronted with high unemployment, several years of economic stagnation and exploding federal budget deficits, they were still adjusting to and debating the impacts of the Canada-US Free Trade Agreement implemented in 1989. In recent years the Canadian economy has experienced significant restructuring as both US and Canadian firms adjust to an increasingly borderless economy and the challenges and opportunities it presents. Additionally, the specter of Quebec's threatened secession and a lingering constitutional crisis has taken its toll on Canadian unity and has diverted attention from the pursuit of freer trade.

Nevertheless, as a small economy Canada is more dependent on international trade than is the United States, and is generally open to the concept of adding more members–trading partners–to NAFTA. Not only is a multilateral agreement likely to increase Canadian trade, but more NAFTA members would dilute the bargaining power of the United States–the largest and most powerful of the three countries–in negotiating the agreement and settling trade disputes. Thus, in 1997, noting that the US Congress was reluctant to add more members to NAFTA, Canada signed a bilateral free trade aggreement with Chile.

Clearly the first five years of NAFTA's implementation have been difficult for the three countries, and much of the blame has been directly or indirectly placed on the agreement itself. Still, it must be remembered that the international economic environment, especially during the 1997–98 period, has been especially difficult with key Asian economies, Russia and Brazil experiencing serious economic problems. While NAFTA does not seem to be in danger of being dismantled at this time, a 'widening' of the agreement to include more members or a 'deepening' to further integrate the three countries certainly appears less likely than in January 1994.

THE NAFTA DEBATES

The road to NAFTA was paved with harsh debates. Critics from the right and the left in all three countries argued, usually for different reasons, that freer trade would reduce national sovereignty and economic autonomy and give large multinational corporations (MNCs) more freedom to exploit the human and natural resources of member countries without regard for the needs of the populace or the environment. Proponents, however, maintained that freer trade would bring increased competition and efficiency, higher living standards and a more competitive North American economy, better able to compete in global markets. Understanding these different perspectives and the events that led up to the implementation of NAFTA is essential to determining what it is and where it might go in the future.

From the perspective of most market-oriented economists, it is quite natural that the three countries of North America negotiated, signed and ratified a treaty to formally integrate their economies. The only question they might ask is, What took them so long? After all, from a purely economic point of view, the fact that Canada, Mexico and the US are close neighbors, with relatively complementary economies,[1] implies that they are natural trading partners. Thus, the three countries, already highly integrated economically would benefit from removing

[1]Economic complementary refers to the countries producing different types of goods and/or using different production techniques. For example, Mexico tends to specialize in basic manufacturing utilizing labor-intensive manufacturing techniques, while the US tends to specialize in products and services using capital- and knowledge-intensive techniques.

barriers to international trade and investment by forcing a more rational geographical redistribution of economic activity throughout the three countries, allowing for a better realization of potential economies of scale and more efficient allocation of resources. (The degree of integration is usually calcuated as the total value of intraregional trade (exports among members) as a percentage of total exports of all the member countries. In the late 1980s, before implementation of either of the two free trade agreements, this was approximately 43 percent for North America, compared to around 59 percent for the then twelve-country European Union which had been involved in economic integration agreements since the late 1950s.)

Of course, economists acknowledge that there will be both winners and losers as international trade and investment expands. They argue, however, that the 'gains from trade' (that is, lower production costs and lower prices to consumers) outweigh the losses that workers and firms in certain sectors of the economy are likely to sustain.

One question that bothered some economists is how to deal with the enormous disparities in economic development between Canada and the United States on the one hand, and Mexico on the other. In the case of the European Union, which in 1992 brought twelve countries into a 'single market' after almost four decades of conscious integration efforts, the disparities between the most advanced countries (Germany and France) and the least developed (Greece and Portugal) were not as great as those between the countries of North America. However, in the European case a 'social fund' was established to transfer resources from rich to poor countries in order to reduce the disparities between them and the instabilities that could result from those disparities. Yet, so sure were market-oriented North American economists that a NAFTA based mainly on market forces would result in significant employment and income gains that such a fund was not seriously considered during the negotiations.[2]

Geographers, like economists, see the three countries of North America as 'natural trading partners'. Close proximity means lower trans-

[2]The main argument against a social fund was that North America was building a 'free trade area', and not an 'economic union'. See Chapter 2.

portation costs and they would expect there to be a high degree of integration in the absence of significant natural or artificial barriers such as rugged mountain ranges or closed border gates. Additionally, they would look at trading patterns in the Canada-US border region. Since 90 percent of all Canadians live within 200 miles of the border, a high proportion of total trade is north-south–international trade with the US as distinguished from interprovincial east-west trade. This same pattern can be found in the US-Mexico border region.

Historians, however, are likely to have a different perspective on NAFTA than mainstream economists or geographers. Given the United States' enormous size and hegemonic behavior, as well as the history of conflict and lack of trust that has characterized North American relations over the last two centuries, historians might very well be astonished that such a treaty even reached the negotiating table. The fact that much of the Southwest region of the US was Mexican territory that was lost as a result of the US-Mexican War of 1848 still angers many Mexicans as does the long history of American intervention in Mexican affairs. While Canada-US relations have been strained at various times, since World War II the two countries have generally worked very closely on a wide variety of economic, political and security issues.

Political scientists also have reason to be uneasy about a NAFTA. They tend to view free trade agreements as problematic issues for political candidates irrespective of their ideological positions. That is, free trade is usually seen by workers in developed countries as a threat to their economic security, especially during periods of stagnating wages and massive restructuring ('downsizing') as was the case in the early 1990s. Nonetheless, firms, especially those in high-tech, export-oriented industries, tend to support freer trade and, through lobbyists, wield considerable influence with political candidates. Hence, politicians may well lose voter support if they support NAFTA, and lose campaign funding if they oppose it–a classic 'no win' situation.

Nevertheless, some political scientists looking at US-Mexico relations, which have fluctuated widely in recent decades, saw NAFTA as a tool for 'normalizing' those relations by institutionalizing the channels of bilateral discussion on a wide range of economic and political issues

Table 1.1 Chronology of Important Events

19th Century	
1854–56	US-Canada Reciprocity Treaty
1856	Treaty abrogated by US
1869–1923	Canada attempts to reinstate Treaty 7 times
1882	US-Mexico Reciprocity Treaty
20th Century	
1965	US-Canada Auto Pact
1979	Mexico rejects GATT membership
1982	Mexico signs an agreement with US on subsidies and countervailing duties
1986	Mexico joins GATT
1987	Framework Agreement on Bilateral Trade (US and Mexico)
1989	Implementation of Canada-US Free Trade Agreement (CUSFTA)
1990	Mexican President Salinas proposes a US-Mexico Trade Agreement
1991	NAFTA negotiations begin
1992	Single Market completed in Europe
1994	Implementation of NAFTA begins

from trade and investment to border relations and drug trafficking.

Thus, from a mainstream economic perspective NAFTA makes sense, but from many others it does not. As noted above, the three countries' economies were already quite integrated before 1994, when NAFTA's fifteen-year process of implementation began. In fact, the United States has been the major trading partner of both Canada and Mexico for many decades and Canada and the United States have had free trade arrangements since the mid 1960s. The United States and Mexico began building a cooperative trading relationship in the mid 1980s (see Table 1.1).

Nevertheless, it is important to note that what is now emerging as a trilateral relationship is being created from two bilateral relationships that exist between the United States and Canada and between the United States and Mexico, respectively. The reality is that the bilateral relationship between Canada and Mexico is not now nor ever will be as important quantitatively or qualitatively as the other two. This is primarily due to the fact that the US economy dwarfs those of Canada and Mexico and therefore serves as the 'hub' in a 'hub-and-spoke' relationship based as much on economic realities as on geography.

This relationship is clearly illustrated in Tables 1.2 and 1.3, which provide an overview of North American trade relationships for the years 1989 (the initial year of CUSFTA) and 1993. For example, Table 1.3 shows that in 1989 US exports to Mexico and Canada were approximately US$25 billion and US$78 billion, respectively, while exports between Canada and Mexico totaled less than US$1 billion combined. It is roughly the same story if you look at imports among the three countries; the Canada-Mexico relationship simply is not as strong as the US-Canada or US-Mexico link, but the two tables demonstrate that the Canada-Mexico relationship is growing rapidly.

The data presented in Table 1.4 reveal why this is so. In 1994 the US population was approximately ten times as large as Canada's and three times that of Mexico, while the absolute size of the US economy was also ten times that of Canada but nearly twenty times that of Mexico. Thus the United States is both the largest producer/exporter and the largest market/importer in the North American region.

Table 1.4 provides additional information on the three countries– most notably, each country's ranking on the United Nation's Human Development Index (HDI). The HDI was developed in the late 1980s by the United Nations Development Programme (UNDP) and introduced in its 1990 annual report. It has since been refined and now combines three basic components of human development: longevity (life expectancy), knowledge (adult literacy and mean years of schooling) and standard of living (real GDP per capita adjusted for local cost of living using purchasing power parity exchange rates).

Table 1.2 North American Trade, 1989 (in millions of $US)

	US imports % of total imports	Canadian imports % of total imports	Mexican imports % of total imports	Total exports to the world	% of exports to NAFTA
		70.93%	72.92%		
US exports		78,266	24,969	370,417	27.87
% of total		21.13%	6.74%		
	18.51%		1.53%		
Canadian exports	85,305		525	123,084	69.73
% of total	69.31%		0.43%		
	3.51%	0.25%			
Mexican exports	16,163	272		51,019	32.21
% of total	31.68%	0.53%			
				544,520	
Total imports					
from the world	460,887	110,345	34,240	605,472	
% of imports					
from NAFTA	22.02	71.17	74.46		

Note: Different accounting methods may lead to inconsistencies.
Source: IMF, *Direction of Trade Statistics Yearbook, 1990*.

Table 1.3 North American Trade, 1997 (in millions of $US)

	US imports % of total imports	Canadian imports % of total imports	Mexican imports % of total imports	Total exports to the world	% of exports to NAFTA
		76.58%	65.00%		
US exports		150,124	71,378	688,697	32.16
% of total exports		21.88%	10.36%		
	19.72%		0.83%		
Canadian exports	177,317		916	214,422	83.12
% of total exports	82.78%		0.43%		
	10.51%	1.10%			
Mexican exports	94,531	2,157		110,431	87.56
% of total exports	85.60%	1.95%			
Total Imports					
from the world	899,020	196,027	109,808		
% of imports					
from NAFTA	30.24%	77.68%	65.84%		

Note: Different accounting methods may lead to inconsistencies.
Source: IMF, *Direction of Trade Statistics Yearbook, 1997.*

Table 1.4 Comparative Statistics: NAFTA Participants

Country	Population (1993 millions)	GDP 1993 US$ millions	GDP per capita US$	External debt 1993 billions	Inflation Inflation 1980–90 %	1998 or latest	Life expectancy (years)	HDI rank
Canada	27.5	618	22,219	435	4.4	0.7	78.1	1
Mexico	90.4	740	8,166	125	70.3	15.9	72.9	52
USA	256.1	6,379	24,715	NA	3.7	1.5	75.9	9
Total	376.3	7,737	20,560	560				

Sources: World Bank (1997); *The Economist*, October 31,1998.

Purchasing power parity is a method of comparing values of currency units of two different countries as defined in the Introduction to Part II. The UNDP holds that, with its latest refinements, the HDI provides a better measure of a country's socioeconomic progress than does simple Gross National Product (GNP) or Gross Domestic Product (GDP). GDP refers to all output produced within the geographic boundaries of a country, by both citizens and foreigners. GNP excludes output produced by foreigners living or working in the country. Furthermore, the HDI can be used to evaluate progress over time and to guide policy making as it provides a wider basis for comparing the experiences of different countries. In this context, note that the United States ranks ninth, while Canada ranks first and Mexico fifty-second, reflecting their enormous disparities not only in income but also in health and education.

Given these asymmetries in the trilateral relationship, the long history of conflict between the United States and its neighbors and the lack of consensus on the desirability of NAFTA in the three countries, we might inquire as to exactly what did bring these three economies together in the early 1990s to draw up this agreement. Many factors, both internal and external, contributed. First, the election of a conservative, free trade proponent (Ronald Reagan) as US President in 1980 and the election of his ideological equivalent in Canada (Brian Mulroney in 1984) certainly was important in bringing the United States and Canada together to negotiate CUSFTA in the late 1980s. Then when Mexico elected Carlos Salinas de Gortari in 1988, another free trader (educated in the United States), the stage was set, politically, for such an agreement.

From an economic perspective there are several factors worth mentioning here. First, the case can be made that the weakening competitive positions of all three countries *vis-à-vis* key European and Asian economies forced the economies of North America to come together to attempt to increase their joint efficiency through increased specialization, market expansion and cooperation. Another factor was that North America was, in fact, becoming more integrated economically and there seemed to be a growing consensus in the three countries that the integration process should be better managed in order to provide clearer 'rules of the game' with respect to both international trade and investment flows. Still another factor was the desire, or rather the need, of both Mexico and Canada to gain guaranteed access to the large and prosperous US market at a time when international trade conflicts, especially between the United States and Japan, were heating up and the European Union was increasingly focusing inward on its own integration process.

To these must be added a number of external forces that played important roles. Why did these three countries, which by the mid 1980s had embraced a multilateral approach to trade negotiations through GATT, decide to take a trilateral/regional approach to lowering trade barriers? After all, GATT had been relatively successful in a series of negotiating rounds over the last three decades. The GATT negotiations had reduced overt protectionism (for example, tariffs and quotas) on manufactured products and introduced a system of rules and arbitration procedures which, although complex and cumbersome, had reduced trade conflicts in much of the world from their high pre-World War II levels. Why was this 'global' approach pushed aside by a regional one in 1990?

Several factors influenced this decision. First, from the perspective of the United States and Canada, in the early 1990s the Uruguay Round of GATT negotiations did not appear particularly promising.[3] Second, other transnational regions (for example, Europe and Asia) were putting together trading blocs that could potentially reduce North America's access to those markets.

Of final note, it was President Salinas of Mexico who initiated negotiations with the United States in 1990 after completing an extensive trip through Europe, during which he concluded that rebuilding Eastern Europe following the collapse of the Soviet bloc would likely absorb much of the financial capital that he had hoped to attract to Mexico.

[3]The agenda of the Uruguay Round (1986–94) focused on reducing tariff and nontariff barriers on a wide spectrum of products (including agricultural products and services) while increasing international protection for 'intellectual property' (that is, patents and royalties). At the same time that the NAFTA negotiations opened in 1990, progress in these areas was particularly slow.

Thus, he turned to the United States for both increased trade and investment. Canada, already in a free trade agreement with the United States, then decided to join the (trilateral) negotiations, primarily to protect its own interests by working with Mexico to counterbalance the excessive power of the United States and to avoid being excluded from a favorable trading relationship with Mexico.

The NAFTA negotiations lasted approximately three years (1991–93). During much of this time a serious global recession increased unemployment and negatively impacted many people's incomes. Large and small firms throughout the world began a process of 'restructuring', usually implementing new management practices such as 'just in time' inventory systems and 'total quality management', and eliminating jobs ('downsizing') at all levels. Suddenly, the long-standing concerns of workers, forepersons and managers, who saw their jobs evaporating, heated up the free trade debates in all three countries. In general there were four sources of criticism of the proposed NAFTA:

- Labor and community groups, mainly in Canada and the United States, decried the loss of jobs in the manufacturing sector and the deteriorating living standards that they predicted would result from freer trade as well as the disruptions to communities that would follow decisions by multinational corporations to move jobs to lower wage cost locations. However, most labor groups in Mexico, long loyal to the official government party, saw job and perhaps wage gains resulting from NAFTA and, therefore, for the most part sided with the government's pro-NAFTA position.

- Environmentalists in all countries, citing the poor environmental enforcement record in Mexico, feared a massive exodus of firms out of Canada and the United States to escape those countries' stricter enforcement policies, aggravating both regional and global pollution as well as driving the job displacements noted above. Additionally, a growing group of environmentalists, who oppose expanding international trade generally, sided with the anti-NAFTA forces. They maintained that increasing 'global interdependence' could have enormous negative effects on both the environment (for example, through oil spills) and 'institutions of community' within national borders.

- Human rights groups in the three countries pointed to the absence of truly democratic processes and the large number of human rights violations in Mexico. They argued that increasing trade links would implicitly condone such behavior. It is widely recognized that, while Mexico had dramatically reformed its economy, political reform had consciously been relegated to the back burner.

- In both Mexico and Canada, NAFTA opponents were concerned with the potential loss of cultural identity, sovereignty and political autonomy that could result from a closer, more open relationship with their much larger and more powerful trading partner.

The opposition to NAFTA produced concrete results: two complementary agreements were generated, one dealing with environmental concerns and another with labor practices.

Understanding NAFTA

Individuals specialize in tasks for which they are best suited. An accountant hires a plumber to do his bathroom and the plumber hires an accountant to do her taxes. In effect, they trade. The same is true for different regions within a country. Florida trades oranges for Washington apples. Just as individuals and regions can gain by trading so can nations. However, there are often barriers to international trade which do not exist between individuals and regions. Economic integration is the process by which two or more countries reduce those barriers in order to gain from the trade which results from international specialization. Economic integration can occur in a variety of forms–from a simple free trade area to a much more complex economic union (see Chapter 2)–but the essence of economic integration is linking national economies through reducing barriers to trade, foreign investment and other cross-border transactions.

From the outset it should be clear that NAFTA is not simply a free trade agreement among the three nations. If it were, it would consist of considerably fewer than the approximately 2,000 pages that were needed to adequately define the new North American economic relationship. NAFTA extends to include rules on foreign investment and the treatment of intellectual property but, significantly, it excludes labor flows. There are provisions for the temporary entry of certain white-collar workers in certain occupations, but in general terms the agreement does not provide for the free movement of workers between member countries, as does, for example, the European Union.

In order to understand NAFTA, its implications and its future development, we have provided–in the next seven chapters–a brief but comprehensive overview of what you need to know, including:

- the economic theory of international trade and economic integration underlying NAFTA and any subsequent agreements that may emerge in the future (Chapter 2),
- the circumstances and the (global) environment that brought the three countries together to negotiate NAFTA and its complementary agreements in the early 1990s (Chapter 3),
- the major points regarding the economic development of each country in the context of the changing global economy and the institutions responsible for managing it (Chapters 4–6),
- what NAFTA does and does not do (Chapter 7) and
- alternative paths for the future development of NAFTA and the likely impacts of NAFTA on business, the environment and other aspects of North American life (Chapter 8).

2. International Integration: Theory and Practice

This chapter has two main objectives: (1) to put the concept of international integration within the context of economic theory; and (2) to describe and provide insights into the international institutions countries have put in place to regulate the process of international integration. Understanding the theoretical basis for economic integration is important because, to a considerable extent, government initiatives regarding trade and other aspects of integration are influenced by theoretical arguments. As with any change in government policy, changes to how nations interact with each other will involve trading off a set of benefits against costs. Theory can provide insights into those benefits and costs. This chapter discusses the major theories of international trade and the insights they provide for policy makers.

International commercial relationships with other countries will impinge on a nation's sovereignty. To provide a commercial environment where firms are willing to invest in trade-related activities requires rules for trade and other aspects of international commercial activity that trading nations accept. As these rules limit nations' sovereignty, a large number of international organizations have been established to facilitate the difficult trade-offs between the need for a secure business environment by those engaged in international commerce and the sovereignty concerns of nations. Of course, trade is not the only arena where international organizations impinge on sovereignty. Political organizations such as the United Nations and military alliances such as the North Atlantic Treaty Organization (NATO) also affect sovereignty. The international organizations which facilitate and regulate international economic relations have evolved over time. They are described and the extent of their role in the process of international integration outlined. The combination of theoretical arguments and institutional arrangements presented in this chapter should provide the background required to understand the complex issues dealt with in the chapters that follow. Without a basic grounding in trade theory and the organizations of international commercial relations, it will not be possible to fully appreciate the impact NAFTA will have on North American integration or the opportunities it creates for individual firms.

INTERNATIONAL TRADE THEORY

International integration is an idea that encompasses a very wide range of institutional arrangements among nations–open borders, coordination of economic strategies, common political institutions and shared responsibility for the well-being of individuals, to name only a few. International integration is also a matter of degree, with many possibilities between the polar cases of a nation-state that does not engage in international trade (practices autarky) and has no relations with other countries (is isolationist), to the complete abrogation of national sovereignty to another level of political authority. While almost all modern nation-states represent, to some degree, an evolutionary process whereby smaller political groups have surrendered sovereignty, no examples of completely isolated countries exist. All nations trade and enter into discourse with other states, however minimally. Most nations are heavily involved economically and politically with other nations and, hence, exhibit a considerable degree of international integration. While international integration encompasses a wide range of institutional arrangements, the fundamental motivation for interaction with other nations is the perceived benefits from engaging in trade. Hence, an understanding of why benefits from trade are expected to arise is essential to any discussion of international integration.

Why Study International Trade Theories?

Even among economists (who are well known for abstract theorizing), the theory of international trade is considered more a purely intellectual exercise than a policy-making tool. The importance of international trade theory, however, lies in its ability to provide fundamental insights into the economic forces underlying nations' trade. The world of international commerce is exceedingly complex and only by stripping away the nonessentials can the basic principles of trade be uncovered. Hence, while the assumptions often imposed in trade theory–for example, only two goods, two countries, two factors of production–often appear extremely unrealistic, it is important to concentrate on the insights provided by the results generated by trade theories.

The insights derived from international trade theory are important because, in spite of the restrictive assumptions of the models, they have weathered the test of critical intellectual scrutiny over a very long period and, hence, have come to be generally accepted by political decision makers. As a result, these propositions represent the underlying basis for trade policy, particularly in the major developed economies. Thus, unless one has a basic understanding of trade theory, it is not possible to comprehend the dynamics of nations' international commercial relations.

The Determinants of International Competitiveness

Since the earliest investigations of economic activity, it has been recognized that firms in different countries initiate transactions with firms in other countries because it will bring them some advantage. This is one of the cornerstones of *The Wealth of Nations*, written by the Scottish economist Adam Smith in 1776. The reasons for exchanges between firms in different countries are no different than those that underlie exchanges between firms in the same country. To understand this fundamental point is extremely important. This is because concerns are often expressed regarding transactions taking place internationally that would not elicit any comment if undertaken by two firms in the same country. This suggests that the source of concerns regarding international transactions must be based on a perception that what may be good for an individual firm may not necessarily be good for the nation. It is also important to realize that nations themselves do not trade, only firms. Of course, in some countries the government or its agents may actually undertake all or part of a nation's international commerce. If this is the case, different types of advantages may be perceived as arising from trade than those associated with the strict commercial interest of private firms. Transactions must, however, still be organized and a nations' trade is only the sum of these transactions. Individuals, as well as firms, may engage in international trade, but the dominant participants in trade are firms (for example, a manufacturer, an import-export company, a transnational corporation). We shall approach the topic of trade as if all trade is carried out by firms. Why then, are international trade issues often so politically charged and trade debates so heated?

The reason lies in the concept of competitiveness. The bundle of goods and services traded and their volumes are determined by the relative competitiveness of the firms in a nation. The types of goods a nation exports or imports are important indicators of that nation's degree of economic development. While the perception of what constitutes a developed country has changed over time–for example, from a producer of iron and steel in the early part of the twentieth century to a producer of automobiles and planes in the middle part of the century to a producer of computer software and microchip designs in the latter decades–a failure to competitively produce the goods and services that conform to the current definition of a developed country gives rise to political concerns. Further, when international competitiveness appears to be declining, political action is often called for to restore it.

The factors that determine a nation's international competitiveness are exceedingly complex. In some cases, competitiveness is related to factors over which nations have little control–the availability of natural resources, geographical location and climate. For the most part, however, competitiveness relates to factors over which governments can exercise some control–the skills of the labor force, higher education, the legal and commercial environment, infrastructure such as roads and ports, entrepreneurial incentives, taxes, research and development activity, the market power exercised by foreign firms and the activities of foreign governments. Trade theories help identify the sources of competitiveness and what causes them to change.

Alternative Theories of International Trade

Trade theory has undergone a long evolution in its quest to explain competitiveness, but as yet no comprehensive theory has been developed. The insights gained along the way, however, are considerable. 'Classical' theories of international trade–most closely associated with the work of Adam Smith in the eighteenth century and David Ricardo in the nineteenth (Smith, 1961; Ricardo, 1951)–were primarily concerned with showing that trade was beneficial to the nations that engaged in it. The two simple proofs of classical trade theory, 'absolute advantage' and 'comparative advantage', still provide much of the popular intellectual underpinnings for belief in trade liberalization.

If two nations voluntarily trade, then both must gain if each country specializes in producing the good for which it has an absolute advantage. Advantage is defined by relative efficiency in resource use. The good that the country produced would then be exchanged in trade for the good in which it had an absolute disadvantage. This intuitive result can best be proved through a simple numeric example. In Table 2.1 we have two countries (Canadiana and Americana) and two goods (oranges and pencils). By expending one unit of labor, Canadiana can produce one orange. Alternatively, Canadiana could use one unit of labor to produce four pencils. For an equal commitment of labor, Americana can produce five oranges or three pencils. Clearly Canadiana has an absolute advantage in producing pencils and Americana has an absolute advantage in producing oranges. Assume that people in Canadiana will exchange one pencil for one orange. Americana could shift one unit of labor from producing pencils to producing oranges (it is beginning to specialize in orange production). If Americana can trade five of its oranges for five pencils produced by Canadiana, it will gain two pencils (that is, by moving one unit of labor from its own production of pencils, three pencils less are produced but five pencils are gained from trading). The five units of oranges Canadiana receives from trading would have required it to expend five units of labor time if they were produced domestically. If Canadiana had used this labor time producing pencils, it could have produced twenty pencils. By specializing and trading,

Table 2.1 Absolute Advantage (output per unit of labor)

	Oranges	Pencils
Canadiana	1	4
Americana	5	3

Table 2.2 Comparative Advantage (output per unit of labor)

	Steel	Silver
Mexicana	1	3
Americana	7	6

Canadiana can make a net gain of fifteen pencils (twenty minus the five pencils it must trade). Of course, people in Canadiana have given up nothing because the five oranges they are no longer producing have been acquired by trading.

Our example has shown that by specializing in the production of the good in which it has an absolute advantage and then engaging in international exchanges, a country can make gains. The next important question that comes to mind is: Should a country trade if it is more efficient in the production of all goods?

The law of 'comparative advantage' states that a country with an absolute advantage in the production of both goods (in a two-good world) should specialize in producing and exporting the good in which its absolute advantage is the greater–importing the other good. This is numerically illustrated in Table 2.2. In this example, Mexicana has an absolute disadvantage in the production of both steel and silver, meaning that Americana is more efficient at producing both goods. Americana is seven times more efficient in producing steel and twice as efficient in producing silver. As its greater advantage is in producing steel, Americana's comparative advantage is in the production of steel. Compared to Americana, Mexicana is less inefficient in producing silver, 3 to 6 versus 1 to 7 and can be said to have a comparative advantage in silver production.

To illustrate the gains from trade, assume Americana can exchange 7 kg of steel for 7 kg of silver. This implies an international exchange ratio of one unit of silver for one unit of steel. If goods had to be exchanged on the basis of labor costs before trade, this implies that one unit of steel would have exchanges for 6/7 of a unit in Americana before trade, while one unit of silver would have exchanged for 1/3 of a unit of steel in Mexicana. The exchange rate with trade lies between the two pre-trade exchange rates with silver relatively cheaper now in Americana and steel relatively cheaper now in Mexicana. If Americana chooses to shift one unit of labor out of the production of silver and into the production of steel, it could produce an extra 7 kg of steel. This extra steel could be traded for 7 kg of silver. As only 6 kg less silver would be produced, Americana would gain one unit of silver compared to its no-trade position. Mexicana would also gain because the 7 kg of steel it received for its silver would have taken seven units of labor time to produce. Mexicana could now use that labor effort to produce 21 kg of silver, trading 7 kg of this extra silver production for an extra 7 kg of steel. Hence it would have the same quantity of steel and an extra 14 kg of silver by specializing and trading. Mexicana gains more (14 kg of silver) than Americana (1 kg of silver), but they both have gained by specializing and entering into trade with one another. This is the fundamental (and somewhat counterintuitive) lesson of the theory of comparative advantage. The potential for exploiting gains from trade arising from comparative advantage remains the most popular justification for trade liberalization to this day.

While classical theories of trade focused on the benefits to be gained from trade, they did not answer the question: What determines comparative advantage? Classical economists suggested that the quality of natural resources or differences in climate led to differences in the efficiency of labor. While this provided a reasonable explanation when trade consisted largely of agricultural and resource-based commodities, it did not seem relevant in the case of industrial goods.

In the 1930s, a new 'neoclassical' theory of trade was developed to explain how comparative advantage could arise (Ohlin, 1933). Neoclassical theory assumed, in addition to the two countries and two goods of the classical economists, two factors of production–usually stylized as capital and labor. Further, the two output goods were assumed to have different factor intensities–one using more capital than labor, the other more labor than capital–but the production technology used was assumed to be the same in both countries. If the countries have different resource endowments–one country has relatively more capital than the other–neoclassical theory predicts that the capital-rich country will specialize in the production of capital-intensive goods and then export them. The labor-intensive country would specialize in and export labor-intensive goods. For example, Mexico, with its abundant labor, would be expected to export labor-intensive goods to the United States and Canada, while labor-short Canada and the United States would export capital-intensive goods to Mexico. A further neoclassical conclusion was that in capital-abundant countries, labor productivity (and hence income) would be high because labor had more capital with which to work. This conclusion of neoclassical trade theory led to a host of government policies designed to increase capital accumulation as a way to improve a country's standard of living. Another important conclusion of neoclassical trade theory was that if countries were opened up to international trade, labor in the capital-intensive country would shift out of the production of labor-intensive goods and into the production of capital-intensive goods–for example, out of producing textiles and into the production of cars.

While it offered powerful arguments to explain comparative advantage, neoclassical trade theory does not provide an all-encompassing explanation of comparative advantage. It has been argued (Keesing, 1966) that nations whose populations include a large proportion of highly skilled labor and professionals will specialize in the export of skill-intensive goods. Countries with large quantities of unskilled labor will export goods requiring little skill, producing little reward for labor. As skills can be altered through education–often called investment in human capital–governments have initiated programs to improve the skills of their workforces.

Efficiency can be affected by the size of industrial enterprises. To a point, large industrial enterprises tend to be more efficient than smaller enterprises–they embody economies of scale. If a country can gain the lead in attaining economies of scale, they will have a lower unit cost than foreign competitors and export those goods. Government intervention in the economy has often been focused on aiding industries to achieve economies of scale, 'picking the winners' and supporting them.

Innovativeness has also been suggested as a means of generating a comparative advantage. Countries that develop new products are able to gain a technological advantage (and possibly economies of scale) over other countries. Profits are gained by exporting before the competition catches up (Posner, 1961). Vernon (1966) postulated that traded industrial goods go through a product life cycle whereby production and exporting ability gradually move from innovating countries to countries with abundant low-skilled labor. This would seem to fit the pattern observed for many electronics goods developed in the United States and other developed countries whose production gradually moves offshore. In part, the *maquiladora* (plants mainly engaged in the assembly of imported components) sector along Mexico's border with the United States is a manifestation of this phenomenon. The mature *stages of production* have moved to Mexico (where wages are relatively low) while the development of new products and manufacture of components remain situated in the United States and other advanced countries.

These theories suggested that comparative advantage could be generated by being more innovative than competitors. Programs designed to encourage or directly fund research and development (R&D) have been put in place by most governments in developed countries.

Neoclassical theory, as well as the theories that followed it, predicted that countries would trade goods produced in different industries–for example, wheat for steel. But during the 1960s, however, it became obvious that trade was growing fastest between advanced industrial countries and that this trade was in goods from the same industries, albeit in differentiated products–for example, Budweiser for Heineken (Balassa, 1975).

Consumer tastes are, at least in part, determined by income. As people become wealthier, they desire better quality goods and greater variety. These are often only available from abroad, but at a premium. As incomes rise, consumers may well be willing to pay these premiums (Barker, 1977). The opening up of trade and the commensurate larger market will allow firms to specialize in the production of varieties. Clearly there is no single trade theory that can explain all aspects of trade (Perdikis and Kerr, 1998). Success as a trading nation is likely to depend on a large number of factors.

Why are Some Countries More Successful in International Commerce?

Some countries' industries continue to be successful even when factors such as labor costs, available resources and so on, work against them. Porter (1990) identified four major determinants of international competitiveness:

- Factor endowments, whether basic (natural resources, labor, and so on) or advanced (labor skills, technical knowledge, infrastructure). Basic factors can give a country a competitive edge in the production of certain goods; it is the availability of the advanced variety that maintains and enhances it.
- The size and composition of the domestic market relative to foreign demand, specifically the demands placed on local firms by domestic consumers relating to the quality and upgrading of their products. If the home market is demanding, firms are often better prepared to sell in international markets.
- The existence of internationally competitive support industries: banking, transportation, communications, information.
- Domestic industrial rivalry which forces firms to adopt innovative organizational structures and managerial strategies. Firms in sleepy, protected industries are unlikely to be international competitors.

These four aspects are mutually reinforcing. A nation's competitiveness in a particular area can be achieved and enhanced if favorable demand conditions coexist with plentiful factor endowments, successful and competitive support industries and a group of producers whose rivalry encouraged them to make full use of the other conditions and to continually upgrade and improve their products. Governments' attitudes toward education, research and development and the provision of advanced communication and infrastructure could affect factor conditions. Their industrial and competitiveness policies, along with taxes and interest rates, can influence firms' strategies, structures and security, as well as those of support industries.

The emphasis on a nation's competitiveness may seem natural, but it is puzzling in light of the classical approach to international trade. There the explanation of trade is in terms of 'comparative' advantage, not 'competitive' advantage. Trade is viewed as a matter of mutually beneficial exchange and the poorest, most inefficient nation on earth and the richest, most efficient can both gain from international trade so long as the relative costs of producing goods differ between the two countries. Moreover, the idea of international competitiveness may lead to the incorrect notion that one nation could became more competitive than any other and, therefore, have an absolute advantage in everything and therefore become the preferred choice for all goods. Remember, however, as the classical theory shows, trade hinges on comparative not absolute advantage and a nation cannot have a 'comparative' advantage in everything.

Hence, the importance of the idea of international competitiveness applies to the specific industries in which a nation has (or hopes to have) a comparative advantage. From this perspective, careful analysis of international competitiveness typically focuses on three related hypothesis:

1. the more efficient an industry is, the more likely that it will be able to survive as an export industry and the higher the gains from trade are likely to be;

2. there may be certain industries for which countries would prefer to have a comparative advantage, for example, those which draw on highly skilled, highly paid labor, or which generate a higher surplus above production cost (higher 'economic rents'); and

3. whether or not a country has a comparative advantage in a particular industry depends not only on the efficiency of production

within the country, but also the efficiency of production in other countries. Thus, changes outside this country may generate a 'decline in competitiveness' for this industry and, hence, shift it from having a comparative advantage in trade to having a comparative disadvantage.

What Conclusions can be Drawn from Trade Theories?

While no comprehensive trade theory has yet been developed, trade theories are useful in explaining trade patterns in certain groups of goods. Those that require unsophisticated labor inputs, a heavy degree of natural resources, or a favorable climate will be traded according to absolute or comparative advantage. Thus, trade in goods coming from the extractive industries (that is, oil and natural gas, minerals, timber) or basic agricultural commodities such as wheat and corn can be explained adequately by classical trade theory. Goods whose production requires standardized technologies and no specific factor inputs will be produced in countries that offer the best combination of factor prices: textiles or unsophisticated electronics will trade according to simple neoclassical trade theory. More sophisticated goods will be produced in innovative countries with highly skilled labor forces. As these goods require efficient supporting industries, they will be produced in advanced countries and exported both to other advanced countries and to developing countries.

Theoretical explanations of trade patterns feed directly into policy debates concerning what governments can do to improve a country's competitiveness. The main classical conclusion–that countries gain from trade–has stood both the test of time and considerable intellectual scrutiny. Totally open economies, however, have not often been observed.

PROTECTIONIST ARGUMENTS AND MANAGED TRADE

While trade theories suggest there are gains to be made from an open international trading regime, protectionist sentiments often win out on election day. They are deeply rooted and have considerable political appeal.

The Benefits of an Open Trade Regime

It is common to think of success in trade as arising from increases in exports. Exports are 'good' while imports are somehow 'bad'. This is a fallacy. A general increase in international exchanges–both imports and exports–is desirable. The 'gains from trade' arise from moving resources out of relatively inefficient industries and into efficient industries, with part of the extra production from efficient industries exchanged internationally for the inefficiently produced goods that have been given up. Over the long run, lowering trade barriers will allow countries to reap benefits from trade. In part, the error may stem from the tendency to think of trade solely in terms of production: exports mean greater production for the economy and therefore look attractive Trade, however, is also about consumption: from this prospective imports are particularly appealing since they increase the goods available to the economy.

Protectionism and Political Economy

One of the longest-ranging debates in economics and politics centers around the degree to which a nation's economy should be protected from the rigors of international competition. This is in spite of the theoretical evidence suggesting that countries gain from trade. Further, few of those who are identified with protectionist sentiments would advocate an autarkic trade policy (that is, that Canada should produce its own bananas rather than importing them). The case for protection is, however, often made for existing industries that find themselves noncompetitive internationally.

The reasons for this are simple. All of the gains that are expected to arise from trade in the models discussed above are based on the premise that resources can move easily (and costlessly) from declining, less competitive to expanding, more competitive industries. Neoclassical trade models are 'timeless' and all adjustments are long run.

Of course, resources do not move easily. Labor employed in textiles one day does not quickly and costlessly switch to making computers the next day. When foreign competition leads to the downsizing or closure of domestic firms, layoffs occur. People become unemployed. Skills applicable to one industry may not be useful in the expanding sector. Even if those let go from declining industries can find work in other sectors, it may require a move to a new location halfway across the country. Moving one's household is not costless. Further, if the declining industry is a locally or regionally important industry, its downturn will mean that the value of the assets–such as housing–of those now unemployed will fall, making it even more difficult to get established somewhere new. Workers may find themselves faced with a costly retraining period.

The owners of existing businesses will also find the value of their productive assets threatened by foreign competition. Support industries, and in some cases whole communities, may be threatened by an industry's decline. Hence, foreign competition creates a coalition of vested interests in the status quo. These vested interests are often difficult for politicians to ignore. Trade theorists argue that as there are considerable gains from trade available, those who are winners in the process should compensate the losers. Unfortunately, in practice, direct compensation is almost impossible to organize and, hence, does not occur.

Governments have three basic policy approaches to the problems created by declining competitiveness. First, they can ignore the problem. Unemployed workers must rely on the social welfare system and bear most of the costs of adjustment themselves. Second, the government can provide retraining, moving assistance and other adjustment packages for displaced workers. Both of these courses of action may require considerable government expenditures. The third option is to attempt to prevent the industry's decline by erecting trade barriers against foreign competitors. Costs are imposed on consumers of the protected goods, but budgetary expenditures are not required unless the protection is temporary and combined with a government restructuring package.

It is often difficult for politicians to ignore the concerns of vested interests. To the extent that declining industries are geographically concentrated, locally elected members of legislative bodies may have to promise expensive adjustment packages or protection to ensure re-election. However, delivering on a protectionist package promised to local constituents may be difficult for individual politicians because they represent only one voice in a larger process of government with national concerns as its priority. For example, in the United States, with its system of divisions of powers, the administration (with its national focus) tends to be 'free-trade' oriented while Congress (with locally elected members) is more 'protectionist'. To improve their effectiveness, members of Congress or Parliament must form strategic voting alliances (log rolling) with members who represent other industries in separate geographic locations seeking protection. These 'I'll vote to protect your industry if you'll vote to protect mine' tactics can lead to protectionism being a major political force.

BACKGROUNDER: PROTECTIONISM AND THE POLITICAL PROCESS

There has been a general long-term trend toward trade liberalization, at least in developed countries, since World War II. Protectionists have, however, been able to secure sector-specific increases in trade barriers and have been particularly effective at delaying the process of liberalization. As there has been little broad-based political support for protection over the period, they have been able to accomplish the ends of vested interests they represent through effective manipulation of the political process. In part, this stems from the stakes involved: the potential losers from a deteriorating competitive position will have a lot to lose and may be geographically concentrated, while the benefits of liberalization tend to be widely spread among the population. Hence, potential losers have a larger incentive to take action to protect their vested interests.

The central focus of political action by protectionists is the formation of groups to lobby governments for the imposition or retention of trade barriers. For a number of reasons, the protectionist lobby is often very effective. First, as suggested above, the pressure to organize is greater because they are a well-defined group. If they are geographically concentrated they are likely to face lower costs of organization. Those who gain may not be as willing and/or may face higher costs to organize to prevent trade restrictions from being put in place. This gives protectionists an advantage in the political process.

Second, the potential losers may be better represented in the congress, parliament, or legislature than the gainers. This is even more pronounced if the losers enjoy a favorable geographic distribution. For example, if the losers command a majority of 51 percent in two out of three constituencies, then only 34 percent of the total vote is needed to secure a majority in the legislature. The same 51 percent majority in thirteen of twenty-five legislative districts means that a majority of seats can be gained through only 27 percent of the total vote. Further, as they have more to lose, potential losers are more likely to vote.

Third, the political power of potential losers can be increased if different lobby groups support one another. A majority in the legislature can be secured if the politicians supporting protection vote strategically. This 'log rolling' works as follows: say there are three seats in the legislature and two industries threatened by proposed trade liberalization legislation. Each threatened group is geographically concentrated and able to elect a politician who advocates their position. Politician A is strongly in favor of import barriers to protect the industry located in his constituency–Bill 1–but weakly in favor of reducing the level of protection afforded to the industry located in the constituency of politician B–Bill 2. Politician B takes the opposite position. Without cooperating, both politicians may be in a minority position and their bills will be voted down; liberalization will result. By combining to support each other, they will be able to form a majority and pass both their propositions.

The result of the ability to act strategically is that there is a political market for protection. Demand for protection will come from groups that can identify a threat to their livelihood from trade liberalization. These groups tend to be domestic firms facing foreign competition in the home market, trade unions representing workers employed in those domestic firms and firms that supply threatened domestic firms with components.

This positive demand for protection will be diminished by opposition from groups that will lose out from protection–firms that rely on an open trading system for access to markets, their component suppliers and workers. Companies involved in the distribution of imports, such as Japanese automobile dealerships in the United States, will work against protection. Finally, consumer groups fearing higher prices will work against protection.

The supply side of the market for protection is made up of politicians and bureaucrats. Politicians wanting to get re-elected may be willing to support protectionist legislation if the protectionist group can deliver more votes than can the free traders.

Although nominally neutral, bureaucrats have an important role in providing a supply of protection. Bureaucrats are often motivated by the prestige, power and influence they enjoy relative to the economic group they serve–for example, the positions of the civil servants in the Department of Energy *vis-à-vis* oil companies. The main constraint that bureaucrats face is the power of elected politicians. As politicians must rely on the civil service for advice, bureaucrats' discretionary power in the supply of protection can be great.

Of course, there may be compelling reasons for not wanting certain industries, or types of industries, to disappear from a nation's economy. Domestic production of strategic military goods–parts for jet aircraft, specialized lubricants, communications electronics, and so on. Even in these cases, however, one must be careful not to confuse true strategic needs with the arguments of vested interests. Often it may be far less expensive to store vital military supplies or civilian necessities than to protect the existence of domestic industries on an ongoing basis. In most cases, domestic production, including food production, can be brought on line relatively quickly in times of crisis, well before carefully managed stockpiles are depleted. When this is not the case and the domestic industry needs to be kept in production, it is usually less costly to provide a direct subsidy than to put up trade barriers with their resulting multisector distortions.

Another common protectionist argument is the 'infant industry' theory. The premise of this theory, and its variants, is that a country could have a comparative advantage in the production of a good if the initial difficulties associated with establishing a new industry could be overcome. The task of establishing a new industry can be much more difficult if the industry is already well established in other countries. As foreign firms already have all the 'teething' problems sorted out, their lower-cost exports make it almost impossible for the infant domestic industry to become established. Hence, the domestic industry requires temporary protection. The evidence would suggest, however, that infant industries fail to grow up and that protection is seldom temporary. There are a number of reasons for this. One is that infant industry firms must rely on the domestic market initially. If there are considerable economies of scale in the industry, the domestic market may not be large enough to justify an efficient scale of operation. As a result, smaller plants with higher unit costs are built. Removal of trade barriers would leave these firms vulnerable to foreign firms already able to gain the cost advantages associated with economies of scale. In Canada, with its small domestic market, industries established under infant industry policies were victims of this dilemma. Once established behind trade barriers, it is often easier for firms to successfully argue for continued protection than to make the cost adjustments necessary to become internationally competitive.

One variant of the infant industry theory is the 'senile industry' argument. The argument is that an industry that has lost its comparative advantage may be able to regain it if it receives temporary protection so that it can re-equip its factories and retrain its workforce. These costs could be recouped if it acquired a greater share of the home market. Whether one can distinguish between a loss of competitiveness due to poor management or a genuine change in a country's comparative advantage is, however, questionable.

A more sophisticated version of the infant industry theory was the basis of many developing countries' industrialization policies from the 1940s through the 1970s. It was argued that to break out of their dependence on low-growth, low-value industries such as agriculture and resource extraction, countries needed to industrialize. As developed countries already had the lead in manufactured goods, it would not be possible for competing industries to become established in the home market of developing countries without protection. In part, this argument hinged on the economies of scale argument underpinning the older infant industry theory. However, more general economies of absolute size and 'learning by doing' were also emphasized. As developing countries gained experience in producing manufactures and developed a skilled labor force, the costs would fall and the industry would be competitive without protection. This strategy became known formally as 'import-substitution industrialization' (ISI)–substituting domestically produced manufactured products for imports–and was particularly popular in Latin America, including Mexico. Many inefficient industries were established as a result. However, the available evidence suggests that most of these industries never become able to compete internationally and, particularly when growth potential of the domestic market was exhausted, these industries acted as a brake on further economic development (Flanders, 1964).

One of the most often expressed arguments, but the least sophisticated, is the 'cheap foreign labor' argument. According to this argument, workers in developing countries are paid much lower wages than is the case in developed countries. Hence, the developed country will be swamped by less-expensive foreign imports, domestic businesses will be bankrupt and workers will be unemployed. While this can be true for any individual firm or even industry, it cannot be true for the whole economy. Imports have to be paid for. Over the long run, the only way imports can be financed is through export sales. This means that other industries in developed countries must expand. Of course, this is simply the normal manifestation of resource reallocation to take advantage of shifting comparative advantage and the benefits that specialization provides to the nation as a whole. These theoretical advantages, however, provide little comfort for those who face unemployment as a result of foreign competition. They will lobby hard to protect their livelihoods. As a result, when dealing with declining comparative advantage, most governments follow policies that are combinations of assistance for adjustment, social welfare benefits and protectionist policies.

The Trade Reality: Managed Trade

The trade policy of any country represents a political compromise between the two forces outlined above–the perceived benefits of an open trade regime and protection conceded to those with a vested interest in the status quo. No country has a completely open trade regime, nor does any country practice total autarky. All countries operate trade regimes that fall within the middle ground of 'managed trade'. Under a wide variety of rationales, certain industries receive protection from trade measures while others operate in a virtually free trade environment. Many of the existing trade restrictions are the result of retaliation for the actions of other countries who found it politically expedient to impose protectionist measures. Protection damages the interests of the countries from which they source their imports. For example, if German a product using high-quality Swedish steel as a major input were excluded from the Japanese market, Sweden as well as Germany might retaliate against the Japanese. These countries often retaliate with protectionist measures of their own. The degree of protectionism and openness that characterizes a nation's economy is seldom static, with swings between more protection and more openness common. This is because politicians seldom envision that the protection they are extending is permanent and because the arguments for trade liberalization are so compelling. As a result, the long-term trend is toward liberalization while the short run can be punctuated with (often dramatic) increases in protection.

BACKGROUNDER: THE INSTRUMENTS OF PROTECTION

How is protection against imports provided? In reality, the structure of protectionist measures is only constrained by the inventiveness of the bureaucrats who think them up. Here we will only discuss the most common instruments used by governments to protect domestic industries. This discussion will be confined to what are generally termed 'border measures', which are designed to disrupt the flow of goods. Other 'nonborder' measures that can be used to improve a domestic industry's competitiveness include subsidies, tax holidays and preferred access to government contracts or public facilities such as transport. These are not discussed.

Border measures are commonly divided into tariffs and nontariff barriers.

Tariffs

Tariffs are a tax on goods collected by the importing country when they cross its border. For example, assume that a tariff is set by the government at $10 per pair of shoes. Assume the price of a pair of shoes when it arrives in customs is $30. The government collects its tax before the shoes enter the domestic market. This effectively increases the price of a pair of shoes to $40 per pair ($30 plus the $10 tariff). Hence, instead of having to compete against $30 shoes, domestic firms only have to compete against $40 shoes. Domestic shoe producers' competitiveness is increased.

Tariffs are generally of two types: (1) flat rate–a set monetary rate per unit imported (as in our shoe example); and (2) *ad valorem*, which is calculated as a fixed percentage of the value of the goods imported. Hence the more valuable the import, the higher the monetary amount of the tariff.

According to internationally agreed rules, tariffs must be fixed and announced in advance. They can only be altered by governments on preannounced schedules. This provides exporters with a degree of certainty when they are making production and investment decisions.

Tariffs are the preferred protection measure of multinational organizations because they are the least distortionary protectionist instrument; if the same tariff rates are applied to the goods of all countries wishing to export a product to a country, then trade will gravitate to the lowest-cost producer. Tariffs are also easily compared, which makes negotiations to reduce them simpler than for other measures.

Nontariff Barriers

Import quotas Import quotas are quantitative restrictions on the number or volume of a commodity that can be imported over a specified time period–for example, 50,000 automobiles per year. By limiting the total quantity that can be imported, the total supply (domestic and foreign) available in the domestic market over the period is reduced. As total supply is reduced, domestic prices rise, which is to the advantage of domestic firms.

Quotas often require complex administrative structures to monitor imports and allocate the total quota among foreign countries wishing to supply the protected market. The latter is required because by restricting quantity, excess demand is created for the right to import. Quotas are apportioned among competing exporters by a variety of methods. Difficulties are encountered when a new potential exporting country with no quota asks for access to the market or when an existing exporting country has considerably improved its competitive position relative to other exporters and desires a larger share of the quota.

According to international agreements, import quotas are to be converted into tariffs giving equivalent protection. The rate at which this conversion is supposed to take place is, however, only vaguely set out.

Health, sanitary and phytosanitary regulations These regulations cover a wide range of rules governing the physical condition of products entering a country. All countries have regulations designed to ensure that products coming from abroad are not hazardous to the environment or the health of humans, animals, or plants (phyto is the Greek term for plants).

In many cases these regulations are legitimate. However, if cleverly designed, they can also act as barriers to trade. As these regulations are developed by each country independently, differences in procedures can impose considerable costs on exporters. A country may specify scientific tests that are different from those used in the exporting country. Testing facilities may not be recognized, or the qualifications of those conducting the tests questioned.

The only effective means to remove this source of trade barriers is to establish internationally accepted standards and harmonize regulations over time. This has, as yet, proved to be a slow and tortuous process. Nations are particularly reluctant to give up sovereignty when the health and safety of their populations are involved.

Consumer protection legislation Countries tend to establish consumer protection legislation independently. Exporters can incur large costs when faced with multiple regulations. These regulations can be used strategically to inhibit trade. For example, the spacing of headlights on cars can be part of consumer protection legislation. Metal stamping presses for car bodies are one of the largest cost items in the production of automobiles. If an exporter's domestic market requires headlights to be three feet apart, an importer requiring a three-foot six-inch spacing for headlights simply excludes the exporter's vehicles from its market. Performance standards for electrical equipment or the resolution of television sets provide other examples. International harmonization of standards is the only effective means of reducing these nontariff barriers.

Variable levies Similar to tariffs, variable levies are taxes collected by customs when products are imported. Unlike tariffs, they are not fixed. As the difference between the domestic price and the foreign supply price of a product increases, so does the variable levy. Hence the domestic market of the importer is totally isolated from changes in international prices. Variable levies have been used very effectively by the European Union to exclude imports of agricultural commodities that have volatile prices. Variable levies make planning by both exporters and importers extremely difficult and potentially costly.

Rules of origin Some countries impose rules of origin requirements on products sold in the domestic market. For example, 60 percent of the value of a car sold in the domestic market might have to have originated within the country. This means that no imported cars can be sold. It would, however, allow a foreign firm to set up an assembly plant and import some of the parts for the same car for assembly. By using local labor and some local parts, the 60 percent rule can be met. This has been a strategy followed by a number of developing countries as part of their industrialization strategy.

When economies are booming, the forces of liberalization tend to gain the upper hand. In part, this is because in a growing economy it is far easier for those in industries whose relative efficiency is declining to find employment in alternative sectors. Industries experiencing rapid growth cannot be as choosy about their labor force and are more willing to make the investment in workers' retraining. Booms also mean that governments have more tax revenues available which can be applied to adjustment policies. On the other hand, during economic slumps, protectionists tend to be on the ascendancy. Those who become unemployed will have difficulty finding employment in alternative industries. Governments faced with declining tax revenues and rising social welfare costs are more prone to opt for the 'cheap' option of raising trade barriers. Many of the trade barriers that have existed between developed countries in the second half of the twentieth century arose out of the Great Depression of the 1930s, when desperate governments initiated a host of protectionist measures in vain attempts to isolate domestic jobs from the worldwide economic decline. The result was a retaliatory 'beggar-thy-neighbor' spiral that both deepened and lengthened the Great Depression.[1] One can view the entire period from the end of World War II until the start of the Uruguay Round of trade negotia-

[1]Under a 'beggar-thy-neighbor' spiral, nations typically do not simply match one another's tariff increases, but retaliate with larger tariff increases than were imposed by its trading partners.

tions in 1986 as a long, tortuous process focused on removing the trade barriers enacted largely on manufactured goods in the 1930s. While in the Uruguay Round the focus of trade negotiations shifted to new issues such as trade in services, international protection for intellectual property and rules for foreign investment, there was still considerable effort put into reducing trade barriers first erected almost half a century before.

Managed trade implies rules for international commerce. If imports are going to be limited or prohibited, there must be rules that firms engaged in international commerce can follow. Governments like to have very flexible systems so that they can react to protectionist pressures easily. Businesses engaged in international commerce, which often requires large investments, desire security against capricious–and unanticipated–acts by governments. An American firm that has made a large investment in exploiting export potential wants to be sure that the Canadian government cannot act to curtail imports once that investment is made. It is not much consolation to the US investors that the US government could retaliate against Canadian exports of some unrelated product; their investment is still lost. Of course, Canadian exporters to the United States are seeking the same assurances. To protect the interests of their exporters, governments are forced to enter into discussions with other governments regarding rules for trade: under what circumstances countries can raise tariffs or impose import quotas? how they will be calculated? how often they can be changed? Firms often engage in international commercial relationships in a number of countries. For them, a common set of rules provides an advantage: they do not have to learn, monitor and possibly alter their production practices to comply with, regulations of many countries. As a result, multinational rules for the conduct of trade are sought.

A host of bilateral, regional and international agreements have been negotiated to facilitate managed trade. These agreements represent a compromise between governments' desires to retain freedom of action and businesses' desires for security in their international dealings.

ECONOMIC INTEGRATION

While the benefits from trade provide the incentive for nations to engage in discussions regarding international commerce, to fully capture the benefits from specialization and commercial interactions, states may consider cooperation on a number of economic fronts. This wider process of international economic cooperation is known as 'economic integration'. All formal international agreements limit the actions of the individual nations taking part in the agreement. Each nation must weigh the expected benefits of closer economic ties against the loss of its sovereignty when deciding what degree of international integration to pursue.

Questions of Sovereignty

The nation-state is still the primary actor on the world economic stage. There is no supranational government that can compel countries to engage in activities that they do not wish to engage in. All countries are, for example, free to leave the United Nations. When nation-states join international organizations, and thereby agree to operate by the rules which have been negotiated, they do so voluntarily. Nation-states guard their sovereignty closely. They are ultimately entrusted with their citizens' security as well as their economic and social well-being. Even when certain elements of sovereignty are temporarily ceded to multilateral organizations, the nation-state still represents and promotes domestic national interests. Although states always have the right to withdraw from their international commitments, if they choose to do so, the benefits from cooperation will also be withdrawn. Hence nation-states must consider carefully what constraints they are willing to accept on their freedom of action when they begin to proceed down the road to economic integration.

Degrees of Economic Integration

While broad multilateral organizations exist to foster international trade and cooperation, progress is often slow, given that the sovereignty concerns of well over one hundred nations must be addressed simultaneously. In some cases, progress is virtually impossible given the range of political ideologies, vested interests and cultures involved. As a result, smaller groupings of nations may attempt to negotiate more wide-ranging agreements concerning economic integration. These are often easier to negotiate given a stronger common incentive, based in many cases on geographic factors or a similar perspective. These 'economic' blocs are allowed within the rules of the major multilateral trade organizations.

An economic bloc can be defined as a grouping of countries that mutually grant trade concessions to each other. Trade blocs can be loosely classified into four categories: (1) 'free trade areas'; (2) 'customs unions'; (3) 'common markets'; and (4) 'full economic unions'.

In a free trade area, trade restrictions between member states are eliminated for most or all of the products traded. Each country is allowed to keep its tariffs and other trade restrictions that are applied to countries that are not members. This means that member countries apply different trade barriers to non-members. As a result, a free trade area must put mechanisms in place to prevent importation of commodities into low-tariff countries that are subsequently transshipped duty free to high-tariff countries. For example, in the Canada-US Trade Agreement there are provisions that require a certain proportion of the value of an automobile shipped from Canada to the United States to be added in Canada. Similar provisions apply to US automobile exports to Canada. These rules of origin prevent cars made in Japan from being exported to Canada and then sent to the United States, avoiding US automobile duties.

In a customs union, the members trade freely among themselves; but unlike in a free trade area, a common external tariff regime is agreed upon. This means that in multilateral trade talks, the member countries must negotiate with nonmembers as a single unit and, hence, there needs to be a coordinating institution.

In a common market, in addition to a common external tariff and free trade in goods among members, there is also free movement of capital and labor. Taxes must be coordinated to prevent industries locating in low-tax countries; and health and safety standards, which impose costs on businesses, must be made roughly equivalent so that firms in different member states face a *level playing field* in their commercial environment. Educational and professional qualifications are recognized as equivalent across member countries. Given that differences in interpretation in these areas of the agreement are likely to arise, a central coordinating body will be required to negotiate common standards and arbitrate any disputes.

A full economic union moves a step beyond a common market and requires the total harmonization of macroeconomic fiscal and monetary policy. Government spending and taxation decisions are made in common and the operations of the member countries' central banks must be coordinated. A single currency may be adopted but is not necessary; fixed exchange rates among currencies will suffice. Government contracts must be open to bids from firms in any member country.

Clearly these are somewhat arbitrary divisions and existing arrangements for economic integration often straddle these divisions. The importance of these divisions may also decrease over time as trade barriers worldwide are removed or reduced through progress made in the multilateral trade organizations. In some cases, trade arrangements among sovereign states may have fewer trade restrictions than those observed between the political subdivisions of nations. For example, professional qualifications are equally recognized throughout the European Union. Hence lawyers or school teachers certified in any country can work in any other country–a condition that does not apply across the individual states in the United States or the provinces of Canada. Hence economic integration may move beyond that which exists in political federations. The fundamental difference, however, is that states in the United States, for example, cannot secede from the union. In the European Union, each state retains the sovereign right to withdraw from the organization at any time.

The central coordinating bodies of trade blocs can become quite formal and take on many characteristics of a 'supranational government'. In the European Union there is a parliament, an executive branch and a European Court. These institutions represent a system that can accommodate the needs of both the major economies such as

Germany, Britain, France and Italy, and those of smaller nations such as Denmark, Belgium and Finland. With a number of relatively equal large member countries, a centralized organization provides a reasonable structure.

In NAFTA, particularly if it is extended to other countries, there will be one dominant economy–the United States. A central body in which the smaller states could gang up on the United States probably represents an unacceptable level of sovereignty reduction for the United States. As a result, the 'hub-and-spoke model' for economic integration in the Western Hemisphere has been favored in the United States. Each member of NAFTA makes an individual treaty with the United States (and each other) so that the United States becomes the hub of a large number of agreements with individual states. Whether this model will continue to be acceptable to other NAFTA members if the bloc expands remains to be seen.

Regional Economic Integration in Theory

Trade blocs, because they are a subgroup of states, will always have benefits as well as costs associated with their formation. There will be benefits gained from 'trade creation' among the members of the bloc as well as losses associated with 'trade diversion' as international commercial transactions with firms in countries outside the bloc are replaced by transactions with firms in countries within the bloc. Trade diversion generally implies a loss to the importing country because the cost of the good now imported from a member of the trade bloc is higher than the cost of the good from outside the trade bloc. However, the individual importer finds the cost from the trade bloc country to be lower than the cost from outside plus the tariff on products from outside the trade bloc. Thus, the individual importer gains but the gain is smaller than the loss of tariff revenue to the government. If the benefits outweigh the costs, then countries should join the regional trade bloc. The factors that determine the relative size of the benefits and costs are: (1) the degree of overlap (production of similar products) in the economies contemplating the formation of an economic bloc; (2) the magnitude of the cost differences among common industries; and

(3) the level of import tariffs between potential member countries prior to the formation of the bloc.

The greater the overlap between the economies, the greater the likelihood that the bloc will be trade-creating in terms of both inter-industry trade and intra-industry trade. This is clearly the case with the United States and Canada. If there are large cost differences between industries in two countries, then the potential for trade creation is large. The Mexican clothing industry has a considerable cost advantage over that in the United States, while the US corn industry has a cost advantage relative to the Mexican industry.

When high tariffs are removed as a result of the formation of an economic bloc, growth in trade will ensue. While much of Canada-US trade was tariff-free prior to NAFTA, those sectors that were protected generally had high levels of protection. In particular, Canadian manufacturing received considerable protection. There were high Mexican tariffs on many Canadian and US goods as a result of Mexico's previous import-substitution development strategy.

While the sovereignty of individual countries will be somewhat reduced, it is also true that collective economic power is increased. As a result, small or medium-sized states may find it beneficial to join or form economic blocs. The combined power of the bloc may enable the member countries to achieve objectives, say, in trade negotiations that would have been impossible had they attempted to achieve them individually. Conversely, the power of a large member of the bloc may be reduced if it must now pay heed to the objectives of the smaller members of the group.

Trade blocs also have a dynamic element. If trade blocs are successful, other nations will want to join. If more nations are accepted, other states in the region will fear they will suffer as they are excluded from the bloc's markets. Worried they will be left out of the bloc and isolated, they have a considerable incentive to join the bloc.

Regional Trade Associations

The process of regional economic integration has probably progressed furthest in Europe. For a long period there were three competing regional economic associations there: the European Union (EU),[2] the European Free Trade Area (EFTA) and the Council for Mutual Economic Assistance (CMEA). The CMEA was the trade grouping comprising most of the communist states in Eastern Europe dominated by the old Soviet Union. With the fall of communism, CMEA ceased to exist.

In Western Europe there has been a long process whereby the more successful EU attracted members from EFTA. As a result, EFTA is no longer an important trade association. The EU has expanded steadily from its original six members–France, Germany, Italy, The Netherlands, Belgium and Luxembourg–to include the United Kingdom, Ireland, Denmark, Greece, Spain, Portugal, Sweden, Finland and Austria. In Western Europe, now only Norway and Switzerland remain outside the EU. Countries in Eastern Europe, particularly the Czech Republic, Slovakia, Hungary, Poland and Slovenia are eager to join.

The EU has been very successful in moving along the road toward full economic integration, with the removal of trade barriers, the virtually free movement of capital and labor and the harmonization of many regulations. In its trade relations, the EU acts as a single nation and has become a powerful voice in global economic affairs.

While regional economic associations exist in Africa and Asia, little real progress toward economic integration has as yet taken place. Countries in these areas still follow independent economic policies. In the Western Hemisphere, there seems to be more positive movement toward economic integration. In addition to the NAFTA, in South America there are MERCOSUR–which includes Argentina, Brazil, Paraguay and Uruguay–and the Andean Common Market (ANCOM)–Bolivia, Columbia, Ecuador, Peru and Venezuela. A Central American Common Market (CACM) has also been established, along with the Caribbean Community and Common Market (CARICOM). These various regional trade associations may provide the embryo of a trade bloc for the Western Hemisphere.

---

[2]Formerly the European Community (EC) and, in yet another previous incarnation, the European Economic Community (EEC).

THE MULTILATERAL INSTITUTIONS OF THE INTERNATIONAL ECONOMY

NAFTA and other regional trade associations operate within the rules agreed to at the multilateral forums that provide the institutional structure for international commercial relations and economic coordination. These institutions arose out of the strong belief in trade liberalization that emerged at the end of World War II, especially in the advanced industrial countries of Europe and North America.

Bretton Woods

There were two major factors that policy makers in many developed nations felt were responsible for the disruptions to international commerce that occurred in the 1930s. These were an absence of any international controls over the erection of trade barriers by countries, and the strategic use of currency devaluations. Negotiations after World War II led to the establishment of the General Agreement on Tariffs and Trade (GATT) in 1948 to provide a set of mutually-agreed-upon rules for the former. Prior to this, in 1944, an agreement was reached among the finance ministers of forty-five nations to establish new international monetary institutions to address the latter problem. The United States and the United Kingdom took the lead in devising the Bretton Woods system, which had as its core institution the International Monetary Fund (IMF).

The International Monetary Fund

The Bretton Woods system was a fixed (pegged) exchange rate regime. While devaluations were still possible, they could not be used as part of strategic macroeconomic policy. Devaluations, when used strategically, can artificially increase exports and discourage imports. They were, for example, used by countries attempting to deal with the 'beggar thy neighbor' tariffs of the early 1930s. The IMF managed a pool of gold and currencies which could be allocated to countries faced with devaluation. The Bretton Woods system of pegged exchange rates could not be sustained, and in 1973 the exchange rates of the major industrial nations began floating. The IMF still has, however, an important role of coordinating broad exchange rate policies.

BACKGROUNDER: THE QUESTION OF EXCHANGE RATES

While the world of international finance and exchange rates is exceedingly complex, acceptance of one idea is the key to understanding the factors that affect exchange rates–a nation's money is no different from any other commodity; its exchange price (rate) is determined by supply and demand. If international transactions are to take place, the currencies of countries must be exchanged. Coffee cannot be purchased with Canadian dollars in Brazil, nor can Mexican pesos be used to buy steel in Sweden. These exchanges take place in international money markets located in cities like London, Zurich, New York and Tokyo, which act as clearinghouses for those wishing to acquire foreign currencies.

There are three sources of supply for a nation's currency in international money markets: (1) domestic firms that wish to buy imports–they supply domestic currency to exchange for the currency of the country from which they wish to buy; (2) investors with funds in the country who wish to invest abroad–they supply domestic currency to exchange for the currency of the country where they wish to make their investment; (3) the government–it supplies domestic currency to acquire a foreign country's currency as part of its foreign reserves.

There are three sources of demand for a nation's currency in international money markets: (1) foreign firms that wish to import products produced in the country–they buy the country's currency (by exchanging their domestic currency) in order to facilitate their purchases; (2) investors with funds in foreign countries who wish to invest in the country–they buy the country's currency in order to be able to undertake their investments; (3) the domestic government that wishes to buy back its domestic currency in the international market–it can only do this by using its foreign exchange reserves.

As with any other commodity, an increase in the supply of a currency in the international market will decrease its price. That is, it takes more Canadian dollars to acquire a specified quantity of Mexican pesos; hence the exchange value of the Canadian dollar has gone down. If there is an increase in demand for a country's currency, the price will rise; it will take fewer Canadian dollars to buy the same quantity of Mexican pesos.

One option countries have is to simply allow the international money market for its currency to operate according to the forces of supply and demand. This is known as a floating or flexible exchange rate policy. Floating exchange rates are, however, unpopular with most domestic firms and investors. Floating exchange rates make it difficult for importers and exporters. As most international transactions are complex, involving payments over varying time periods, changes in exchange rates alter the profitability of an international transaction. For example, let us assume a Mexican businessman contracts to buy goods worth 1,000 Canadian dollars when the peso exchanges at 3 new pesos to the Canadian dollar; the expected cost of the imports is 3,000 new pesos. If, when the time comes to pay for the goods, the exchange rate of the new peso to the Canadian dollar has changed to 5 new pesos per Canadian dollar, the price of the imports has increased to 5,000 pesos.

Investors do not like flexible exchange rates because their return on investment can be adversely affected by changes in the exchange rate. Assume a Canadian firm invested a million Canadian dollars in Mexican government bonds when the rate of exchange was 3 new pesos to the dollar. It acquires bonds worth 3 million pesos. If the exchange rate changes to 5 pesos to the dollar after the bonds are purchased, when the Canadian firm wishes to sell its bonds and bring its investment home, 3 million pesos will only buy 600,000 Canadian dollars. The Canadian firm has lost 400,000 Canadian dollars on the investment. Allowing exchange rates to float can inhibit both trade in commodities and foreign investment because of the risks it creates.

An alternative is for governments to put in place a fixed exchange rate policy where it guarantees the rate at which its currency can be exchanged for foreign currencies. Hence the exchange rate risk is removed for investors and those wishing to engage in foreign trade. The government has two ways to ensure that the exchange rate remains at the established level. First, it can use its foreign exchange reserves to buy back domestic currency when there is excess supply at the fixed exchange rate. It can also sell domestic currency in the international money market (acquiring additional foreign reserves when there is excess demand at the official exchange rate). Second, the government can raise interest rates so that investments in their bonds and other securities look more attractive. This will increase the demand for its currency when it is in excess supply, thereby keeping the exchange rate at its announced level. Lowering interest rates has the opposite effect.

While firms and investors like fixed exchange rates, governments may be less enthusiastic. Keeping the rate fixed by selling foreign reserves will only work so long as there are reserves to sell. If there is consistent excess supply, reserves will eventually run out, forcing a 'devaluation'–a formal, government-announced change in the rate. Devaluations tend to shake the confidence of both investors and domestic firms. Using the interest rate to keep the exchange rate at its fixed level may also work against other macroeconomic objectives. Raising interest rates may choke off domestic investment, slowing the economy. High interest rates on government debt will make the management of budget deficits more difficult.

As there are a number of supply and demand factors affecting the exchange rate, it may be possible to run, for example, trade deficits over a long period. An unfavorable balance of trade means that imports exceed exports at the fixed exchange rate. If trade in goods were the only factor affecting the supply and demand for a currency, then supply would exceed demand and the exchange rate would have to change. However, if there was sufficient foreign investment (an increase in demand) at the fixed exchange rate to offset the excess imports, there would be no need for a change in exchange rates. Similarly, as long as the government is willing to sell foreign reserves to increase demand for its currency sufficient to offset the surplus generated by the unfavorable balance of trade, there is no need for a devaluation.

All of these ideas can be used to explain the Mexican devaluation crisis of December 1994. The Mexican government had been following a variant of a fixed exchange rate regime for a number of years; for our purpose it is sufficient to think of it as fixed at approximately 3 new pesos to the US dollar. With the peso fixed, Mexico was exhibiting strong economic growth; inflation was low and exports were growing very strongly (22 percent annually). As a result, Mexico was receiving a great deal of foreign investment, increasing demand for the peso. This strong demand for the peso allowed an unfavorable balance of trade to be maintained (–US$23 billion in 1993 and –US$29 billion in 1994). In the United States, interest rates began to rise, making investments in the United States look more attractive. The Mexican government did not wish to follow the United States in raising its interest rates, fearful that economic growth would be inhibited. As foreign investment demand for pesos declined, the government stepped in, buying pesos with foreign reserves. The growing unfavorable balance of trade in goods, however, meant that Mexico's foreign reserves were depleted from US$24.5 billion at the end of 1993 to US$17 billion in October 1994 and to US$6.5 billion in mid December 1994. To prevent the total depletion of its reserves,

Mexico attempted a small devaluation on December 20, 1994. This precipitated a crisis. Investors, fearful of further devaluations, began to move their money out of Mexico in huge amounts. This put a very large supply of pesos on the international market. With no reserves and an investor panic meaning that they would not respond to increased interest rates, two days later the Mexican government had to let the peso float. The peso immediately fell to approximately 5 new pesos per US dollar and it continued to fall.

The value at which a country's currency is exchanged for foreign currencies is often a source of national pride and closely scrutinized by the international commercial community as a barometer of the country's economic performance. Hence, many governments attempt to regulate their exchange rates. Governments may not wish the exchange value of their currency to fall, for example, and interfere in the currency market to keep the exchange rate above that which market forces would produce. If this practice continues over a long period, it is known as having an 'overvalued' currency. This means that more imports can be purchased and exports appear expensive to foreigners. More imports will be desired than there is demand for exports. In international exchange markets, hence, there will be more demand for foreign currency by importers than can be supplied by exporters wishing to buy currency. The government must either limit access to foreign currency by importers or encourage sufficient foreign investment to increase the supply of foreign currency to make up the shortfall. In the former case, a method of determining who gains access to foreign exchange must be put in place. These allocation measures distort domestic markets. For example, the government may decide that machinery but no foreign luxury cars can be imported. To encourage the inflow of investment, interest rates on securities will have to be increased to make them attractive to foreign investors. High interest rates, however, may inhibit economic growth.

An 'undervalued' currency makes exports look cheap to foreigners– they can exchange a relatively small amount of their currency for a relatively large amount of the currency of the country whose currency is undervalued. Imports, on the other hand, are expensive. This may inhibit economic growth if key sectors of the economy are dependent on imports. The government must either encourage its nationals to invest abroad–thereby supplying more domestic currency into exchange markets to keep its value down or it must sell its domestic currency and build up reserves of foreign currency. While there may be good reasons to hold some reserves of foreign exchange, large and ever growing holdings of foreign exchange is not desirable. While it is true that the foreign currency can be used to buy foreign goods and services at any time, holding foreign currency means that real goods and services have been exported to the country which issued the foreign currency. In simplistic terms, real goods have been exchanged for money which has no value unless it can be spent.

In general, policies which keep a country's currency overvalued or undervalued create situations which are either unsustainable over the long run or require policies which impose distortions on other markets thereby causing widespread inefficiencies throughout the economy. For example, the attempt by the Mexican government to keep the exchange value of the peso overvalued required large inflows of foreign capital. To sustain those inflows would have required Mexico to raise interest rates which would have slowed economic growth–a distortion which the Mexican government could not accept. The inflow of foreign capital was not sustainable and the peso crisis of 1994 ensued.

The International Bank for Reconstruction and Development

As part of the new world economic order established after World War II, there was a recognition that international prosperity could be threatened by differences in levels of economic development. Countries suffering from high levels of unemployment, low levels of investment and impoverishment tended to be politically unstable and governments perceiving themselves in desperate situations often adopted disruptive economic policies.

To aid in overcoming these problems, the International Bank for Reconstruction and Development (IBRD)–or, as it is more commonly known, the World Bank–was established. Initially the World Bank's chief concern was with the reconstruction of Europe in the wake of the devastation of World War II.

Once Europe recovered, the World Bank transferred its focus to the problems of developing countries. Recently it has been heavily involved in aiding the transition from command economies to market economies in Central and Eastern Europe and the former Soviet Union.

The World Bank finances a wide variety of projects in developing countries and the former command economies. Its financing is mainly in the form of loans and, hence, does not represent transfers of aid funds. The World Bank applies commercial criteria to its loans and is often criticized for this limitation in its development activities. Nevertheless, the World Bank is still the major multilateral policy instrument for fostering international development.

The World Trade Organization

An attempt was made to negotiate a comprehensive International Trade Organization (ITO) as part of the new international order after World War II. The ITO, along with the IMF and the World Bank, was expected to be a major pillar of the international economic system. The ITO was never ratified by the US Congress. Agreement could not be reached except on the limited subset of trade matters that had been negotiated in the General Agreement on Tariffs and Trade (GATT). As a result, GATT, by default, became the principal multilateral organization regulating trade. GATT's original mandate, however, was limited to trade in goods. While it had considerable success in removing barriers to trade in goods, nations became interested in regulating other aspects of international commerce–in particular, trade in services and the international protection of intellectual property. As GATT's structure was not designed for this wider role, in 1993 an agreement was reached to establish the World Trade Organization (WTO). Members of GATT automatically became members of the WTO.

The WTO is guided by a regularly scheduled conference of ministers from all WTO members. The day-to-day administration of the WTO is the responsibility of the General Council. The General Council settles trade disputes between members and reviews, on a regular basis, their trade policies. The WTO oversees three organizations: GATT and two new organizations negotiated at the same time as the WTO–the

General Agreement on Trade in Services (GATS) and the Agreement on Trade-Related Aspects of Intellectual Property Rights (TRIPS).

GATT, now administered by the Goods Council of the WTO, remains the primary international organization establishing the rules for trade in goods. High tariffs had been erected in the beggar-thy-neighbor period of the 1930s and these were still in place at the end of World War II. Reducing these tariffs was the primary role envisioned for GATT. Hence tariff reduction combined with 'tariffication' are the major liberalizing mechanisms of GATT. Tariffication is a process whereby alternative trade-restricting practices such as import quotas are converted to tariffs giving an equivalent degree of protection. When trade restrictions are in the form of tariffs they can be directly compared, which facilitates the negotiation process. A major GATT principle is that once a tariff is lowered by a country it becomes 'bound'–cannot be raised–at the new level.

'Nondiscrimination' is another major GATT principle. This means that tariff concessions given to any GATT member must be extended to all GATT members. This prevents countries from being able to single out, for increased trade barriers, a particular trading partner whose comparative advantage is improving.

'Transparency' is a third GATT principle. This means that there can be no secret trade arrangements between countries. This helps strengthen the nondiscrimination principle. Any trade action taken by a country must be brought before the WTO, where other nations have the right to express any concerns they may have.

The fourth principle of GATT is 'accepted retaliation'. To protect their sovereignty, it has been agreed that individual countries can ignore GATT's trade rules in ways that could injure other countries. There is a recognition that politicians may have to acquiesce to domestic protectionist pressures in certain circumstances; hence these actions must be accommodated in GATT. It is also agreed, however, that injured countries have the right to retaliate up to an amount of equivalent value without fear of second-round retaliation. Hence, beggar-thy-neighbor retaliations are prevented.

Regional trade agreements are also allowed in GATT. Regional trade agreements must abide by GATT principles but are free to exceed the degree of trade liberalization that has been accomplished at GATT. Hence NAFTA and the European Union, for example, have gone beyond GATT protocols on a wide range of trade issues.

Members of the new General Agreement on Trade in Services (GATS) have made a commitment to improve the transparency of regulations concerning services. Countries have agreed to open the services market to varying degrees. Future negotiations will take place regarding reductions to restrictions in the cross-border movement of individuals providing services, the harmonization of professional standards and the control of trade-distorting subsidies in service industries.

The central theme of (TRIPS) is that countries agree to enforce the property rights of other countries' firms and citizens. This commitment extends to patents, trademarks, films, sound recordings, computer software, integrated computer circuits, trade secrets and test data.

BACKGROUNDER: INTELLECTUAL PROPERTY RIGHTS AND TRADE

Strictly speaking, the issue of protecting the property rights of foreign individuals or companies and the rules of international trade are topics that are only tangentially related at best. They are, however, both part of the broader issue of rules for international commercial relations. It is true in some cases that counterfeit or pirated goods–where no payment has been made for the use of intellectual property–become imported competitors in the markets where the intellectual property was developed. In these cases, however, domestic intellectual property laws are sufficient to exclude imports of counterfeit goods. The question then arises as to why intellectual property rights were included in the recent Uruguay Round of trade talks and why TRIPS was included under the umbrella of the new WTO.

The international protection of intellectual property rights has become a major concern of developed countries over the last few decades. Most of the new intellectual property in the world is produced in developed countries. There are a large number of reasons for this: higher levels of education; large amounts of government resources put into research infrastructure, including universities; populations with sufficient incomes to create large markets for new products; and the strong enforcement of property rights. Much of the new intellectual property developed requires large amounts of risky investment. Without the ability to capture the rents that accrue from the sale of products embodying new intellectual property, the investments will not be made. In the case of films, recording artists, and so on, large investments in production and marketing have to be made. Firms invest a great deal in their reputations, often visually represented by their trademark.

While the protection of intellectual property rights is strong in developed countries, in many developing countries such protection is weak, partially due to the limited abilities of developing countries' governments and partially by design. Some developing countries have argued that, because most of the development of intellectual property takes place in rich countries, they will never be able to close the development gap. Other countries have argued that in the case of pharmaceuticals and agricultural technology, for example, their citizens are too poor to pay high prices for essential drugs or farm inputs. For other governments, the effort to enforce the property rights of foreigners did not seem justified given other activities they could undertake which would lead to higher domestic benefits. The net result was that the returns for those who develop new technology were reduced relative to their true potential. Poor protection of intellectual property in developing countries has, however, been a fact of life for a very long time. The question is, Why has it become a major issue in the last quarter of the twentieth century?

There are two reasons for the current prominence of intellectual property issues. The first relates to the revolution in electronic technology which ushered in the computer era. In previous eras, the intellectual property component of goods was small relative to the total price when manufacturing processes were complex. This meant that counterfeiting provided few rewards given the small intellectual property value. Manufacturing processes were often too complex to be undertaken in poorly developed economies. One result of the revolution in electronic technology, however, is that manufacturing these new products is relatively simple and can take place almost anywhere in the world. Low-cost labor provides competitive advantage. At the same time, the cost of developing new computer chips, computer programs, and so on, represents a very high proportion of the value of output. Once developed, computer chips or programs can be copied easily, meaning that the rewards for counterfeiting are very large when protection of intellectual property is lax. As a result, large-scale pirating began to take place in developing countries.

The second problem that brought the issue of international property rights protection to the fore was the general slowdown in economic growth in most developed countries. Investment in new technology is fundamental to economic growth. The corporations involved in research and development argued that their investment efforts were reduced as a result of the inability to capture the full benefits from the development of new technology. Only by extending intellectual property rights internationally could this problem be corrected.

The governments of developed countries, however, had no means by which they could influence developing countries. No effective international rules for intellectual property rights enforcement was in place, and no mechanism to exert economic pressure on nations refusing to enact and/or enforce intellectual property rights existed. To gain leverage over developing countries, developed countries decided to make intellectual property rights protection part of the Uruguay Round of GATT negotiations. By tying intellectual property rights to the threat of trade retaliation, the developed countries gained a lever which could be used to influence the behavior of developing countries. Having GATT and TRIPS linked directly in the WTO will allow the withdrawal of trade concessions to be used as a weapon against those nations who do not live up to their TRIPS commitments regarding the enforcement of foreigners' intellectual property rights.

The United Nations Conference on Trade and Development

GATT was often seen as a 'rich nations' club' by developing countries, many of whom were still colonies when it was originally negotiated. It was felt that GATT was not responsive to the needs and concerns of developing countries. In response to this frustration, the United Nations Conference on Trade and Development (UNCTAD) was established in the early 1960s. It deals exclusively with issues concerning trade relations between developing and developed countries. Its scope is very wide, dealing with many aspects of trade that are outside the GATT mandate. The mandate of UNCTAD is to attempt to enhance nations' development prospects by improving their trade opportunities. While UNCTAD's mandate is broad, it has not been endowed with any real power and, hence, remains primarily a forum for the presentation of ideas and concerns as well as the exchange of information on trade problems. It attempts to reform trade through the use of persuasive arguments based on the ideas of obligation and responsibility.

The major policy-making forum of UNCTAD is conferences convened every four years, commonly referred to by their chronological order, such as UNCTAD VI. The major concerns of UNCTAD have been attempts to raise and/or stabilize the prices of developing countries' primary exports, to improve market access in developed countries for developing countries' manufacturers, to enhance technology transfer, and to facilitate the solution of developing countries' debt problems.

Hemispheric Multilateral Organizations

In addition to truly international organizations, there are also multilateral organizations which span the Western Hemisphere. These organizations attempt to capitalize on recognized commonalities of interests within the region. This has not always been easy as various nations have tended to perceive that there was more to be gained from focusing their attention on other political and economic ties. Further, many of the states in Latin America as well as Canada were wary of US hegemony in any hemisphere-based organization. Canada, in particular, was focused on ties with Europe and its North American Treaty Organization (NATO) obligations for most of the period after World War II. Argentina, Brazil and some other South American countries felt closer ties with Europe than with their northern neighbors. After the Castro revolution, Cuba was increasingly drawn into closer relations with the Soviet Union and other Eastern European countries. In recent years, the attention of the United States and Canada has shifted toward the Asian-Pacific Rim in response to the trade opportunities presented by the rapid rates of economic growth in that region. Still, hemisphere-wide organizations have had an important role to play.

The major multilateral organization in the region is the Organization of American States (OAS), founded in Bogota, Columbia, in 1948. Its mission is to foster peace, security, mutual understanding and cooperation among the nations of the Western Hemisphere. The OAS has never lived up to its potential largely because it could not rise above Cold War politics. The organization's credibility with many Latin American states was damaged due to the perception that it was an instrument of the United States in the East-West conflict (Muñhoz, 1994). The ending of the Cold War has revitalized the OAS to some extent, and it may have an increasingly important role in the control of drug trafficking and protection of the hemisphere's environment.

The Inter-American Development Bank (IDB) was founded in 1959 and is the hemisphere's rough equivalent of the World Bank. The IDB provides financing for economic and social development projects as well as technical assistance. Projects may be cooperative efforts among nations or they may be confined to an individual country. The most important UN organization in the hemisphere is the Economic Commission for Latin America and the Caribbean (ECLAC). Founded in 1948, it promotes coordination of economic development in the Latin American region in conjunction with other UN organizations.

Thus, there are a number of multilateral and hemispheric organizations that operate in conjunction with subhemispheric trade organizations such as NAFTA.

CAN AN ECONOMIC BLOC TAKE SHAPE IN THE WESTERN HEMISPHERE?

The success of NAFTA in bringing together three large and diverse economies has put in motion two forces. The first force is momentum. If NAFTA appears to be 'a winner', then other nations will want to join to capture the economic benefits of 'trade creation' that are available. Second, there is the fear of being left out. Nations who do not join may see their trading opportunities drying up as other states join NAFTA and reorient their economic focus (that is, they may be hurt by 'trade diversion'). Each nation must weigh the benefits from joining against the reduction in sovereignty that will inevitably ensue. Other states in the hemisphere are watching NAFTA closely.

The likelihood of a successful expansion of NAFTA is higher now than it would have been in the past. With the obvious failure of 'import substitution' as a means of providing sustained economic growth, most nations in Latin America have embraced an open trading policy as part of their development strategies. The real question is whether the founding members of NAFTA, particularly the United States, wish for a further expansion. More countries will mean more complex coordination and more consultation. This will inevitably mean pressure to create new institutions. These regional institutions will begin to limit the freedom of action of national governments–to reduce economic sovereignty. Whether an acceptable compromise can be found remains the major question mark in the future expansion of NAFTA.

SUMMARY

Currently, trade liberalization is in ascendance. Protectionism is largely discounted as a policy associated with the 'national good'. This does not mean that vested interests cannot mobilize considerable political support in aid of their individual industry, but the protection granted is now largely identified with the particular vested interest it serves.

There is a general consensus among the developed countries that the long process of trade liberalization that followed World War II was a major contributor to the long period of sustained growth through the 1950s, 1960s and 1970s. If sustained growth is to return, then many of the remaining trade barriers must be removed. This means removing barriers in areas of commercial relations not traditionally dealt with in international trade–services, investment, protection of intellectual property and macroeconomic coordination. These new aspects of liberalization suggest that a greater degree of economic integration among nations may be required than in the past. While progress is being made in multilateral negotiations, it is slow. Nations seeking to garner the gains available from economic integration have been increasingly seeking regional economic associations with smaller, more tractable groups of countries.

3. The Global Economy after World War II

In the last chapter we briefly examined theories of international trade and economic integration, as well as the various multilateral institutions that have managed the global economy throughout the post-World War II period. In this chapter we explore the evolution of the main features of the global economy over that period, especially as it relates to North American integration. The main objective is to show the relationship between important international events and the development of international multilateral institutions and economic theory in the entire post-World War II period, on the one hand, and the emergence of NAFTA in the 1990s, on the other. We believe that an understanding of this link is necessary in order to understand: (1) the forces that have shaped current economic integration efforts in North America, and (2) the nature of the current controversies that divide proponents and opponents of the integration process. We also give special attention to events and trends in Latin America, the most likely region to become associated with NAFTA in the near future. History is important because it has conditioned current economic policies and institutions as well as our thinking regarding what can or should be done now and in the future.

Some of the ideas discussed in this chapter have been touched on already in the preceding chapters. However, they reappear here in a different context, as part of the evolution of the global economy and the intellectual thought that attempts to explain that evolution. In order to facilitate this discussion we invite the reader to follow the time line illustrated in Table 3.1, as we believe it will help to organize and synthesize the concepts more effectively.[1]

THE LEGACY OF THE PAST

Economic historians of the twenty-first century will probably look back on the 1980s as a crucial (watershed) decade in the history of modern economics and in the history of economic thought because the internationalist Keynesian paradigm was (partially) supplanted by a neoconservative one stressing the limitations of government policies and the strengths of freer markets. In fact, not since the 1930s, the decade of the Great Depression, were there such far-reaching changes in economic life and the way we view it, especially in Mexico where the state had been a major actor in the economy for several decades.

Prior to the 1930s, most economists viewed the 'free market' as an efficient and equitable mechanism for guiding capitalist economies in their quest for growth and development. Consequently, governments were usually viewed as 'necessary evils', and most businessmen believed that 'the best government is that which governs least', as Adam Smith had said–except, perhaps, when their own interests could be advanced by government policies.

In this framework, which we now call the 'conservative' or 'classic liberal' view, national governments are regarded for the most part as passive caretakers of an active market system, which is expected to adjust automatically to changing conditions through the actions of the 'invisible hand' of market forces. Of course, in practice governments historically played important roles in most market economies by providing economic infrastructure (for example, highways, port facilities and other 'public goods') and laying out the 'rules of the game' through regulatory agencies (for example, anti-trust laws and public utility regulations). Nevertheless, the proper role of government in conservative economic theory is very limited.

---

[1] *World Development Report 1991: The Challenge of Development* (World Bank, 1991) presents an interesting view of the global economy and economic development over the last century.

Table 3.1 Time Line: 1930 to Present

Events	Institutions	Economic Perspectives
1930s		
Great Depression (1929–41)		
International economic	Bank for International	Demise of neoclassical
collapse	Settlements (BIS)	macroeconomics
Gold standard		Keynesian theory
abandoned		emerges
1940s and 1950s		
WWII (1939–45)		Acceptance for a
Reconstruction after WWII	Marshall and	greater role by
US major economic and	Dodge Plans	government
political power	Bretton Woods	Economic planning
	IMF and GATT	
Korean War (1951–53)	UN and IDB	Emergence in Latin
Cold war begins	European Coal and	America of
Expansion of US MNCs	Steel Community	Structuralism
Europe and Japan rebuild	EEC	Theories (ISI)
1960s and 1970s		
Vietnam War (1963–1975)	OECD	Development economics
Petrodollar stagflation	OPEC	Countercyclical fiscal
Decline in US	Alliance for Progress	monetary policy
competitiveness	North/South Dialogue	Fine tuning
		Welfare state
1980s and 1990s		
Global recession (1981–82)	Baker Plan (1985)	Supply-side economics
Third World debt	Brady Plan	Neo-conservative
crisis (1982)	CUSTRA (1989)	stabilization policies
'Lost Decade' for Latin	Enterprise of	in Latin America
America	the Americas	Growing critiques of
Economic reconstruction	begins (1990s)	Keynesian economics
in Latin America	EU (1992)	and structuralism
Soviet reforms	End of Uruguay Round	industrialization
Reforms in Eastern	NAFTA (1994)	Export-oriented
Europe	Economic Summit of	(EOI) and neo-
End of Cold War	the Americas (1994)	structuralism
Steps toward trade	Global Conference on	*Perestroiska*
liberalization	Economic Growth	*Glasnost*
Economic reconstruction	and the	Growth of
continues in Latin	Environment (1992)	international
American	Global Conference on	monetarism
	Population (1994)	

All of that dramatically changed, however, with the Great Depression of the 1930s. The Depression brought falling living standards, rising unemployment and increased political instability in most countries of the world. It also stimulated higher tariffs as countries, especially the US, attempted to protect their domestic industries from foreign competition. These protectionist policies, however, were met with retaliation in the form of higher tariffs in other countries. As a result of these 'beggar-thy-neighbor' trade wars, international trade fell dramatically which in turn aggravated the depression. Largely as a response to that crisis, and due mainly to the concepts pioneered by the most influential economist of modern times–the English economist, John Maynard Keynes (1883–1946)–national governments gradually began to assume a more active role in the management of their economies. This new, expanded role for governments that began during the 1930s came about simply because there was no other entity in the economy that could or would, according to Keynes, provide the analysis, resources and actions necessary to revive the severely depressed economies of both the advanced, industrialized and the poor, raw material-producing economies of the capitalist world.

Thus in the short period of a decade, from the mid 1930s to the mid 1940s, governments became major actors in guiding the economic development of most capitalist, market-oriented countries. Although the degree of government management varied greatly from country to country there was a general tendency for governments to: increase their regulation of businesses; to assume responsibility for stabilizing the 'boom and bust' fluctuations of the business cycle; to implement some sort of social welfare system; and in some countries to implement planning systems for promoting national economic growth and development. The expansion of the governmental role in the economy, according to this new 'modern liberal' (Keynesian) view, would reduce the risks and uncertainties inherent in a continually changing market economy, and provide for a more efficient and equitable use of scarce resources so as to maximize long-term growth and development.

THE 1940s

War and Reconstruction

World War II (1939–45) conveniently gave a demonstration of Keynes's contention that large amounts of government spending could lift an economy out of depression and into prosperity. In the United States, for example, in 1940 before its entry into the war, labor unemployment was still approximately 15 percent, down somewhat from the 25 percent level at the height of the Depression in 1933. However, by 1944, after three years of large government expenditures and budget deficits to finance the war effort, unemployment stood at a mere 1.2 percent. During the same three-year period, total production (GNP) almost doubled, demonstrating that a country could, by increasing budget deficits, at least for a limited time, spend itself into prosperity. This provided a powerful argument for increasing the participation of the federal government in economic affairs.

In addition, it is important to note that the increased demand for all types of goods and services during World War II spread beyond the economies of the Allied countries. For example, it stimulated some Latin American countries' export markets, including those of Mexico, which in turn stimulated the growth of their domestic industrialization processes. The war also limited exports from the United States and Europe and thereby provided domestic manufacturing firms in Latin America with an opportunity to expand and develop without having to compete with the lower priced imports that frequently had appeared to thwart their industrialization attempts in the past.

Immediately after World War II the war-torn countries of Asia and Europe began the process of rebuilding their economies. They were assisted by the United States through the now famous Marshall Plan in Europe (and the lesser known Dodge Plan in Japan) which were designed to provide loans and grants to the advanced western economies to strengthen them economically and militarily against the perceived threat of Soviet expansion and domination.

The reconstruction process was carried out very quickly, and within a decade or so the economies of Japan and Western Europe emerged with new factories and equipment which frequently were more efficient than those of their principal competitor and benefactor, the United States.

By the 1950s, buoyed by the successful reconstruction of Europe and Japan, economists throughout the capitalist world turned their attention to the poor, 'underdeveloped' economies of Africa, Asia and Latin America. What these countries needed, they concluded, was capital accumulation which could, in part, be provided by aid from developed countries and foreign investment via multinational (transnational) corporations (MNCs or TNCs) operating in more than one country. Such financial and technical assistance from the advanced industrial countries would be accompanied by a vast transformation of the economic and cultural values and institutions of these 'backward' countries. In short, the traditional economies of the 'underdeveloped' world should be restructured, replacing traditional ways with market-oriented, capitalist institutions.

About this same time representatives from many developing countries in Africa, Asia and Latin America began to meet in a variety of contexts to discuss their common economic and political problems and interests as ex-colonial, relatively backward, raw material-producing countries. After much deliberation one popular view that emerged was that their own interests and their relative position in the global economy were generally different from those of the industrial, developed countries. Out of these meetings came the term 'Third World' to describe these emerging nations whose history, economies and social structures were significantly different from those of the advanced, industrial, capitalist countries–the First World–and from the industrializing countries of the socialist bloc–the Second World.

PREBISCH-ECLA THESIS

The economist who provided the first and most widely accepted view of the economic condition of the Third World generally, and Latin America specifically, was the Argentine Raùl Prebisch (1901–86). Prebisch, who began his career as an economist in Argentina's banking sector, became interested in the uniqueness of economic conditions in the 'underdeveloped' economies of Latin America. His works were widely published during the 1940s, and in 1948 he became the first Secretary General of the United Nations Economic Commission for Latin America (ECLA). Later he held the same position with the United Nations Conference on Trade and Development (UNCTAD), founded in 1963.

His main argument, now usually referred to as the Prebisch-ECLA thesis, was that the traditional 'international division of labor'–based on trade between developed, industrial 'center' countries and underdeveloped, raw material-producing 'periphery' countries–tends to result in an 'unequal exchange' that, according to Prebisch, historically favoured the center countries at the expense of the periphery countries (refer to the time line of the global economy in Table 3.1). Extensive studies carried out by Prebisch and others showed that not only do commodity prices suffer wide fluctuations, but over time Latin America had to sell (export) more and more primary products (for example, coffee or copper) in order to buy (import) the same quantity of manufactured products from its more industrialized trading partners in the center. In economic terms this represents a 'deterioration' of the periphery's terms of trade–prices of exports (mainly primary products) in comparison with prices of imports (mainly manufactured products)–with the center. While this point has been debated interminably throughout the last four decades, Prebisch's position still seems to have validity: 'whether we look at the last 40, 120, or 150 years, a deterioration of primary product prices in relation to prices of manufactures is beyond doubt' (Avramovic, 1994, p. 109.)

The implication here is that the international trading system has, since colonial times, contributed to the 'underdevelopment' of Latin America and other periphery regions while subsidizing the 'development' of its major trading partners, the industrialized center countries.

In order to correct this systemic deficiency, Prebisch and others suggested that periphery countries abandon the market-oriented development strategy based on traditional primary product exports–the 'primary export model' (PEM)–and adopt independent development strategies based on the creation of a domestic manufacturing base.

Such strategies came to be known as import-substitution industrialization (ISI)–industrialization by domestically producing consumer goods that previously had been imported from First World economies. Such inward-directed strategies, Prebisch argued, would require both increased government support and protection of domestic industry in order to keep cheaper foreign goods from displacing domestically produced goods. Such protection, it was believed, would give emerging domestic industries some time to achieve the same level of efficiency as industries in the First World. Meanwhile, it would be necessary to carry out certain 'structural' changes both within Latin America (for example, agrarian reforms and regional economic integration) and internationally (for example, commodity cartels to prop up commodity prices as well as economic and technical aid) in order to enable periphery economies to compete in the global economy.

Prebisch's views eventually provided the basis for what is often called the 'ECLA school of economic thought', which had an enormous effect on economists in Latin America throughout the post-World War II era. His theories, although hotly contested by many economists, especially those in the center countries, also contributed to the development of the 'structuralism' and 'dependency' theories that subsequently enjoyed considerable popularity in Latin America and other periphery areas. An excellent survey of traditional structuralism (that prevailed from the 1940s until the early 1980s) in comparison with the contemporary 'neostructuralism' (which has emerged in the 1990s) can be found in Sunkel (1993). For an overview of dependency views, see Chilcote and Edelstein (1986). Both of these theories, in varying degrees, supported the protection of national industries, at least in their 'infant' stages.[2]

The new theories of Keynes and Prebisch led to policies that over the next few decades would transform capitalist economies from market economies to 'mixed economies'. This meant that the market forces of supply and demand were increasingly modified and/or complemented by governmental actions. Governments became committed to active

[2]The idea of temporary protection for 'infant industries' is discussed in Chapter 2.

policies in pursuit of objectives such as full employment, price stability, sustained rates of growth and economic development. Achievement of these objectives, it was assumed, would translate into increased job opportunities and rising living standards for all sectors of the population through appropriate management of the budgetary (fiscal), credit (monetary) and trade and foreign exchange policies of the national government while maintaining the essential aspects of a market economy (that is, market allocation of most goods and services through the price mechanism).

The new policies took on a variety of forms, depending on the particular circumstances of each country. In most Third World countries, in an attempt to utilize scarce resources more effectively, governments became planners, regulators and in many cases producers of those goods and services considered essential to the process of rapid industrialization and modernization.

Meanwhile, in the First World, where resources were more plentiful and living standards higher, there was more emphasis on countercyclical, stabilization policies–monetary and fiscal actions designed to smooth out the wide swings of the business cycle. However, many countries also implemented various types of industrial policies–coordinated actions between private firms and government agencies to increase international competitiveness. Additionally, political pressures applied by liberal politicians and sometimes grassroots movements of workers and the poor spurred the creation and expansion of a modern welfare state–large expenditures on social security, unemployment insurance, basic medical care and so on–that provided a safety net for those people unable to work and/or support themselves. The welfare state was supposed to humanize the capitalist system by reducing the risks and uncertainties inherent in an unrestrained market system and to provide macroeconomic stability to the system itself.

During the same period, the emergence of the Cold War between the East and the West, mainly between the United States and the Soviet Union, stimulated the emergence of what is referred to by some as a 'warfare state'–with high levels of government expenditures made in order to assure a constant state of military preparedness, even during peacetime. The warfare state was supported by a large and politically effective 'military-industrial complex' (military officers and weapons manufacturers) in the United States, the Soviet Union and many other countries of the capitalist and socialist blocs. Unfortunately, large military expenditures diverted resources away from economic and social development and spawned an international arms race that endured until the collapse of the Soviet Union in the 1990s.

The decade of the 1940s also is important at the international level for it was during this period that the major center countries, led by the United States and the United Kingdom, began to construct a new version of the international trade and monetary system which had virtually disintegrated during the Great Depression and World War II. Thus, during the period 1944–48 a group of multilateral economic institutions was created that was designed to provide new 'rules of the game' for international trade and financial transactions in order to facilitate the expansion of the global trading system.

As noted in Chapter 2, these new institutions included the IMF, the IBRD and GATT. All of these agencies are attached to the UN, established at the end of World War II to promote international peace and security. These institutions, along with the Bank for International Settlements (BIS)–'the central bank for central banks', founded in 1930, are still in existence; however, over time their operations have expanded and changed considerably in order to keep up with the needs of the continually evolving global economy. In many ways the evolution of the international trade system has been quite successful. Between 1950 and 1990 the volume of world exports increased ninefold, while the volume of world output increased fivefold. GATT, which now has become part of the WTO and has some 150 members and encompasses some four-fifths of world trade, has played a major role in lowering the average tariffs on manufactured goods among the major capitalist countries from about 50 percent in the 1930s to about 5 percent in the late 1980s. Nevertheless, as we shall see, the international trading system still has many problems.

Because of the dominant position of the United States immediately after World War II, the US dollar became the foundation of the new international monetary system, usually referred to as the Bretton Woods system, which lasted from 1944 to 1971. However, since 1971 the US dollar, and the US economy in general, have lost much of their dominance in the global economy, and the international monetary system has changed considerably. Nevertheless, the United States is still a major actor in the global economic system, and the US dollar is still a key international reserve currency along with the German mark (likely soon to be replaced by the Euro) and the Japanese yen.

THE 1950s AND 1960s

A Long Period of Economic Expansion

During the 1950s and 1960s the economies of many First and Third World countries enjoyed relatively high rates of economic growth, and international trade expanded even faster. For some countries the new policies were associated with a mixed economy, together with the rapidly expanding international trade system, meant rising prosperity and employment opportunities accompanied by increased industrialization. At this time two more important economic institutions came into existence. The Inter-American Development Bank (IDB), with its headquarters in Washington, DC (see Chapter 2) and the Organization for Economic Co-operation and Development (OECD), located in Paris. The OECD was created in 1960 to achieve a greater degree of economic consultation and harmonization between the advanced, market economies of Europe, North America and Asia.

Still, throughout the period many Third World countries continued to stagnate and became even poorer as their rapidly growing populations made it more difficult than ever to translate modest economic growth rates into rising living standards for all. In recent years this group of very low income countries–mainly in Africa and Asia–has come to be known as least developed countries (and unofficially as the Fourth World).

Meanwhile, during the 1950s and 1960s, another much smaller group of Third World countries, utilizing varying degrees of state-directed (government-directed) development strategies, was relatively successful in terms of achieving higher levels of industrialization. The strategy usually followed in Latin America, including Mexico, was that of import-substitution industrialization, based on the model suggested by Raùl Prebisch. During this period, ISI policies produced many benefits by generating new jobs, higher incomes and higher levels of industrialization. There were, however, costs as well. Import substitution industrialization strategies focused mainly on development of the domestic manufacturing industries while neglecting agricultural and export sectors. Moreover, the fruits of progress largely benefited the middle and upper classes and did not reach the poor who, in many cases, saw their plight worsen. The poor suffered from the lack of public expenditures in rural areas as well as the relatively high cost of domestically produced manufactured goods.

While the inward-directed development policies of ISI did bring industrialization to many Latin American countries, they fell short of the objective of reducing their 'dependency' with respect to center countries. In some countries multinational corporations came to dominate the most dynamic sectors of the economy (for example, automobiles and other manufactured goods); and while imports of consumer goods generally decreased, imports of capital and intermediate goods (goods used in the production of other goods) from developed countries increased.[3]

By the late 1960s some Latin American countries began to study the outward-directed policies implemented by Asian countries like Taiwan, Singapore and South Korea, which were following more outward-directed policies of integrating with the international economy by exporting nontraditional products, including labor-intensive manufactured goods. The strategy of export-oriented industrialization–deliberate opening up of the domestic economy to international trade as a means of increasing the efficiency of domestic firms and stimulating production for export as a means to deepening the industrialization process–seemed to produce a more balanced development process and a more equal distribution of income than ISI in Latin America.

[3]For an excellent overview of the impacts of ISI policies in Latin America, see the special issue of *World Development Report: Latin America in the Post Importation Era*, (World Bank, 1977).

During this period, the economies of a group of relatively open, newly industrializing countries (NICs) were transformed by the phenomenon of 'global production sharing'. This phenomenon refers mainly to the labor-intensive assembly operations that have been shifted out of First World countries to Third or Fourth World countries where operations can be carried out with low-skilled, low-waged labor. Most of the assembled components or final products are then exported to be sold in First World markets. This geographical dispersion of manufacturing activities occurred primarily because of two factors: (1) the availability of new, more efficient communications and transportation technology, which dramatically cut shipping and communications time and costs, and (2) the existence of large and growing wage differentials between the rich and poor countries of the world. These factors have allowed MNCs to organize their manufacturing activities to take advantage of significant cost and/or tax differences. Thus, labor-intensive phases of production tend either to be automated or relocated to virtually any part of the world where low labor costs and adequate infrastructure exists, while capital- and knowledge-intensive phases of research and development, manufacture of components, final testing and distribution usually remain in the high-wage core countries where skilled personnel and instrumentation are readily available. The developing countries that participate in this arrangement often create special 'export-processing zones' (EPZs)–designated areas providing special tariff treatment and infrastructure to firms performing labor-intensive assembly operations. They do so in the expectation of generating new jobs, foreign exchange and technology transfer as part of their export-led development strategy. Mexico has become the most important Latin American country pursuing this type of activity, mainly because of its close proximity to the United States. However, the effectiveness of the *maquiladora*, as the EPZ is called there, as a tool of regional and national development has been quite limited. For an overview of this global industry, see Grunwald and Flamm (1985).

BACKGROUNDER: MEXICO'S MAQUILADORA INDUSTRY

Each day offshore export processing zones (EPZ's) become a more integral part of the international economy, playing a larger part in the manufacture and assembly of a growing array of goods and services. Goods displaying labels with 'Made in the USA' or 'Made in Japan' are less common now than ten years ago. These days they are being replaced with 'Made in China', or 'Assembled in Mexico'. These labels indicate more than a geographical shift in the production of some consumer goods. They represent a deliberate thrust towards a new development strategy for a growing number of large and small nations scattered throughout the world.

For the United Sates, the use of 'offshore sourcing' began as a side effect of establishing manufacturing facilities behind tariff walls in Europe, in order to increase sales to the European Union. For Japan, frequently called a nation of *maquiladoras* because of its elaborate subcontracting system, the decision to use offshore EPZ's apparently was a part of a deliberate strategy to gain market share from the United States. Mexico created the *maquiladora* industry as an EPZ because of both the demonstrated success of other EPZ's in the Far East, such as Taiwan and Singapore, and Mexico's need to solve pressing social and economic problems.

The Border Industrialization Program, which gave birth to the industry in the mid 1960s, was designed to reduce unemployment in Mexico's northern border region, generate foreign exchange, provide higher skill levels for workers and stimulate technology transfer to Mexico by attracting foreign manufacturing firms there to establish assembly operations. Since then, and especially as a consequence of the peso devaluations in the 1980s (and again in 1994), the industry has grown rapidly.

The term *maquiladora* comes from the Spanish word *maquila*, which in colonial Mexico was the charge that millers collected for processing grain. Today *maquiladora* stands as a generic term for those firms which 'process' (assemble and/or transform in some way) components imported into Mexico which are then re-exported. Alternatively, it can be said that *maquiladora* is an economic unit for the production of goods or services based on the temporary importation of raw materials and equipment to be transformed in Mexico and subsequently sold abroad.

The term 'in-bond industry' comes from the fact that those components which are imported into Mexico are imported under a bonded status in order to insure that they are not sold in Mexico's markets, but are reexported for sale in foreign markets.

The industry has evolved dramatically since it's beginning in 1965. While it is still located mainly in Mexico's northern border region–almost two thirds of the 4,000 *maquiladora* plants are located in the states next to the US–many of the plants now utilize modern, automated technology and require high skill levels from their one million workers. The ownership of plants has become more diversified, as many large Asian electronic manufacturers established facilities there in order to take advantage of the tariff benefits offered to firms who produce within North America under the provisions of NAFTA (see Chapters 7 and 8).

The success of the *maquila* can best be illustrated by looking at its annual growth rate in recent years–10–20 percent by most indicators–and the fact that it now brings in more foreign exchange for Mexico than any other single sector except for petroleum. The major shortfall of the industry, however, has been its inability to link up with the rest of the nation's economy–only about 2 percent of the industry's inputs are 'sourced' from Mexican suppliers.

Thus the phenomenon of global production sharing, along with the emergence of the NICs, has led to a gradual but continual modification of the international division of labor that traditionally condemned the periphery to being producers/exporters of primary products while the center produced/exported manufactured goods. Today we increasingly find center-based MNCs searching the Third World for stable, low-wage areas where the labor-intensive phases of production can more efficiently (and more profitably) be carried out. As a result, more and more basic manufacturing is being carried out in countries like Brazil, Mexico, Taiwan and Korea, while Japan, the United States and Europe increasingly tend to specialize in high-quality, high-tech manufacturing and service special 'niche' markets throughout the world economy. The export of services, largely based on high investment in human capital, now constitute a large proportion of developed countries' exports. Nevertheless, for most very poor developing countries, the traditional international division of labor continues and their prosperity remains tied to (often) volatile primary product prices.

While there are certain disadvantages inherent in 'outward-directed' strategies, they have in the past proved to be more successful than inward-directed ISI strategies. There is, however, some question as to whether or not such strategies can be duplicated by each and every developing country, given the high degree of saturation of First World markets and increased competition that characterizes the global environment of the 1990s.

Finally, it should be noted here that it was during the 1960s that the United States, spurred by the 1959 socialist revolution in Cuba, undertook a major aid effort in Latin America, the Alliance for Progress. After ten years of pouring billions of dollars into development projects, many economists and statesmen alike concluded that a 'Marshall Plan for Latin America' could neither build developed countries as rapidly nor as successfully as the original Marshall Plan had rebuilt the war-torn countries of Asia and Europe after World War II.

The Unique Role of the United States

Throughout the 1950s and 1960s the US economy expanded at relatively high rates. Aided by increased expenditures on armaments during the Korean War (1950–53), economic growth was interrupted by only two minor recessions in the 1950s and one in the early 1960s. Thereafter the economy expanded continually, fueled by large military expenditures during the Vietnam War (1963–75) and by social expenditures on the domestic 'War on Poverty' (1963–68).

The main problem with the US economy during the last half of the 1960s was a relatively high rate of inflation, and this problem continued to plague both the US and other developed countries over the next decade. Nevertheless, given the fact that the US economy was, and still is, the largest national economy in the world, its growth fueled the rapid economic expansion throughout this period, and it became widely recognized as the 'engine of growth' for the entire global economy. When the US economy expanded its demand for imports, the exports of its major trading partners grew as well. Of course, this also meant that when the US economy contracted, its imports also contracted, negatively affecting the exports of its trading partners. It also meant that inflation in the United States was transferred to the global economy through trade and financial links.

Throughout this period the United States was regarded as the undisputed economic and military leader of the global system. The special position of the US dollar as the 'key international currency' gave US-based MNCs an unusual advantage which stimulated their sometimes not-so-welcome expansion throughout the capitalist world. Thus, after World War II, MNCs from many First World countries, but mainly the United States, replaced national corporations as the major actors in the global economy, accounting for roughly one-third of the total world production of goods and services. Prior to World War II, MNCs operating in developing countries invested mainly in the primary sector–extractive industries such as mining, fishing, forestry and agriculture–but after World War II they moved more heavily into the secondary sector–manufacturing and construction–as well as the tertiary sector–commerce, finance and other services–operating in a variety of organizational forms.

The impacts of MNCs on both sending (that is, First World) and host (largely Third World) countries has been widely debated. On the one hand, it has been argued that they generate jobs and foreign exchange in host countries and provide access to new technology, capital, markets and skills. On the other hand, they also sometimes exert a considerable degree of political pressure on host governments, transfer profits out of host countries and act as independent agents without regard for the economic or social needs of the host country. In the process of looking after their own private business interests, the activities of many MNCs can act as a destabilizing influence on small developing economies. The major difficulty for the sending (center) countries, where most MNCs are based, is the costs associated with labor market adjustments as jobs are moved offshore, while the major benefit is the income that accrues to the sending country from the profits and other fees earned abroad by the MNC.

The growth of US MNCs, together with the emergence of the US military as the Western world's police force and protector of US interests around the globe, gave the United States an inordinate degree of economic and political power and engendered a great deal of both criticism and emulation.

By the mid-1950s, the economies of Asia and Europe that had been decimated during World War II were substantially rebuilt and quickly began to challenge US economic hegemony. Increasingly, Japanese and European products displaced US-made goods throughout the global economy, including in the United States itself. During the 1960s the once large US trade surplus dwindled, to become a trade deficit in the early 1970s, signaling the demise of the United States' 'golden era' as the world's undisputed provider of manufactured goods. In 1945, the United States' share of world production was over 50 percent. However, by 1980 this figure had dropped to about 32 percent. Currently the United States produces approximately 20 to 25 percent of Gross World Product.

While much of this decline was inevitable as other countries grew rapidly and developed, some of it has probably been due to poor management and the fact that in the US so many resources were diverted from productivity enhancing activities to military uses during the Cold War. Now in the post Cold War era relatively fewer resources are utilized in such 'non-productive' sectors. The world has changed, however, and the US, while still powerful, will not regain the strong hegemonic role it played in the world economy during the 1950s and 1960s.

THE 1970s

As was discussed above, in the 1960s several developing countries–most notably Mexico, Brazil, Taiwan, Hong Kong, Singapore and South Korea–began to manufacture and export products such as steel, automobiles, textiles and consumer electronic products that previously had been produced only in First World or Second World countries. Not only did these Newly Industrializing Countries (NICs) achieve high levels of economic growth during this period, but they made serious inroads into markets that previously had been the exclusive domain of the advanced industrial economies of the First World.

The 1970s brought another very significant change in the Third

World: the emergence of the Organization of Petroleum Exporting Countries (OPEC) as an effective cartel for securing monopoly profits for member countries. Dramatic increases in oil prices–first in 1973 and again in 1979–made most oil-exporting countries richer. However, the oil price hikes created serious disruptions in the international economy, especially for oil-importing countries, many of which contracted large external debts to finance their imports while keeping their economies growing. The oil price increases also aggravated existing inflationary pressures and shocked the global economy into two worldwide economic downturns, one in 1974–75 and another in 1981–82. The latter turned out to be the most severe since the Great Depression.

This combination of economic stagnation–low or negative rates of economic growth–combined with relatively high inflation, rising prices, led to a new term to describe the situation: stagflation. After World War II, First World economies had experienced either stagnation or inflation, but not both simultaneously. The 1970s stagflation, therefore, presented a serious challenge to the Keynesian macroeconomic stabilization theory which had guided economic policy makers throughout the global economy since the 1940s. Ultimately the problems surrounding stagflation stimulated economists to reassess Keynesian theory and led to significant criticisms and modifications of the original theory.

Throughout this decade the economic situation of most oil-importing Third and Fourth World countries became increasingly difficult. Not only did their energy costs skyrocket due to the OPEC price increases, but First World demand for their exports of primary products such as food, fibers, forestry products and minerals fell. This resulted in lower prices, lower volume of exports and substantially decreased foreign exchange earnings. Thus their ability to finance the imports necessary for economic development was severely curtailed. There is evidence that the demand for primary products will rise at a slower rate in the future than in the past, and that periphery countries will therefore have to depend on other types of exports to finance their economic development needs. Thus, due primarily to technological developments in the use of new materials, manufacturing processes no longer use the same quantities of resources per unit of output as they did ten, twenty, or thirty years ago. The same thing is happening with respect to labor; new production processes now utilize more computers and more automated processes than they did ten years ago, thereby reducing the demand for labor. If this trend continues, it will have enormous effects on the development of periphery countries. Historically, most Latin American countries relied on the export of primary products to generate foreign exchange. This foreign exchange financed the imports needed for industrialization which, it was assumed, would generate enough jobs to absorb new entrants into the labor force. Now, because of less labor intensive manufacturing technology this strategy for development will probably work even less well than in the past.

The 1970s were also marked by the rise and demise of the so-called North-South Dialogue. As noted above, during the 1950s and 1960s a number of United Nations organizations were established (for example, ECLA and UNCTAD) to systematically examine the special problems of the periphery countries, particularly with respect to their economic relations with the center. Then in the 1960s and 1970s, at the insistence of periphery country governments, a number of important conferences were held under the auspices of the United Nations between the main center and periphery nations. At issue were the many structural deficiencies of the global economic system discussed above with respect to the Prebisch-ECLA thesis.

In this extended 'dialogue' between the North (center) and the South (periphery), the South argued, as had Prebisch, that the global economy systematically favors the North. Subsequently the South formulated and then presented its proposals for a New International Economic Order (NIEO). The thrust of their argument was that the center countries should make special concessions to periphery countries, such as lower tariffs on periphery exports of manufactured goods, and provide higher levels of economic and technical assistance with the objective of accelerating industrialization in the periphery. Out of these deliberations came a few special programs such as the Generalized System of Preferences (GSP) which eliminates or lowers duties on a range of products imported into the advantaged industrial economies, including the United States and Canada. In general, however, the developed countries were occupied with their poor economic performance and the proposals of the Third World bloc were not taken seriously.

THE 1980s

While the countries of the North were reluctant to negotiate with the South as a bloc, nevertheless many discussions did take place during the 1970s. Then, in the early 1980s, falling oil prices and the Third World debt crisis significantly changed the negotiating environment in favor of the North. Suddenly many countries of the South found themselves reluctantly responding to the IMF's conditions for restructuring their debt instead of pushing for the reforms of a global system they considered to be unfair and detrimental to their future development.

Throughout the 1970s many Third World countries had sought to stimulate their stagnating economies and pay for their rising oil bills by borrowing increasingly large amounts of recycled petrodollars–dollars deposited by OPEC countries in US, European and Japanese banks–from commercial banks in the First World. The banks, flush with large deposits of petrodollars, were in a position to satisfy the demands of developing countries for credit. With the 1981–82 recession, triggered mainly by anti-inflationary monetary policies in the United States, many Third World countries found their export markets disappearing and the payments on their external debt rising. The tight monetary policy in the US and most developed countries led to higher interest rates and, consequently, higher debt service costs. Additionally, oil prices reached a peak in 1981 and then began to fall sharply, so that even many oil-exporting countries, including Mexico, found themselves with serious debt service problems. Many of the other Third World countries had by now taken steps to reduce their dependence on imported oil, so they did not benefit from oil price reductions to the same extent that they had been hurt by the oil prices increases of the 1970s.

The combination of large debts, stagnating exports and rising interest rates led to a dramatic decline in the ability of Third World debtor countries to service their debts–make scheduled interest and principal payments–and many countries throughout the Third World found themselves on the verge of international bankruptcy. In 1982 a 'debt crisis' was formally declared. In 1981 Costa Rica declared a moratorium on debt payments, but it was not until the larger countries of the region found themselves in similar positions (Mexico in August and Brazil in November) that the debt crisis was formally recognized. Despite formal recognition, however, there has been no clear definition of the debt problem nor a definitive strategy for resolving it. Early definitions referred to it as a 'liquidity crisis' (a temporary scarcity of foreign exchange), but later definitions focused on 'insolvency' (the inability to amortize the debt).

Widespread default on the debts owed would have threatened the viability of the international financial system which, in turn, would have had a significant disruptive effect on the global economy. Not wanting to risk such drastic consequences, First World governments, large commercial banks (mainly in the United States, Japan and Europe) and the IMF began a long series of negotiations with debtor countries to temporarily resolve the debt payments problems and prop up the commercial banks whose 'exposure', particularly in Latin America, was dangerously high. This was done by restructuring Third World external debt–lengthening the payback period, reducing fees and sometimes the interest rates charged, and extending more loans–so that they could pay the debt service due (interest plus principal).

Meanwhile many First World economies, following the leadership of Margaret Thatcher's Britain, began to carry out extensive market-oriented reforms, ranging from tax cuts and deregulation of key industry sectors to financial liberalization and privatization of state-owned industries, based on the main principles of supply-side economics–cutting both taxes and the role of government in the economy in order to stimulate economic growth. In the US this bundle of policies was associated with the administration of President Ronald Reagan and was dubbed 'Reaganomics'. This switch back to *laissez-faire* economic policies was also embraced by the IMF and the World Bank, which used the Third World debt crisis as an opportunity to impose market-oriented reforms on many developing economies which had relied for decades on 'statist' economic policies based on a high level of government involvement in and regulation of economic activity at both the macro and micro levels.

IMF assistance in 'bailing out' distressed, debt-ridden countries was therefore conditional on those countries' acceptance of the IMF's 'austerity policies'. At first, these policies routinely required governments to cut government expenditures and devalue their exchange rate. Such policies, argued the IMF, would cut inflation, increase exports and decrease imports, thereby increasing earnings of foreign exchange and, in turn, improve countries' ability to service their (external) debts and attract the new investment needed to stimulate long-term economic growth.

Rapid restructuring combined with tight budgetary discipline, however, can impose significant adjustment costs on countries while tight monetary and fiscal policies can lead to recessions. Additionally, devaluations can put upward pressure on prices by making imports more expensive. Thus, such programs–in the short run, at least–frequently led to lower living standards, increased unemployment, continued inflation and, in turn, political instability as the poor and middle classes protest their deteriorating circumstances.

Meanwhile, with the emergence of the debt crisis in 1982, First World commercial bank loans to periphery countries virtually disappeared. Official development assistance from First World governments also fell as they transferred resources previously devoted to international assistance to domestic priorities. So, while loans from multilateral lending agencies like the IMF, World Bank and the Inter-American Development Bank increased somewhat–although they were not sufficient to make up the decrease in other categories–they became virtually the only available source of long-term funding, increasing the leverage of those agencies. After a few years the IMF and the creditor countries recognized not only that political instability was increasing throughout the Third World but also that First World exports were falling, resulting in fewer jobs and lower incomes in center countries. Therefore, after some deliberation, the United States came up with a new plan in 1985: the Baker Plan, named after former US Treasury Secretary

James Baker III. New loans and assistance, combined with continued debt restructuring, were to be provided by the commercial banks and the US government, together with the IMF and the World Bank. Again, such assistance was conditional on implementing a set of policies which would allow the market to work more effectively without the burdens of excessive government control.

Specifically, this meant that debtor countries would have to carry out short-term 'stabilization policies' and market-oriented, 'structural reforms'–long-term changes in economic policy including reducing government subsidies and bureaucratic regulations, overhauling the tax system and selling state enterprises to private entities, as well as opening up their economies to increased foreign trade and investment by abolishing import quotas and permits and lowering tariffs and barriers to foreign investment. It was argued that, over the long term, such reforms would stimulate economic growth and the size of their debt in relation to the size of their economies would become smaller. Debtor nations would be able eventually to pay off their debts, which by the mid-1980s totaled about US$1 trillion for the entire Third World and US$400 billion for Latin America, one-fourth of which was owed by Mexico alone.

While most debtor countries endeavored to comply with the conditions set out above, they also criticized the major theme of the Baker Plan: that new, restructured loan packages, together with internal reforms in the debtor countries, would allow their economies to grow at the same time they serviced their debts. In fact, the debtor countries repeatedly asserted that paying off their external debts was inconsistent with achieving long-run economic growth and development.

Periphery countries also complained that while center countries, especially the United States, urged them to restructure their economies along free market lines in order to increase the efficiency of resource use and exports, barriers to trade in center countries, which had been reduced in the 1950s and 1960s, were once again increasing. Concern was also expressed about the potential negative effects on global trade of the formation of regional trading blocs like the Canada-US Free Trade Agreement in 1989 and the commitment of the Europeans to form a 'single market' by 1992.

By 1989 it was clear that the new loans promised under the Baker Plan would not be forthcoming; commercial banks, for example, were still reluctant to 'throw good money after bad'. So a new plan was put forth, the Brady Plan, named after another US treasury secretary, Nicholas Brady. This plan provided that the IMF and the World Bank would back debt reduction agreements (with funding and repayment guarantees), again assuming that debtor countries implement market-oriented reforms. Several countries–the first was Mexico–subsequently obtained some debt relief (that is, lower debt service payments), but total external debt still increased. In Mexico, for example, total external debt rose from approximately US$94 billion in 1989 to US$119 billion in 1993.

Thus, from one perspective, for most Latin American countries the decade of the 1980s was a 'lost decade'. Living standards for most Latin Americans fell significantly. Meanwhile, political instability rose in many of the newly democratized nations of Central and South America as governments attempted simultaneously to service their external debts, restructure their national economies and adjust to rapidly changing international conditions. In the post-World War II period many Latin American countries experienced military dicatorships (e.g. Paraguary, Brazil, Peru, Uruguay, Chile and Argentina) and civil wars that became associated with military regimes (such as Bolivia, Cuba, Nicaragua, El Salvador and Guatemala). Since the beginning of the 1990s most of these have returned, at least nominally, to democratic systems. Latin America's debt crisis was never really resolved. While the overall health of First World commercial banks and the international monetary system has improved and debt service burdens have been reduced since 1982, the size of the external debt has increased and theoretically must still be repaid, someday. Nonetheless, from another perspective the 1980s was a decade of dramatic change in the thinking of economists and policy makers–a 'silent revolution' of market-oriented reforms that has continued into the 1990s (Inter-American Development Bank, 1992).

Meanwhile, in North America and Europe a different kind of 'crisis' emerged: how to deal with the competitive challenge emanating from Japan and the Asian NICs and the negative effects of globalization itself (that is, the adjustment costs associated with export of manufacturing jobs to low-wage countries and the emergence of domestic manufacturing capabilities in the NICs).[4]

The response to the competitiveness crisis in the United States was twofold. First, President Reagan (1980–88) introduced a series of measures–'supply-side' tax cuts and deregulation of business, on the one hand, and large increases in military spending, on the other–in order to increase efficiency, jobs and economic growth and restore US military superiority. It is difficult to assess objectively the success of these policies; conservatives claim that the increased military spending was responsible for the ending of the Cold War, while liberals claim that Reagonomics was responsible for quadrupling the US national debt in one decade while neglecting US international competitiveness. Nevertheless, during this period the United States became a net debtor country. Second, the United States renewed efforts to lower protectionist measures throughout the world by expanding GATT's coverage to agricultural products, services and intellectual property rights protection–the latter a new area of competitive advantage for the United States–and by negotiating a free trade agreement with Canada, its main trading partner. In Europe the response focused on renewed efforts to create an economic union, coupled with infrastructure modernization.

Before proceeding to the 1990s we must note the enormous changes in the political-economic landscape of Eastern Europe in the final years of the 1980s. The policies of *perestroika* (economic restructuring) and *glasnost* (democratization) introduced by the Gorbachev regime in the Soviet Union during the late 1980s brought profound changes in it and

[4]The concept of the 'product life cycle' is helpful in understanding this situation. As discussed in Chapter 2, this theory maintains that certain countries (those with advanced R&D capabilities) tend to specialize in the development of new products, while others specialize in the production of old (mature) products. Thus each product moves through a life cycle from new to old while the geographical location of production also changes. In practice this has meant that new products are usually developed and initially produced in the center countries; as they mature they move offshore to be produced in the low-wage periphery.

the other central and eastern European countries. The infamous 'wall' between East and West Germany was dismantled, and a process of transition from state-planned to market-oriented economies was initiated in most former Soviet bloc countries. This process imposed high social costs, mainly on the poor and middle classes who had the fewest resources available.

BACKGROUNDER: THE MANY DIMENSIONS OF GLOBALIZATION

Before exploring the many dimensions of globalization it might be helpful to clarify what is usually meant by the term. Globalization in the sense we will be using it here refers to 'the widening and deepening of international flows of trade, finance and information in a single, integrated global market' (United Nations Development Programme 1997, p. 82). The time period in which this market has developed is generally taken to be the post-World War II period; however, its roots go back much further and there is evidence that elementary forms of globalization were present in the earlier centuries.

It is generally acknowledged that the General Agreement on Trade and Tariffs (GATT), created in 1948, has performed a catalytic but not a casual role in the liberalizing international trade. GATT was designed to liberalize national and global markets for goods in the belief that free markets would increase efficiency and in turn increase economic growth and human welfare (see Chapter 2). Nevertheless, the principles of free trade have been applied more to goods and capital than unskilled labor with the result that the increased flows of goods and certain types of services is usually praised while the massive movements of 'illegal aliens' is condemned.

Some of the most impressive aspects of the globalization process are dramatically illustrated by the following:

1. Huge declines in transport and communication costs have reduced natural barriers to trade.

- Between 1920 and 1990 maritime transport costs fell by more than two-thirds.
- Between 1960 and 1990 operating costs per mile for the world's airlines fell by 60 percent.
- Between 1940 and 1970 the cost of an international telephone call fell by more than 80 percent and between 1970 and 1990 by 90 percent.

- In the 1980s telecommunication traffic was expanding by 20 percent per year.

2. Artificial barriers have been eased with the reduction in trade barriers (tariffs, quotas and so on) and exchange controls.

- In 1947 the average tariff on manufactured imports was 47 percent; by 1980 it was only 6 percent per year and with full implementation of the Uruguay Round, it should fall to 3 percent.
- Other artificial barriers were removed with the resolution of political conflicts that have divided the world for decades, such as the Cold War and the apartheid system in South Africa.

3. Spurred by the fall of barriers, global trade grew twelve-fold in the postwar period. It is expected to grow 6 percent for the next 10 years. The expansion of capital flows has been even more dramatic.

- Flows of foreign direct investment in 1995 reached US$315 billion, nearly a sixfold increase over the level for 1981–85.

While there are many other dimensions to globalization (for example, the development of a global culture) the main point that should be emphasized here is that technological and institutional changes have made it possible for firms to do business (that is, export, import, invest, speculate) quickly and cheaply anywhere in the world where adequate infrastructure exists. This globalization in turn is dramatically changing virtually every other aspect of economic life.

THE 1990s

At the global level the most significant event of the early 1990s was the end of the Cold War which had started in the mid 1940s. The cost to both the Soviet bloc and the western economies in terms of the resources used to maintain their respective 'warfare states' had been enormous. With the disintegration of the Soviet Union and the demise of the Warsaw Pact (for military cooperation) and the socialist trading bloc (CEMA, Council for Mutual Economic Assistance) came new possibilities to use the freed up resources for peaceful uses. Nonetheless, the optimism that marked the first few months following the ousting of communist parties from power soon evaporated when it was realized that democratizing and rebuilding the former communist countries' economies along market lines would be costly, painful and frequently violent. Additionally, the transition to capitalism in Central and Eastern Europe and the former Soviet Union–and to some extent in China and India, which are now undergoing market-oriented reforms–implies that over the next few decades another two billion people will be incorporated into the global market system as consumers and low-cost producers.

The 1990s also brought a new fascination with regional trading groups and international trade liberalization. In Latin America the 'Enterprise of the Americas' proposal to create a hemispheric free trade zone, announced by US President George Bush in June 1990, focused attention on regional integration. The overall process of market-oriented reform that began in the 1980s with macroeconomic stabilization and structural adjustment programs now began to focus on opening up national economies through regional trading groups in order to force domestic efficiency, reduce inflation and foster international competitiveness.

As noted previously, in North America negotiations began in 1990 to create the three-country NAFTA, building on the Canada-US Free Trade Agreement. By 1993 the agreement was negotiated, and implementation began in January 1994.

In Latin America, the three main regional trading groups (the Central American Common Market, the Andean Common Market and the Southern Cone Common Market) also made significant progress toward increased integration, and at the Summit of the Americas in Miami, Florida, in 1994 an agenda was established to create a hemispheric free trade area by 2005.

Meanwhile, in Europe considerable progress was made toward political and economic unification with the negotiation and ratification by fifteen countries of the Treaty on European Union. In Asia a less formal regional trade bloc had been suggested. However, the dramatic deterioration of many Asian economies in the late 1990s has interrupted this process.

Finally, as noted in the previous chapter, progress toward global trade liberalization occurred with the completion of the Uruguay Round of GATT negotiations in 1993, just before the Summit of the Americas meetings in Miami. The new agreement broadened coverage from manufactured goods to agricultural goods and services, protected trademarks and patents (that is, 'intellectual property') and created a new World Trade Organization (WTO) with more power to enforce the new 'rules of the game' for international trade.

Even though 'free trade', a major theme of the 1990s in the Western Hemisphere, still stimulates heated controversies, an enormous amount of activity is being expended in virtually every country (except the United States) to expand trade relations through new agreements.

Nevertheless, there are still some formidable obstacles to expanding NAFTA. Despite significant economic growth in recent years, most Latin American countries are still in the early stages of the reform process. Most still have significant trade barriers and their macroeconomic stability is still far from ensured. Since the early 1990s, however, many Latin American countries have received considerable attention from the international financial community as 'emerging markets', and private capital has begun to flow back into the region as stock markets have boomed and MNCs have attempted to position themselves for taking advantage of the region's growing and increasingly open markets.

Nevertheless, the December 1994 peso crisis in Mexico and the 1997–98 problems in Asia and Russia have dampened growth prospects throughout the world and have dramatically affected regional economic integration prospects in North America and Europe and have increased resistance to new trade agreements in the United States.

CONCLUSIONS

During the time period covered in this chapter, from the 1930s to the late-1990s, the global economy and our way of thinking about it have changed in several ways.

First, technological developments in communications, transportation and information systems have made globalization of economic activity a reality. Consequently, manufacturing has become more dispersed geographically, and more countries have undergone a degree of industrialization. Developed countries are now more specialized in high technology manufacturing and service industries. The international division of labor has been significantly modified with a resulting change in the comparative advantage of both advanced industrial and newly industrializing countries. Protectionism has diminished considerably during this period and most countries are more 'open' now than at the beginning of the period. The global system is somewhat more 'managed' than it was at the outset of the period, due to the actions of a handful of multilateral economic institutions, including the WTO and the IMF.

Second, the role of government in the economy has changed considerably, twice within the time period examined here. Prior to the 1930s the best government was considered one that governed least. After the Great Depression, the theories of Keynes and Prebisch challenged that premise, and industrial and developing economies entered a period of active government participation in economic affairs. This changed once again with stagflation, the Third World debt crisis and the emergence of supply-side economics in the 1980s. Despite the many social and economic problems that now characterize virtually all countries of the world, there are strong ideological biases against using government to alleviate them and fewer resources readily available to the government for this purpose, even when the political will is present.

Another important change is the relative waning of US hegemony in global affairs. The United States, which emerged from World War II as the dominant power in the global economic system, has experienced serious challenges–from both Japan and the newly constituted European Union–to its competitive position in global markets and to its leadership in international economic institutions. In the post-Cold War era it is not yet clear how the world order will function–economically, militarily and politically.

Finally, the general deterioration of the environment has emerged as an issue to be reckoned with if global living standards are to be improved or even maintained. In this context, the 'good news' is that the level of awareness and discussion of environmental issues and the role of population growth as a contributing factor are rising as evidenced by the global conferences in the early 1990s. The 'bad news' is that environmental destruction still occurs every day and may be getting worse. In this context local, national and global systems must be fashioned to regulate the often wanton misuse of the earth's resources. (World Bank, 1992)

It is in this context that NAFTA has emerged. The world is a very different one than existed in the immediate post-World War II period. Some of the countries that were struggling simply to survive then have emerged as economic powerhouses. Firms in the US must now compete with those in Japan and the EU in the high quality, high technology segments of global markets while firms in the NICs are now capable of producing a wide range of low-cost consumer goods and in some cases intermediate and producer goods.

Increasingly, the nationality of firms and their products has become irrelevant as North American firms enter into strategic alliances with Asian and European companies and international trade increasingly becomes 'intra-firm', with components and final goods moving between different divisions of the same multinational firm. Additionally, firms have become increasingly mobile as they relocate production plants from one place on the globe to another in order to cut costs or better serve a new, emerging market.

Traditional economic analysis suggests that these changes–the reduction of tariff barriers, the increased mobility of capital and increased reliance on free markets–will serve to increase the efficiency of the world economy and, hence, to stimulate economic growth and improve living standards. However, the changes are not costless. In many cases the casualties of such moves are displaced workers and sometimes the demise of their communities. In other cases, it is the environment that suffers, underscoring the need to develop new public policies to effectively minimize these social and economic costs.

As new technology increasingly makes globalization possible, economic borders become less relevant. Individual countries have responded by increasing their integration with others, thereby creating regional trade blocs. The management of international economic relationships is currently conducted by a melange of overlapping trade blocs struggling to find some sort of overriding order under the auspices of the WTO.

PART II

Introduction

In this section we will look at the economic background of the three NAFTA countries, focusing on some of the key factors explaining their development (or lack of it) as well as their trade relations with the rest of the world. Each of the three countries has developed in its own way, struggling with its unique endowment of geographic, climatic, demographic, social and political characteristics which, in turn, led to different development and international trade policies.

One factor that was common to all the countries was a colonial experience; however, that experience was certainly different for each. The United States began as a colony of Great Britain in the early 1600s and was, in the 1770s, the first to break its colonial ties. Mexico was colonized by Spain in the early 1500s. It did not break its ties until the early 1800s. Europeans have fished off Canada's east coast since the early 1500s–possibily even earlier, but more permanent settlements did not come until the French settled in the early 1600s. British settlers did not come until even later. The Peace of Paris in 1763 resulted in Canada becoming a British colony. Canada was the last to gain its independence.

While it clearly goes too far to say that Mexico's colonial experience was 'bad' and those of the United States and Canada 'good', it is certainly true that Spain's administration of Mexico, with its focus on gold and silver extraction, left Mexico with fewer possibilities for economic development than did Britain's looser administration of its North American colonies. Many other factors, however, contributed to the differences between the three countries' current level of development. Since this is not a text on economic development, it is sufficient to say that theories of economic development center on a wide variety of factors, ranging from religion, culture and entrepreneurship to capital investment, education and institutional development.

In the next few pages we will present a series of figures to describe the current economic differences between the three countries and some of the factors which underline these differences. Most of the indicators used are fairly standard (for example, GDP per capita) and may not need explanation; however, others (for example, openness) may be somewhat less familiar. We have provided a brief description for each indicator and then interpreted what the differences mean within the context of this book.

The three chapters following this graphical introduction provide an overview of the development experience of each of the three NAFTA partners within the context of the global economy generally, and more specially within the context of NAFTA. As we have already seen in earlier chapters, NAFTA has from the very beginning been strongly debated in each country. As the agreement is fully implemented over the next decade or so, we can expect both the intensity and nature of the debates to change, depending on the performance (and its perception) of each country's economy, the rulings on trade disputes by the various trilateral institutions and what is happening with other international institutions such as the WTO and other trade blocs such as the EU. Nevertheless, a basic understanding of each country's economy and related politics is necessary to understand the dynamics of NAFTA over the long term.

GROSS DOMESTIC PRODUCT PER CAPITA

Gross domestic product, or GDP, is defined as the market value of all final goods and services produced in a nation over the course of a year. When GDP is divided by population, it is GDP per capita. This is one of the simplest indicators of living standards that is available. Of course, no single number can capture all the subtleties of a nation's quality of life. For example, GDP and GDP per capita ignore a number of important issues such as the distribution of income, the condition of the environment, the degree of congestion and the state of personal safety, to name just a few.

Figure II.1 Real GDP Per Capita at Market Exchange Rates, 1997

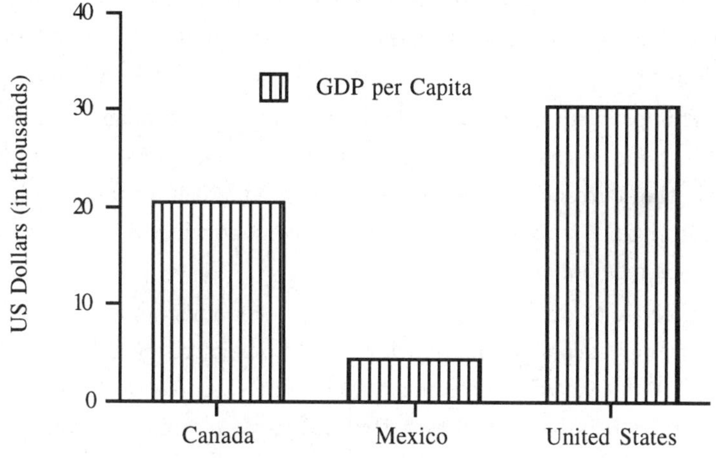

Source: International Monetary Fund (1998), *International Financial Statistics*, August.

Nevertheless, if the total value of the nation's output were to be evenly divided among all its inhabitants, then they would each have an amount equal to GDP per capita. Figure II.1 compares the level of this indicator for the three NAFTA nations. In order to make this comparison, Canadian dollars and Mexican pesos are converted to US dollars. As described in the next indicator, this is a source of bias when international comparisons are made.

PURCHASING POWER PARITY GDP

International comparisons of living standards such as those in the previous graph encounter the problem of radically different prices for similar goods. For example, if the US dollar is chosen as the standard for comparing Canadian, Mexican and US incomes, then Canadian and Mexican GDP are converted into dollars. This is what the previous graph did. This may not always give an accurate impression of living standards, however, because prices are usually vary between countries. For example, Mexico has a surplus of labor and consequently personal services such as haircuts, housecleaning, and cooking are relatively cheaper than they are in the United States or Canada. Consequently the peso equivalent of a dollar goes farther in Mexico than a dollar will in the United States.

This problem is compounded by the fact that sudden shifts in the value of one currency will dramatically alter the number of units it buys of another currency. For example, if the peso falls in value, it looks like Mexican GDP is falling by the same percentage when we convert it out of pesos into dollars.

In order to overcome these problems, economists have constructed an artificial exchange rate which converts one currency into another at a constant level of purchasing power. For example, 1,000 pesos will convert into dollars at a rate that keeps their ability to buy goods and services constant, whether in Mexico in pesos, or in the US in dollars. These artificial exchange rates are called purchasing power parity exchange rates.

The comparisons of real GDP per capita in Figure II.2 is based on purchasing power parity (PPP) conversions of Canadian dollars and Mexican pesos into US dollars. Note the difference between this and the previous graph. In terms of market exchange rates, average incomes in Canada were about 68 percent of the US level and in Mexico they were abut 14 percent. In terms of the purchasing power of Canadian and Mexican income this is an understatement, however. In the purchasing power parity graph, Canadian incomes are about 78 percent of the US level and Mexican ones are around 24 percent.

Which graph is more accurate, the first one or this one? The answer depends on the purpose to which the numbers will be applied. If we want to know something about the ability of countries to buy foreign goods, then we should use an income estimate that is converted at market exchange rates since that tells us their ability to buy goods in another currency. If, however, we want to know something about the ability of citizens to buy goods domestically, then purchasing power parity rates are better because they tell us about the ability to buy goods in one's own currency. Therefore economists generally regard

Figure II.2 GDP Per Capita at Market vs PPP Exchange Rates, 1996

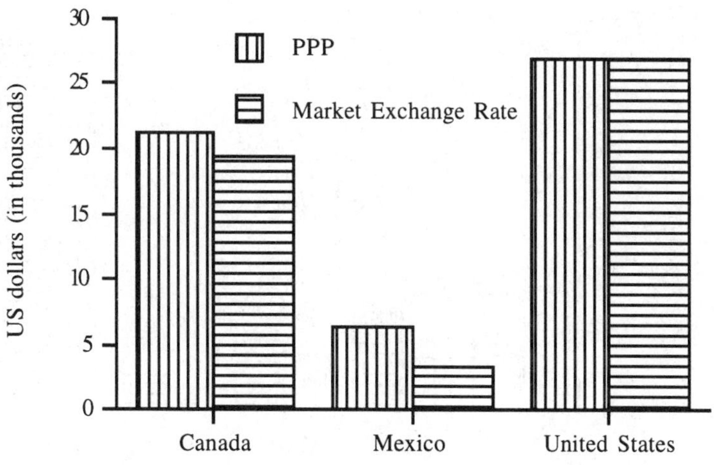

Source: World Bank (1997b).

purchasing power parity exchange rates as a better measure of economic welfare.

TRADING PARTNERS: CANADA, MEXICO AND THE UNITED STATES

The Canada-United States trade relationship is the single largest bilateral trading relationship between any two countries in the world. Exports and imports of merchandise trade totaled well over US$300 billion in 1997 (see Figure II.3).

Both Canada and Mexico are dependent on their trade with the United States to a much greater extent than the US depends on them. Canada sent about 83 percent of its merchandise exports to the United States in 1997. Mexico sent about 85 percent of its exports to the US. The US is also by far the greatest source of both countries' imports. About 68 percent of Canada's imports come from the US and 75 percent of Mexico's (see Figures II.4 and II.5).

Figure II.3 US Trading Partners (Merchandise), 1997

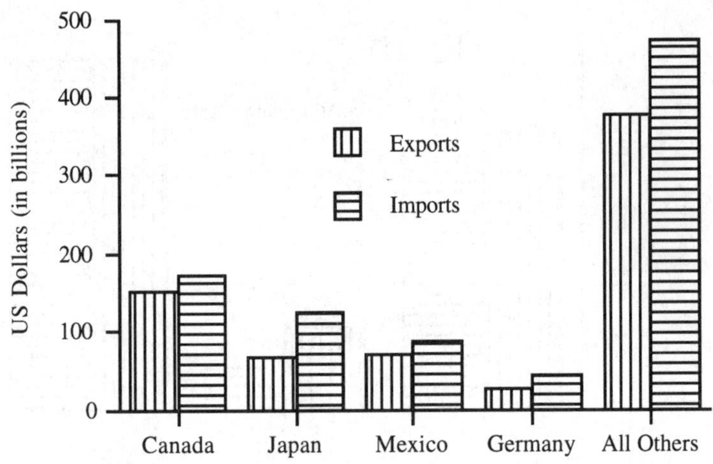

Source: International Monetary Fund (1998), *Direction of Trade Statistics*, June.

While US trade is less concentrated with Canada and/or Mexico, both nations are important to overall US trade. Canada is the single largest consumer of US exports (22 percent) and the most important supplier of US imports (19 percent).

The pattern of trade indicates that the large US market is a hub for North American trade which radiates both north and south, into Canada and Mexico. Although Canadian-Mexican trade is relatively undeveloped, trade with the US is so large and so important that NAFTA can be viewed as an extension of a naturally occurring North American trading pattern that has been developing over the last several decades. Consequently, NAFTA is not likely to divert very much trade from third parties but, rather, is more likely to extend trade relations in the same direction they would go with or without the agreement.

OPENNESS

Openness is defined by trade economists as exports plus imports divided by GDP: (Exports + Imports)/GDP. Openness does not measure the

Figure II.4 Canadian Trading Partners (Merchandise), 1997

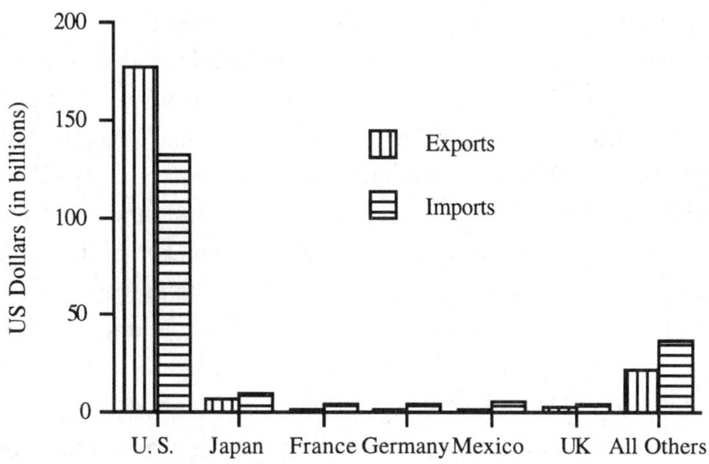

Source: International Monetary Fund (1998), *Direction of Trade Statistics*, June.

Figure II.5 Mexican Trading Partners (Merchandise), 1997

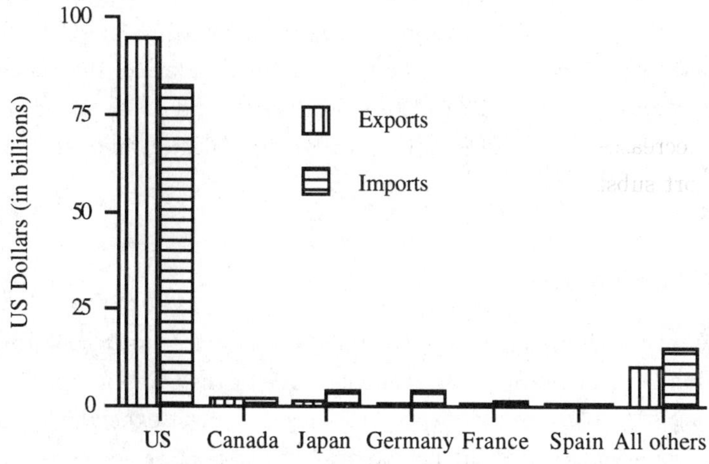

Source: International Monetary Fund (1998), *Direction of Trade Statistics*, June.

trade policies or rules of trade, but rather it conveys a sense of how important trade is to a national economy. The larger the number, the greater its importance.

As can be seen from Figure II.6, Canada is by far the most open economy of the three NAFTA countries, although trade is of increasing importance to Mexico's economy. The patterns exhibited by the openness indicators are not coincidental given that Canada has the smallest population, the US the largest and Mexico's is intermediate. Canada's smaller population leads it to depend more on international trade because by focusing its production on a fewer number of items, it can capture the scale economies that come to firms as they grow larger. If Canada tried to produce more goods for its own consumption, it would have to produce on a smaller scale and, in some industries, would lose the efficiencies that are derived from large scale production.

At the other end of the spectrum, the US has a huge internal market. In many cases, US firms can produce solely for the domestic market and still achieve a sufficiently large production scale to obtain the benefits of size. Consequently, in order to achieve scale efficiencies, US firms are not required to search out additional markets in foreign lands for their goods.

Notice also that a large share of the change in the openness measure happened in the 1970s. In the US, the 1970s explain almost all the increase in the importance of trade since 1950. In Mexico, the increasing importance of trade in the 1970s, late 1980s and 1990s made up for its decreased importance in the 1950s and 1960s during the years of import substitution industrialization.

INVESTMENT

The ratio of investment to GDP tells economists a great deal about a nation's economy. Since investment is one of the components of GDP (along with consumption expenditures, government expenditures on final goods and services and net exports) the ratio must be between 0 (no investment) and 100 percent (GDP = investment). For most countries in the world, the ratio varies between 10 percent and 40 percent.

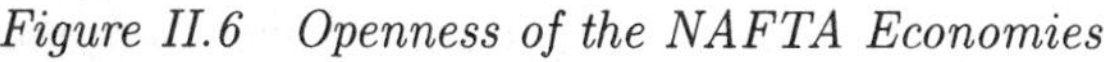

Figure II.6 Openness of the NAFTA Economies

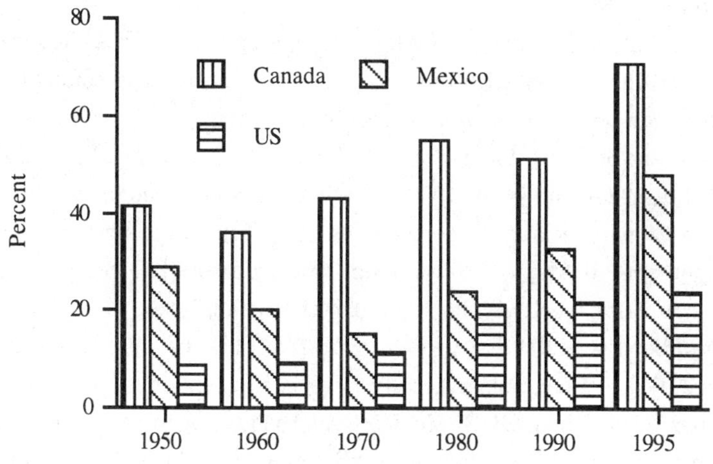

Source: Heston, A. *et al.* (1994); World Bank (1997b).

Investment is defined as expenditures on relatively long lasting goods and services that increase the ability of the economy to produce more goods and services. In other words, investment is the purchase of new factories and machines to go in them. Since houses and apartments are very long lasting, they are included as well, as are the inventories of firms that are necessary to conduct business. To recap, the main items of investment are new plant, new equipment such as machines and computers for businesses, new residences and any additions to business inventories.

The down side to investment is that the higher the level, the lower the level of consumption, government spending and exports. In other words, the cost of investment is that we give up some consumption, government spending, or net sales to foreigners. The up side, however, is that investment will ultimately enable an economy to produce more of all goods.

There are essentially two sources of funds for investment. There are domestic savings which are created whenever households, businesses or government bring in more income than they spend, and there are foreign savings that can be borrowed from abroad but must eventually be paid back.

One of the key pieces of Mexico's strategy within NAFTA was to increase the amount of foreign savings that entered the country. The reason can be clearly seen in in Figure II.7 which shows real investment as a share of GDP. Mexico invested around 16 percent of its GDP in the late 1980s and early 1990s. By comparison, Canada invested between 25 percent and 28 percent and the US invested between 20 and 23 percent. If Mexico's investment were compared to other developing countries, such as the high-growth economies of East Asia, the comparison would be even less favorable. The newly industrializing economies of East Asia typically have investment levels equal to 30–40 percent of their GDP. Mexico's relatively lower investment rate is ultimately a result of lower levels of domestic savings. Its rate of economic growth could be higher if it supplemented its investment with some other source of savings. Hence the strategy of trying to pull in the savings of foreigners through increasing capital flows into Mexico.

HUMAN CAPITAL INVESTMENT

Human capital is defined as the education, skills and expertise of the labor force. The data in Figure II.7 focused only on physical things that add to an economy's capacity to produce goods and services but in reality the accumulation of human capital has the same effect. Human capital is particularly important for countries that want to raise their living standards and for countries that already are industrially developed but that wish to hold on to a comparative advantage in high technology goods and services. That is, human capital is important for every economy.

Measures of human capital are varied. In Figure II.8 school enrollments are used as a measure of new investment in human capital. The numbers are derived by taking the ratio of enrollment in primary schools (or the other levels) to the population in a particular age group. For primary, all 6–11 year olds are in the numerator, secondary includes

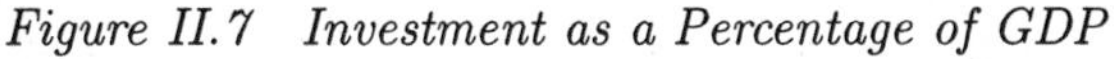

Figure II.7 Investment as a Percentage of GDP

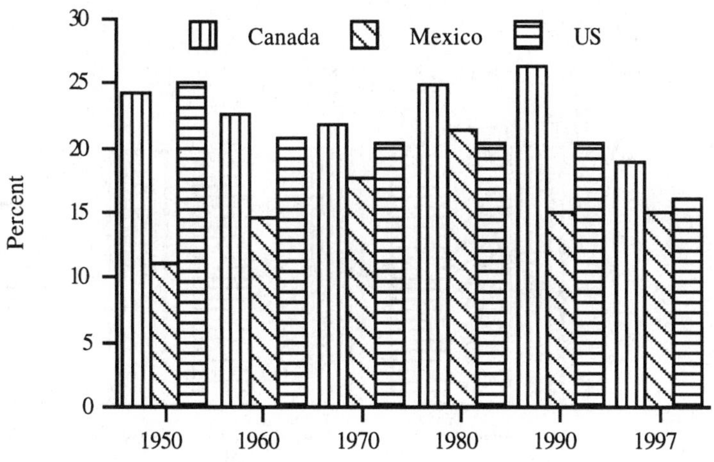

Source: World Bank (1997b).

12–17 year olds and tertiary includes 20–24 year olds. Note that this method allows the ratio to exceed 100 percent since many of the students enrolled may come from other age groups. Nevertheless, it gives a picture of the situation with respect to education and the higher the number, the greater the economy's investment in human capital.

POPULATION

The United States is by far the most populous of the NAFTA nations (see Figure II.9). Canada, on the other hand, is only about 10 percent of the size of the US. The United States' large population has made it the least dependent on trade of the NAFTA countries. Mexico is intermediate between the US and Canada with a population which is over one-third the size of the US. It is important to note how these relative sizes have changed. In 1950, Mexico's population was approximately one-sixth that of the US. Forty years later, in 1990, it had grown fast enough to equal about one-third of the US's population.

It is interesting to note that Mexico's rapid population growth dur-

Figure II.8 School Enrollment, 1993

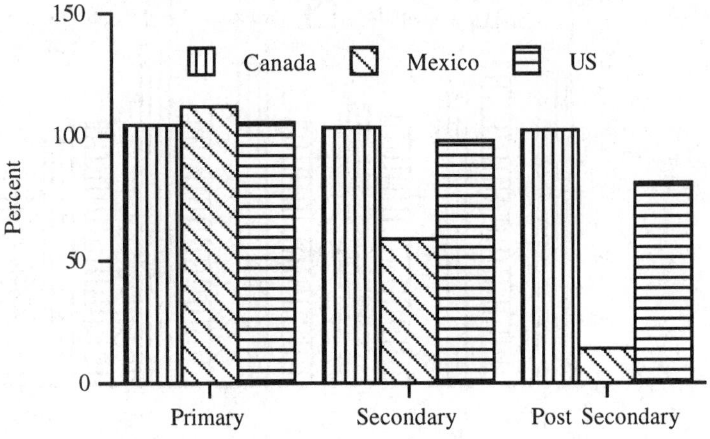

Source: World Bank (1997b).

Figure II.9 Population (in millions)

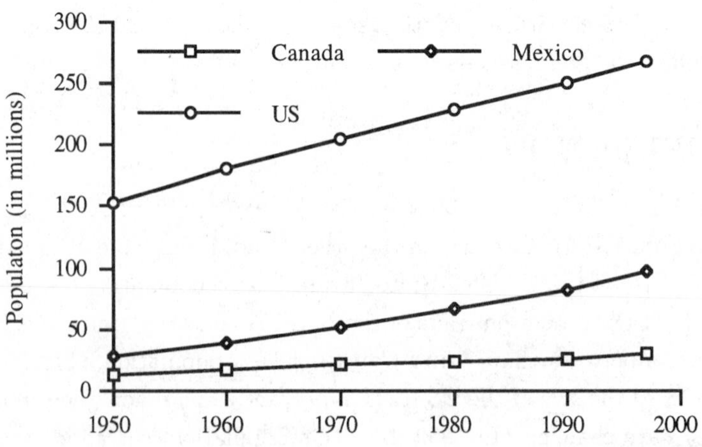

Source: Heston, A. *et al.* (1994); IMF (1998), *International Financial Statistics*, August.

ing the last fifty years is no faster than the growth that the US experienced in the nineteenth century. Nevertheless, relatively rapid population growth puts additional strains on savings and investment when economic growth and rising standards of living are goals. Mexico's ability to save is probably much less than the rates that were achieved in the US a century earlier.

4. The United States after World War II

This chapter surveys the last fifty years of United States economic history. The purpose is to place the economic integration project of the US, Canada and Mexico within an historical perspective. From this long-run point of view, NAFTA represents both continuity and change in the economic policies of the United States. On the one hand, NAFTA is an expression of tendencies in the United States to seek out bilateral solutions to trade issues. Nevertheless, it is also a reflection of broader forces in the international economy which are bringing all three NAFTA countries into closer economic proximity. In terms of both US policy and the apparent commercial evolution of North America, NAFTA is a continuation of ongoing forces. On the other hand, as a harbinger of increased Western Hemispheric and North Atlantic economic integration, NAFTA could mark the beginning of a trend towards a much wider and deeper integration which will have profound implications for national economic conditions. This is particularly true insofar as it applies to US-Mexico relations. In spite of the 2,000 mile common border, history, culture and politics have conspired to make US-Mexican relations far less cordial and trusting than US-Canadian relations. NAFTA in this context represents the possibility for change.

BEFORE INDUSTRIALIZATION

From the vantage point of the post-World War II era, it is frequently assumed that the United States has always favored free and open markets. It is often noted that the Declaration of Independence, proclaiming the separation of the thirteen colonies from Great Britain, was written in the same year (1776) as the publication of Adam Smith's *The Wealth of Nations*, proclaiming the benefits of nonintervention by governments into economic matters (*laissez faire*). Still, the idea that the Founding Fathers of the Republic were believers in the free market could not be farther from the truth. Adam Smith's ideas were considered too radical for adoption by most American leaders and they were interpreted to imply a dereliction of the government's responsibility to foster economic development through support for industry and infrastructure construction. In 1791, Alexander Hamilton, the first Secretary of Treasury, issued *The Report on Manufactures* which remains to this day a classic statement of the infant industry argument in favor of government support for industry and high tariffs. Although direct subsidies for industry were rare, the federal government took seriously its responsibility to regulate international commerce as spelled out by the US Constitution and maintained a high tariff on imports, in part for revenue reasons but also in the belief that it would foster economic development. At the same time, individual US states worked to create an environment in which commerce would grow and both the state and federal governments were a major source of backing for the construction of roads and canals in the first fifty years of the Republic. In the era of the railroad, which began in the 1840s, but took off in the 1850s, the federal government (and some states) provided large tracts of land that were used by the railroad companies both to site their tracks and to sell in order to finance construction.

From the standpoint of the new Republic, the construction of pathways for commerce made sense both economically and politically. In the interior of North America, the British along with the Spanish and French still held sway. The US feared that without settlement and commerce, the interior of the great continent would be lost to foreign powers. In terms of legislation, no other issue consumed as much time or led to the passage of as many bills as the settlement of the West. Should the land be given away or sold and, if sold, for how much? Should the government supply credit, or require cash? Should speculation be permitted on frontier land, and how would surveys be done to reduce conflict and fraud? These issues consumed the attention of nineteenth century congresses more than any other single issue.

Obviously, the abundance of land together with a relatively sparse population meant that there were shortages of labor. In the pre-Revolutionary era, the labor shortages had been minimized by preventing settlement west of the Appalachian mountains and by recruiting large numbers of indentured servants from England, Ireland, Scotland and Wales. In return for passage to the New World and a modest cash settlement at the end of their term of labor, these individuals agreed to work for three to seven years as quasi members of the family. They worked on farms, in shops and in businesses of every sort and more than a third of all Europeans who came to the thirteen colonies, came as indentured servants. Their role in the settlement and economic development of the United States was curtailed, however, by the invention of the cotton gin in 1797 which led to the development of a much expanded slave trade. Few free workers would voluntarily enter a labor market in which they competed with slaves.

The introduction of the cotton gin mechanized the removal of cottonseed from cotton fibers and made it economical to grow the hardier but relatively lower quality short fiber cotton. The significance of this technological advance was that it suddenly expanded the demand for slaves and slave labor. Prior to the spread of cotton, slavery was probably a dying institution but cotton production gave it a new economic base. Through the first five decades of the nineteenth century, cotton and slavery spread from the seaboard of the Southeast across Alabama and Mississippi and as far west as Texas. By most accounts, it led to the overspecialization of the Southern economy and limited the growth of urban centers and manufacturing. The South's failure to develop manufacturing capabilities and cities on a par with the North (together with its smaller share of the total population) were decisive in determining the outcome of the Civil War (1861–65).

While the Civil War was fought in the decade before industrialization began its takeoff into sustained growth, one business enterprise had already begun its ascent into the industrial world–the railroad. Historians debate the importance of railroads as contributors to US economic growth, but several facts are beyond question. First, and perhaps most significantly, the railroads were the first modern business enterprise in the US. All previous enterprises, including textile mills (which were the largest industrial operations in the US before the railroads) were small-scale businesses by comparison, raising capital locally or within the family. By contrast, the railroads required outside financing due to their huge fixed costs and the struggle to satisfy their investment needs ultimately led to the development of stock and bond markets in the United States. In addition to creating modern financial institutions, the railroads were the first enterprises to require professional management. Unlike every previous business enterprise, they crossed regional boundaries and involved many levels of control and coordination in order to avoid accidents while keeping to tight schedules with well maintained equipment and roadbeds. By the mid-1850s, the first interregional networks were constructed, connecting the East Coast as far inland as Chicago.

The success of new businesses, especially ones like the railroad that turned economic relations upside down, is due in part to an institutional environment that protects innovation against entrenched interests. Economic policy in the first century and a half of the Republic may have been shaped by protectionist thought but the legal framework of the United States has usually favored markets over the demands of special interests (Hurst, 1981). In practice, this has meant that it is difficult for established firms or individuals to legally block change, even when the change runs counter to their interests.

In effect, the US Constitution and its interpreters have favored the rights of innovators over the rights of those that were financially harmed by innovation. This aspect of the institutional environment is part of a larger set of rules that lower the costs of doing business in the United States. Transaction costs are one aspect of business costs and it is these that are most directly affected by the institutional environment. Transaction costs are the costs of finding market information (where the market is, what it wants, how to get inputs to produce it and so forth), of negotiating a contract, and of enforcing the contract, if necessary. In countries or circumstances in which one or more of these break down, the costs of doing business rise significantly. For example, if contract enforcement is lax or nonexistent, then businesses are reluctant to transact without some expenditure of private efforts to insure against loss through noncompliance with the terms of the contract. Otherwise, firms in losing contracts can simply walk away from the deal and never worry about the possible consequences. In the United States, the overwhelmingly dominant interpretation of the US Constitution favors the agreement struck in a contract over the breaking of a contract. Enforcement through the courts is relatively certain and sanctions carry penalties. All parties recognize this and hence, once a contract is signed, enforcement costs are relatively small.

In addition to favoring the enforcement of contracts and to making it difficult to block change, the US institutional environment also limits the erecting of barriers to internal trade by subnational level governments. While there are some exceptions (alcohol and certification of skills are the main ones), states are very limited in their ability to restrict commerce across state lines. As a result, the barriers to the creation of a national market have been mostly geographical and as transportation and communication advances occurred, these too dropped away. Consequently, US institutions have enabled the country to reap the full advantage of reduced uncertainty and economies of scale in a single national market.

DEMOGRAPHY AND INCOME

The income and the size of the United States placed it at the forefront of the world's industrial nations sometime around the start of the twentieth century. In this section, we look at the growth of both population and income over the course of the last century.

Population and Immigration

The US market in the twentieth century has had the considerable advantage of being large and therefore benefiting from internal economies of scale. By 1913, the US had more than twice as many inhabitants as its nearest economic competitor and over the course of the twentieth century the population advantage grew to more than four times more

Table 4.1 International Comparisons of Population (in thousands)

Country	1913	1995
United States	97,606	263,100
Canada	7,582	29,600
Mexico	14,971	91,800
France	41,690	58,100
Germany	40,835	81,900
Italy	37,248	57,200
Japan	51,672	125,200
United Kingdom	42,622	58,500

Source: Maddison (1994); World Bank (1997b).

Table 4.2 Immigrants in the US Population

Period	Percent of population foreign born at the beginning of period	Immigration as a percentage of population growth
1910–30	14.6	32.7
1930–50	11.6	5.6
1950–70	6.9	11.2
1970–90	4.7	26.9
1990	7.9	NA

Source: Borjas (1994).

people than each of the leading industrial economies, except Japan (Table 4.1).

Population growth in the US has been fueled in part by immigration. In the half century prior to 1930, between 25 percent and 54 percent of each decade's increase in population was a result of immigrants (Borjas, 1994). As can be seen in Table 4.2 after the passage of immigration restrictions in the 1920s, the immigrant flow as a percentage of the net change in population fell dramatically until the 1960s when it began to increase once again. During the 1980s, immigrants accounted for more than one-third of the total increase in population.

Table 4.3 International Comparisons of Per Capita GDP

Country	1890	1913	1950	1995
United States	3,101	4,846	8,772	19,693
Canada	1,846	3,515	6,380	15,419
	(59.5)	(72.5)	(72.7)	(78.3)
Mexico	762	1,121	2,198	4,667
	(24.6)	(23.1)	(25.1)	(23.7)
France	1,955	2,746	4,176	15,360
	(63.0)	(56.7)	(47.7)	(78.0)
Germany	1,660	2,506	3,295	14,651
	(53.5)	(51.7)	(37.6)	(74.4)
Italy	1,352	2,079	2,840	14,514
	(43.6)	(42.9)	(32.4)	(73.7)
Japan	842	1,153	1,620	16,148
	(27.2)	(23.8)	(18.5)	(82.0)
United Kingdom	3,383	4,152	5,651	14,061
	(109.1)	(85.7)	(64.4)	(71.4)

Source: Maddison (1994); World Bank (1997b); author's calculations.

US GDP

Table 4.3 shows per capita real GDP, measured in 1985 US dollars. The numbers in parentheses are per capita GDP as a percentage of the US value. Between 1890 and 1913, the income level of the United States passed the United Kingdom, making it the richest economy in the world. To be precise, Australia had the highest per person GDP of any country in the world until approximately 1920. Although the countries in Table 4.3 are a small sample, they represent NAFTA nations and leading industrial economies; between 1890 and 1950 the gap between the US and most other nations continued to widen (with the exceptions of Canada and Mexico); after 1950, the difference narrows.

The US Economic Growth since 1950

The economist Angus Maddison (1991) coined the term 'The Golden Age' to refer to the period from 1950 to 1973. The beginning and ending years are somewhat arbitrary but it is clear that they bracket the most extraordinary years of world economic growth. Nearly all countries in all regions of the world experienced rates of real economic growth that were greater than their long-run average rates and that were, in most cases, their fastest rates for any period of the twentieth century.

The United States (and Canada and Mexico) followed this pattern. From 1913 to 1950, real US per capita GDP rose at the average annual rate of 1.6 percent (Canada, 1.5 percent; Mexico, 1.0 percent). During the Golden Age, the US rate increased to 2.2 percent (Canada, 2.9 percent; Mexico, 3.1 percent). After 1973, the real per capita growth rate fell in all nations with some notable Asian exceptions (Maddison, 1994). The reasons for the increase in growth rates during the Golden Age and their subsequent decline, are explored below.

Sources of Strength in the Golden Age and before

Around 1950, the income gap between the United States and other leading industrial nations reached its zenith. The United States' lead in per capita GDP was built around three main factors: (1) an early commitment to mass production; (2) an abundant base of natural resources; and (3) the existence of a large, unified, single market. Each of these will be discussed in turn.

The United States was the first country to develop widespread applications of mass production technology. Beginning in the 1870s, the US entered the period known as the second industrial revolution, a period characterized by rapid technological change and the intense application of energy to manufacturing. One of the main characteristics of the second industrial revolution was the replacement of traditional systems of craft production with new systems of mass production. Table 4.4 compares and contrasts the two production systems.

In the view of many, a third type of production system has recently appeared on the world stage. Variously known as lean production or flexible manufacturing, it combines the speed and machinery of mass production with the small batch size of craft production. This enables producers to have the low average costs of mass producers with the individualized attention to customer needs of craft producers. The system first developed in the Japanese auto and machinery industries.

As late as the beginning of World War II, most European countries were far behind the United States in the application of mass production techniques. In fact, the United States' ability to produce planes, trucks and ships at a rate much faster than Germany or Japan was the key to Allied success in the war. The reasons are not difficult to understand. Mass production requires far greater investments of capital than craft production, and in order to pay for itself the volume of production must be on a much greater scale. That is, the more units of output there are, the wider the capital costs of the expensive machinery can be spread and the lower the cost of production per unit.

To make the system work, machinery must be kept running as much as possible. The huge fixed costs of the physical capital do not disappear in the same way that labor costs do whenever the machinery is shut down. Workers can be laid off and wage costs reduced, but interest on bank loans must be paid regardless of whether the machines sit idle or not. Therefore, bottlenecks or other disruptions in the supply lines are potentially disastrous. In addition to a continuous supply of

Table 4.4 A Comparison of Craft and Mass Production

Characteristics	Craft	Mass
Workers	Wide use of skilled craftmen	Wide use of unskilled workers
Management	Owners are managers, few are professionals	A professional managerial class
Production runs	Small batches of output	Huge batches of output
Nature of product	Each item slightly different	Standardized items
Capital equipment	Simple tools	Heavy use of sophisticated machinery
Cost structure	Low fixed costs, relatively high variable costs	Very high fixed costs
Geographic location of market	Local market with little or no distribution outside of well-defined geographic regions	National and international markets

inputs, firms also need an assured outlet to markets. That is, if goods cannot be brought to market, it has the same threatening effect on the firm's economic health as a disruption in the supply of inputs.

The US is unique in that it has (1) an abundant resource base and, therefore, did not have to go across national boundaries for its inputs (making the supply of inputs more secure), and (2) a large market, and therefore did not have to export in order to sell all of its output (making output markets more secure). Consequently, the investment of enormous sums of financial capital in mass production machinery was less risky in the United States than anywhere else in the world. European producers lacked the same access to resources and to output markets because, in both cases, they had to cross national boundaries. This was particularly a problem during the period (1913–50) when two world wars and a major worldwide depression caused nations to turn inward and to cut their linkages with each other.

After World War II, the situation changed dramatically for manufacturers in all the advanced industrial nations. The IMF, the World Bank and the Bretton Woods system of fixed exchange rates, together with GATT and US military and political hegemony, created a stable set of liberalizing institutions in which there was a high probability of secure access to both input and output markets. Naturally, as European and Japanese producers moved towards greater reliance on mass production systems, they began to catch up to the United States in terms of both their GDP per capita and labor productivity. In statistical terms, the catch up is represented by the strong negative correlation between the rate of growth from 1950 to the present and the initial level of real per capita GDP. In other words, the pattern of growth (among advanced industrial nations) since 1950 is that the countries with the lowest per capita GDP in 1950 grew the fastest (Baumol, Blackman and Wolff, 1989). In the US, the high per capita GDP in 1950 was correlated with relatively slower growth than in other nations.

Relative Economic Decline after 1973

One of the unsettled mysteries of economic growth in the twentieth century is the cause of the growth slowdown after approximately 1973.

The slowdown occurred throughout the Western Hemisphere, across the whole European continent and in Africa, Australia, New Zealand and Japan. The only exceptions were some East and South Asian countries where a combination of good policies, stable institutions and unknown positive factors coincided to produce a growth surge after 1973. Four explanations for the growth slowdown are commonly offered, and all but the first one seem plausible: (1) the oil price increases of 1973–74 and 1979; (2) the decline in investment; (3) a decline in technological innovation; and (4) a shift in economic policy. Each will be briefly discussed.

Given that 1973 is also the year of the first of two artificial oil shortages engineered by OPEC and price hikes (the other occurred in 1979) most people's first thought is to blame the energy crises for the growth slowdown. Between January of 1973 and the end of 1974, the price of oil increased by nearly a factor of five. For example, gas at the pump which had been US$0.25 a gallon in the US in 1973 was almost US$1.25 by the end of 1974. The problem with this fact as an explanation for the growth slowdown is that when the world price of oil collapsed in the early 1980s, growth rates in the US and abroad did not return to their former levels. One conclusion is that there is no clear relation between oil prices and economic growth rates.

In the United States, a more reasonable explanation for the growth slowdown is the decline in savings and investment rates. For example, the US stock of machinery, equipment and buildings used by producers grew at an average annual rate of 3.38 percent from 1950 to 1973, and 2.2 percent from 1973 to 1989.[1] Similar slowdowns in the rate of accumulation of capital occurred in most places around the world, including Mexico and Canada (Maddison, 1989; Maddison, 1994).

Adding to the mystery of slower growth since 1973 is the fact that the contribution of technology appears to have shrunk. Economists use a technique known as growth accounting to measure the contribution of labor and capital to economic growth. The part of growth that re-

[1] Economists refer to this conglomeration of inputs as the 'nonresidential fixed capital stock'. It goes without saying that when investment falls, the rate at which new capital is added to the economy falls too.

mains to be explained after all the measurable factors have been taken into account (for example, the quantity of labor and capital, the level of education, the change in the structure of the economy and so forth) is usually attributed to technological improvements that cannot be directly measured. For some reason, the contribution of technological improvements fell dramatically after 1973, implying that there was a slowdown in the rate at which industries were able to introduce new technologies. This is a long-run trend and while some have speculated that in the late 1980s and early 1990s we were at last beginning to see increases in economic growth coming from new computer and information technologies, it is too early to say for certain if this is occurring. It may seem odd to assert that computers have not yet improved productivity much. New technologies, however, require new organizational forms, and these often take decades to develop. The contribution of electricity to growth, for example, took approximately 40 years from its introduction in the 1880s until it had measurable affects in the 1920s. Today, many businesses use their computers to do what a secretary with a pencil used to do–write memos. The fonts may be prettier, but there is no gain in productivity or economic growth.

A final factor used to explain the growth slowdown after 1973 (in both the United States and the rest of the world) is a permanent shift in economic policies. Between the end of World War II and the late 1970s, the two primary goals of US macroeconomic policies were low rates of unemployment and high levels of economic growth. In other words, the United States (and most advanced industrial economies) pursued Keynesian economic policies of demand management.[2] In the Keynesian system, governments ran deficits during recessions in order to stimulate the level of aggregate demand; during expansions they were expected to run budget surpluses in order to prevent the economy

[2]As pointed out in Chapter 3, the British economist John Maynard Keynes is the most important economic thinker of the twentieth century. Keynes's major contribution was to show that national governments could manage the level of aggregate demand as a means to smoothing out the business cycle and to counteract recessions. In the context of most political systems, these ideas proved to have an inflationary bias, for which reason many governments rejected Keynesianism in the 1970s and 1980s.

Figure 4.1 Annual Changes in Consumer Prices, 1965–97

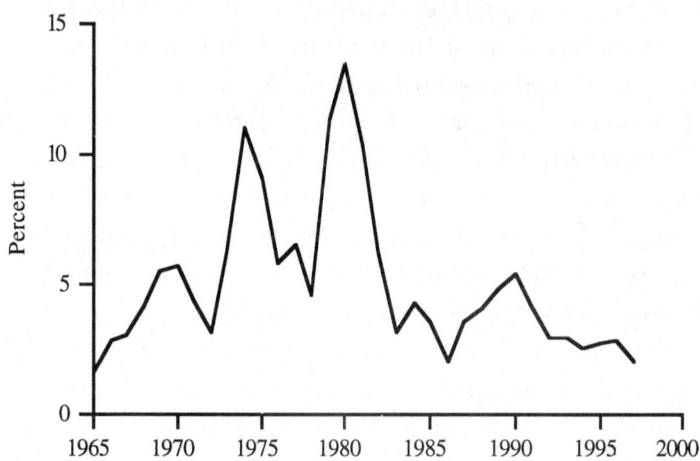

Source: *Economic Report of the President, 1997.*

from growing too fast and to pay off the deficits accumulated in the recession. In practice, most governments were fully capable of running deficits but since surpluses involved cuts in government programs (or higher taxes), few had the political courage to run surpluses during economic expansions.

Inflation became a serious problem in most advanced industrial economies during the 1970s. In part this was due to the inflationary bias of Keynesian policies as practiced by most countries, and in part it was a result of the oil shortages of 1973–74. In addition, large-scale crop failures in 1973 in the Soviet Union pushed up world grain and food prices. Furthermore, in the United States, the Vietnam War continued to be fought with borrowed funds rather than tax increases, and a significant growth in social spending on anti-poverty programs added to government expenditures beginning in the late 1960s and early 1970s.

Figure 4.1 shows how inflation rose dramatically (by US standards) after 1972, reaching its first spike of 11.0 percent in 1974, and its second spike of 13.5 percent in 1980 (*Economic Report of the President,*

1997). The unprecedented increase in inflation caused a shift in the focus of US economic policy from an emphasis on maintaining high levels of economic growth to an emphasis on reducing inflation. The shift in policy was signaled in 1979 by the central bank of the United States, the Federal Reserve (the Fed). The Chair of the Fed, economist Paul Volcker, announced that he would focus on controlling the money supply rather than on interest rates. High levels of inflation push up nominal interest rates and the switch by the Fed to a more restrictive monetary policy reinforced this tendency. The result was that the US economy went into recession, briefly in 1980, and more severely in 1981–82.

The shift in macroeconomic policy from fighting slow growth and high unemployment to fighting inflation did not occur only in the United States. Most other industrial nations followed this pattern, although the exact timing varied by country. While it has not been proven that this shift is related to the growth slowdown in North America and Europe, it remains a viable hypothesis. In addition, the slowing of growth in the industrial economies spilled over into the economies of developing nations. One channel through which the impacts were felt was a decrease in demand for the products of less-developed countries.

US GOALS IN THE EARLY POST-WORLD WAR II PERIOD

The early years of the post-World War II period mark the zenith of the United States' political hegemony and the period of the largest gap between the income of the US and other industrial nations. It is important to note that the differences in income levels between the US and other nations did not stem solely from the destruction of Europe and Japan in World War II, but had been growing throughout the twentieth century. World War II was important to the emergence of the US as a world leader, however, because it created a vacuum in world leadership which the United States' economic and military power made it the natural choice to fill.

In the international economy, the postwar policies of the US included four interrelated goals: (1) to insure that nations did not repeat the mistakes of the 1920s and 1930s by re-establishing protectionist trade regimes after the war; (2) to create stable international institutions to smooth over the problems of international payments imbalances and to act as an international lender of last resort; (3) to ensure the rebuilding and return to prosperity of the war-torn economies of Western Europe and Japan; and (4) to contain the spread of communism, partly through military means, but also through the demonstration effects of prosperity in advanced industrial economies. Needless to say, these goals were interdependent and none of them could succeed in isolation from the others.

Learning the Lessons of the 1920s and 1930s

One of the first goals of the United States in the postwar period was to avoid the mistakes of the 1920s and 1930s. With respect to international trade, this meant the avoidance of a return to the policy of trade restrictions that had characterized most industrial economies between the world wars. This was a significant policy shift for the United States because the country had been highly protectionist throughout most of the nineteenth and early twentieth centuries. The capstone of US protectionism was the Tariff Bill of 1930, better known as the Hawley-Smoot Tariff. Hawley-Smoot was similar to the tariff policies of many industrial economies in that it was a misguided attempt to discourage imports in order to protect the domestic economy from the worst effects of the general economic downturn that had begun in 1929. The resulting downward spiral in US and world trade did not help any nation since most countries introduced similar restrictions on imports. This led to a decline in export industries that offset any gains in employment in industries that were protected from imports.[3]

In 1934, near the depth of the Great Depression, President Roose-

[3]Between 1929 and 1933, US imports fell from US$5.9 billion to US$2.1 billion; as nations retaliated against US trade restrictions, exports fell from US$7.1 billion to US$2.4 billion. The net effect on the US economy, a drop in net exports of US$0.7 billion, is too small to have played a significant role in causing the Great Depression.

velt succeeded in passing the Reciprocal Trade Agreement Act (RTAA), amending the Tariff Bill of 1930.[4] The RTAA was a watershed in the United States' commercial policy because it is the first legislative enactment of a bill that reflects a liberal bias in favor of free trade. The chief architect of the bill, Secretary of State Cordell Hull, favored free trade less for its economic advantages, however, than for political reasons. Hull shared the view common to political liberals that free trade and economic integration reduced international tensions and made wars far less likely. In Hull's mind, part of the blame for World War II was the collapse of trade during the 1930s.

The RTAA emphasized reciprocity as the basis for bilateral trade relations. Reciprocity is a familiar theme in the history of US commercial policy. Essentially, it implies equal treatment, or that the US would provide access to its market in exactly the same way and to the same degree that other countries provided access to US producers. In practice, throughout the 1950s and 1960s, the US was willing to forego complete reciprocity in cases in which sensitive industries of politically friendly trading partners were involved. In other words, the prosperity of foreign producers was a part of US foreign policy goals, and it often took precedent over equal market access. In the 1950s and 1960s, the cost of this tradeoff was low because the US enjoyed large productivity advantages (and quite often, large comparative advantages as well) in most industries. This cost of the tradeoff seems to have changed in the period of the growth slowdown, from the 1970s to the present. In particular, with the ending of the Cold War in 1989, equal market access moved to the front of US concerns and the willingness to tradeoff market access in order to achieve foreign policy goals was greatly diminished.

The US thrust towards liberalizing trade relations in the half-century after World War II was made easier by an important institutional feature of the presidency and Congress. From the passage of the RTAA in

[4]In the United States, the Great Depression is dated from mid-1929, through 1933. After 1933, the economy began to recover, but slipped back into a serious recession in 1937–38. For this reason, people often refer to the entire decade of the 1930s as the Great Depression.

the mid-1930s until the early 1970s, the US president was automatically given the authority by Congress to negotiate bilateral and multilateral reciprocal reductions in US tariff rates without seeking congressional approval. This system insulated Congress from the pressures of industry lobbyists and moved the US towards a far more liberal trade regime than had existed before the war. In the 1970s, however, Congressional reforms altered the committee structure of Congress and had the side-effect of exposing legislators more directly to the pressure of industry sponsored lobbyists. At the same time, the authority granted to the president to negotiate reciprocal tariff cuts was altered. In its place, Congress gave the president a broader power to negotiate with other nations while it limited itself to voting up or down (yes or no) without amendment on the agreements that result from the negotiations. This is what has come to be called fast track authority. Fast track is usually granted for a period of several years after which the president must seek renewal of the authority. It was the failure of the president to seek a renewal for two years after it expired in 1994, together with the refusal by Congress to grant it when it was finally requested in 1997, that delayed the opening of negotiations to expand NAFTA.

It should also be apparent that the concept of reciprocity as used by the United States does not mean free trade, and that the goal of US policy was not to remove all trade barriers but rather to gradually move in the direction of more open markets. In US policy circles the distinction was made between a liberal trade regime and a free trade regime, a distinction that was carried over into the US position in the multilateral forum of the General Agreement on Tariffs and Trade (GATT). Every GATT round of tariff cuts, from the first round in 1947 until the most recent round in 1986, have had liberalization and not free trade as their primary objective. The same can be said for CUSFTA, NAFTA and other US trade negotiations.

Bretton Woods and the Desire for Stable International Institutions

In addition to avoiding the mistake of creating closed economies, the United States sought to encourage the development of a stable international economic order through the creation of institutions that would oversee international monetary arrangements. The most important efforts in this arena led to the creation of the International Monetary Fund (IMF) and the International Bank for Reconstruction and Development (World Bank), both of which developed out of the talks held in Bretton Woods, New Hampshire, in July, 1944. Forty-four nations attended the Bretton Woods Conference, although much of the work of the conference had been done before it took place and the institutions which resulted were largely the creation of the United States and, to a lesser degree, Great Britain.

Again, the US goal was to avoid the mistakes of the 1920s and 1930s when international debt and payments problems coupled with the lack of a lender of last resort had resulted in international default and financial chaos. One primary function of the new IMF was to act like a bank for countries that found themselves unable to honor their international obligations. The US and other industrial economies recognized that private capital markets were incapable of filling this role, and that a multilateral agency that was (at least partially) independent of national governments had the best chance of succeeding.

A second goal of the United States in the creation of the IMF and the Bretton Woods exchange rate system was to reduce the possibility for countries to engage in the kind of competitive devaluations that they had in the 1920s and 1930s. A competitive devaluation is when a country devalues its currency in order to gain competitive advantages for its exports and import-competing industries. The Bretton Woods exchange rate system was a fixed exchange rate system in which nations specified the value of their currency in terms of dollars, and the dollar was valued in terms of gold at US$35 per ounce. The US stood ready to exchange dollars for gold, while other countries could settle their international payments in either gold or dollars. In practice, all nations (including the US) settled nearly all payments in dollars. From the US perspective, this meant that US dollars were widely accepted in the international economy. In turn, this removed the incentive to practice restraint in the printing of money, and by the early 1970s was a contributing factor in the rise of inflation. In theory, nations were to be limited in their ability to devalue their currencies, although in practice this turned out not to be important. It was widely recognized, however, that the goal of preventing competitive devaluations was highly desirable since this use of currency devaluation was a primary source of international economic tension.

Rebuilding of Europe and Japan

In addition to the goals of creating a more liberal international trading system and creating a stable international monetary system, the United States sought to rebuild the war-torn economies of Europe and Japan. Originally, the World Bank was designed to handle the financial flows for reconstruction but it was soon apparent that the Bank's funding would prove inadequate to the task. Accordingly, the United States established the Marshall Plan as a system of financial grants and loans to the nations of Western Europe, and created the Organization of European Economic Cooperation to handle the disbursement of funds provided through the Marshall Plan. The Marshall Plan was named after its originator, the US Secretary of State in the administration of President Truman, General George Marshall. The OEEC later became the Organization for Economic Cooperation and Development, or OECD. Theoretically, aid could have been provided through the IMF or the World Bank, but it would have meant increasing dramatically the flow of US funds through those organizations, as well as explicitly granting them permission to make loans that had no chance of being repaid. The expansion of the IMF and the World Bank along these lines was controversial and it was deemed best not to channel the bulk of the reconstruction funds through them. The Marshall Plan was in effect between 1947 and 1953, during which time it provided funds equal to about 2.5 percent of European GNP, or almost 20 times more than the IMF and World Bank (Eichengreen and Kenen, 1994).

Japan received US aid under the US military occupation. Initially, transfers were much less than under the Marshall Plan for Europe; nevertheless, a similar plan, called the Dodge Plan succeeded in controlling inflation in 1949 and helped set the conditions for Japan's take-off into sustained growth. In addition, the beginning of the Korean War in

1950 proved to be a boon for Japan, as the US encouraged Japanese suppliers to fill the demand for war goods.

In both Europe and Japan, US aid smoothed the transition towards more open markets by providing funds which helped to reduce the internal conflict over economic distribution. In turn, this helped to minimize the dissension of people that found themselves on the losing end of the market liberalization, and to limit the influence of those that offered a more radical critique of trade and markets.

Containing Communism

The primary security and defense issue for US foreign policy in the postwar period was to contain communism. The onset of the Cold War in 1947 coincided with the first round of tariff reductions under GATT accord, and the beginning of Marshall Plan aid to Europe. The Marshall Plan was followed by the Dodge plan aimed at the economic reconstruction of Japan. Although it is unlikely that the establishment of GATT was directly related to the Cold War, there is little doubt that the Marshall and Dodge Plans were. European and Japanese prosperity became much higher priorities with the onset of the Cold War, while at the same time there was an increase in the United States' willingness to trade some of its economic gains from trade liberalization in exchange for support for its political objectives. In addition to the humanitarian element of the Marshall and other aid packages, US policy was designed under the assumption that renewed prosperity in Japan and Europe would limit the influence of communism in those regions and also serve as a demonstration to communist nations of the material benefits of capitalism. For today's perspective it seems very likely that the Marshall and Dodge Plans were in fact very effective weapons in the Cold War.

TRADE AND FOREIGN INVESTMENT AFTER WORLD WAR II

International trade has been less important to the US economy than in most other industrial nations. One reason is that as the technological leader, the US economy was capable of producing most of the sophisticated and complex goods that were available through trade. Note that technological leadership is not the same as economic leadership. However, the United States' development of industrial laboratories and close university-business relations in the first decades of the twentieth century meant that its technological capacities were at the frontier of most manufacturing sectors. There were exceptions, however; Germany had clear technological advantages in chemical industries, for example. A second reason for the relative unimportance of trade is the size of the US market. The United States is capable of attaining sufficient size to produce at the point of minimum average cost in most of its domestic industries. Producers in less populous countries (for example, Canada) were unable to attain the scale economies associated with large output volumes without selling outside the national market. A third reason is geography. The US has a wide variety of climates and soils and is capable of low-cost production of a wide variety of agricultural products. Hence, it is less dependent on imports of basic grains and other staples.

Trade and Investment during the Golden Age

Figure 4.2 illustrates the growth of goods and services exports and imports as a share of GDP from 1950 to 1997. Between 1950 and 1973, exports averaged 4.8 percent of GDP, while imports averaged 4.3 percent. As can be seen in Figure 4.2, before 1972 there is no tendency for exports to increase as a share of GDP. By contrast, imports began a gradual rise in the early 1960s, but did not surpass the level of exports until 1971.

In general, between 1950 and 1973, the United States ran small trade surpluses and trade remained relatively inconsequential to US economic conditions. At the same time, the United States was successful in the pursuit of its trade agenda of steady liberalization of world markets through GATT. Progress towards liberalization was relatively easy since in 1947 most nations began from a starting point of high tariffs and this allowed room for successive rounds of cuts. It was not until the 1980s, when tariffs were low, that further liberalization required more difficult negotiations and GATT process came close to

Figure 4.2 Imports and Exports as a Percentage of GDP, 1950–97

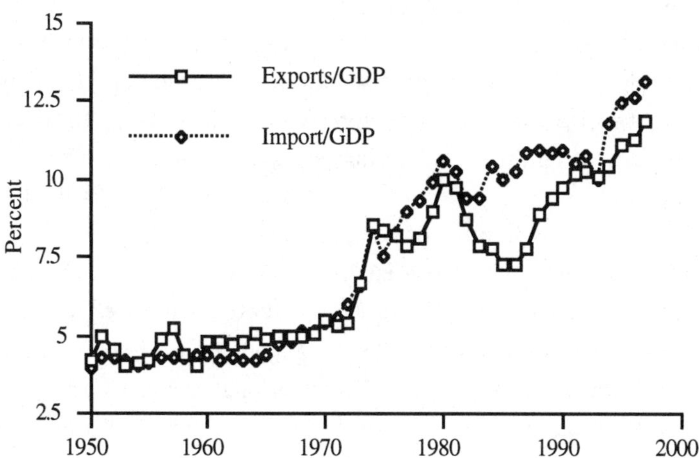

Source: Bureau of Economic Analysis, August 1998.

breaking down.

One feature of US international economic relations in the 1950–73 period was the slow and steady growth of outward foreign investment. As a trade surplus nation, the United States continued to invest more abroad than foreigners invested in the United States. The trade surplus was not the only factor influencing foreign investment, however. Many US-based multinational corporations found that they could more efficiently supply goods abroad with foreign manufacturing plants than they could through trade. That is, rather than export from US-based plants, many multinationals chose to locate production facilities in the markets they wanted to sell to. This decision to invest abroad rather than export is particularly strong in cases in which the foreign market and its resource endowments (labor, capital and natural resources) are similar to the home market. The general result is that the more similar countries are, the more important are their investment relations relative to their trade relations.[5]

The general rule should not be interpreted to mean that trade is

[5]A formal explanation of this general rule can be found in Markusen (1995).

unimportant, but rather that we should look for foreign investment to grow most rapidly between countries with relatively similar resource endowments and income levels. In the case of the United States, outward foreign investment grew most rapidly in Europe and Canada. In Canada, the US auto industry spread from its base in the US into the province of Ontario, and ultimately grew large enough to become instrumental in the creation of the US-Canadian Auto Pact of 1965, creating free trade in autos and automobile parts. The Auto Pact permitted the industry to rationalize its investments between the US and Canada by consolidating production where it was most efficient.

Canada is the second most important location of US outward investment. The United Kingdom is number one, and Europe as a whole dominates all other regions as a location for outward US investment. This point is important because it is often mistakenly assumed that most US foreign investment flows to less-developed countries of the world but the reality is just the opposite. The locational disadvantages of developing nations usually make it easier for US multinationals to supply those markets through exports rather than through local production in the developing country.[6] Furthermore, the differences between advanced industrial economies and developing economies cause most trade between them to be based on differences in resource endowments (comparative advantage). Given the differences in land, labor and capital, production systems which are suitable for the United States are less suitable for developing countries and vice versa.

Figure 4.3 illustrates this point. Total assets of US-owned firms outside the United States are compared by their region of location. Europe was the location of 49 percent of US foreign direct investment in 1997. The advanced industrial nations of the world (Europe, Canada, Japan, Australia and New Zealand) accounted for 68 percent of all US foreign investment. To return to the earlier point about the relative importance of trade and investment, the total value of US exports of goods and services to Europe in 1995 was US$248.5 billion, while sales

[6]Locational disadvantages include scarcities of local capital and skilled labor, along with inadequate infrastructure. In some cases, the small size of the market is another disadvantage

Figure 4.3 The Distribution of US Investment Abroad, 1997

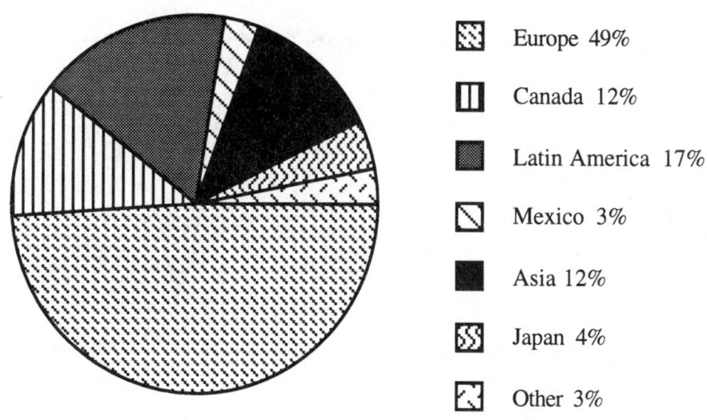

Source: Bureau of Economic Analysis, July, 1998.

by US-owned firms located in Europe totaled US$1,060.9 billion in the same year, more than four times as large (Bureau of Economic Analysis, October, 1997 and July, 1998).

Trade Deficits and Budget Deficits

Figure 4.2 illustrated the opening of the US trade deficit after about 1972. The broader measurement of the trade balance, called the current account balance, shows that US trade began its greatest deterioration around 1982 or 1983, about a decade after the first appearance of the merchandise trade deficit.[7] Figure 4.4 shows the dramatic decline in the United States' current account balance after 1982–83. The year 1991 stands out in Figure 4.4 as a year in which the US almost returned to balance. In reality, 1991 was an exception because the US received about US$40 billion dollars in transfer payments from nations that contributed to the cost of fighting the Persian Gulf War. It bottomed

[7]The current account balance includes: (1) merchandise trade; (2) trade in services; (3) investment income received from abroad minus income paid to foreigners; and (4) net transfers from foreigners. In practice, for most countries, the first two categories make up the vast majority of the current account balance.

Figure 4.4 US Current Account Balance, 1946–97

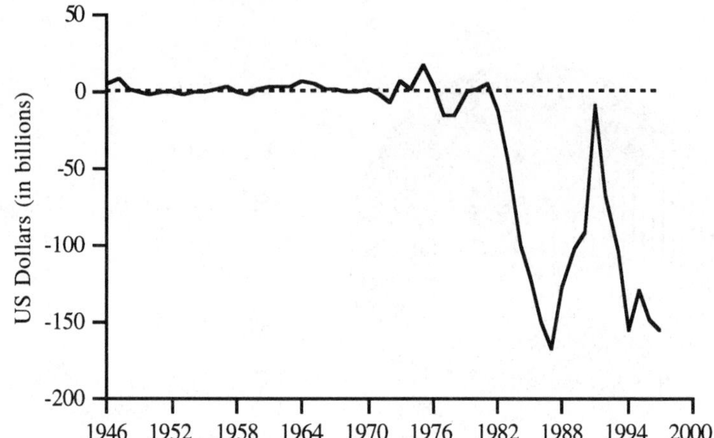

Source: Bureau of Economic Analysis, July, 1998.

out in 1987 at US$167.3 billion, from which it improved until it began to deteriorate once again in 1992. By 1997 it was US$155 billion and growing.

The more or less simultaneous deterioration in the accounts of the US federal government led many to assert that the trade and current account deficits were the result of the sudden surge in the federal budget deficit. In 1982, the US federal budget deficit jumped to $127.9 billion from US$78.9 billion in 1981. Throughout the 1980s and early 1990s it rarely fell below US$100 billion and reached US$282 billion in 1992. After 1992, however, the health of the US economy together with budgetary reforms in federal expenditures caused it to begin to shrink. By 1998, there was a slight surplus.

While it is correct to argue that the growth in the federal budget deficit put additional pressures on an already low level of US private savings, it is incorrect to think that there is a one-to-one correspondence between budget deficits and current account deficits. Private savings and investment are additional macroeconomic variables in the relationship and if savings are sufficiently large, or domestic investment sufficiently small, then the US could finance both a budget deficit, and maintain a current account surplus (which is equivalent to financing net foreign investment). In other words, let S_p equal private savings by households and businesses and S_g equal public or government savings. If S_g is positive, then the government budget is in surplus; if negative, then it is in deficit. $S_p + S_g$ is the total supply of domestic savings available to an economy. It can be shown that the relationship between domestic savings, investment and the current account balance is as follows:[8]

$$S_p + S_g = I + CA,$$

where I is domestic investment and CA is the current account balance. If S_g is negative, the budget is in deficit, and it reduces the supply of savings available to finance investment (I), and the current account (CA). In the US case, the relatively low level of private savings (around 18 percent of GNP) together with the budget deficits of 2–4 percent of GNP in the 1980s, limited the supply of funds available for domestic investment. In the end, the US had to run large current account deficits (negative CA) in order to maintain its level of investment. Current account deficits are equivalent to capital inflows, which is to say that foreign capital was used to finance investment equal to about 1–2 percent of GNP. Note that this is essentially the same sort of problem encountered by Mexico in 1994 and that resulted in the peso crash of December 1994. In both cases, the US and Mexico were trying to invest more than their pool of savings permitted and the difference was made up by a large inflow of foreign capital. In the US case, however, the outcome has been much less debilitating, partly because the inflow of capital was smaller relative to US GNP and because the US has continued to attract foreign capital.

By the late 1990s, the US budget deficit had disappeared and a small surplus took its place. All else equal, this bodes well for the elimination

[8]Let $Y = GNP$; then $Y = C + I + G + CA$, where C is consumption, I is investment, G is government spending on final goods and services, and CA is the current account balance. The definition of private national savings is $S_p = Y - C - T$, where T is (net) taxes. Then $Y = C + S_p + T$. Setting the two definitions of GNP equal to each other results in: $S_p + (T - G) = I + CA$. But $T - G$ is government receipts minus government expenditures, or government (public) savings, S_g. Therefore, $S_p + S_g = I + CA$.

of the current account deficit since private savings rates (S_p) could now be used to finance domestic investment (I) instead of the government deficit (negative S_g). At the same time as the disappearance of the budget imbalance, however, private savings have continued to be low while a strong economy has pushed up investment. A large current account deficit naturally follows according to the accounting identity given above. The strengthening of the US dollar after 1995, together with the voracious US demand for consumer goods (low S_p) and the collapse of several East Asian economies in 1997 (causing imports to be cheaper in dollar terms) have caused large current account deficits to appear for as far as anyone dares predict into the future.

Trade Conflict with Japan

The US trade and budget deficits did not occur in a vacuum. One of the most significant domestic events that happened simultaneously in the early 1980s was the decline of the US auto industry. In the early 1980s, US cars cost more, got worse mileage, and were of a lower quality than Japanese imports. Autos appeared to be on the same path downward as the consumer electronics industry which disappeared in the 1970s, and the steel industry which began widespread downsizing and restructuring, also in the 1970s. Given that the auto industry and related sectors employed tens of millions of Americans, it was politically impossible to ignore their cries for government intervention. Intervention came in several forms, most notably the implementation of a voluntary restraint agreement (VRA) with Japan which was equivalent to a set of quotas on US imports of Japanese motor vehicles.

The desire to limit Japanese vehicle imports was encouraged by more than the penetration of the US car market. A persistent and large trade deficit had opened with Japan (Figure 4.5) at around the same time as the VRA was implemented and the overall US trade deficit expanded. Between 1980 and 1987, the US merchandise trade deficit with Japan jumped from approximately US$12 billion to almost US$60 billion. Since 1987 it has varied somewhat, but has more or less stayed in the range of US$45–US$65 billion.

It is difficult to argue that this increase in the deficit is entirely

Figure 4.5 *US-Japanese Trade, 1975–97*

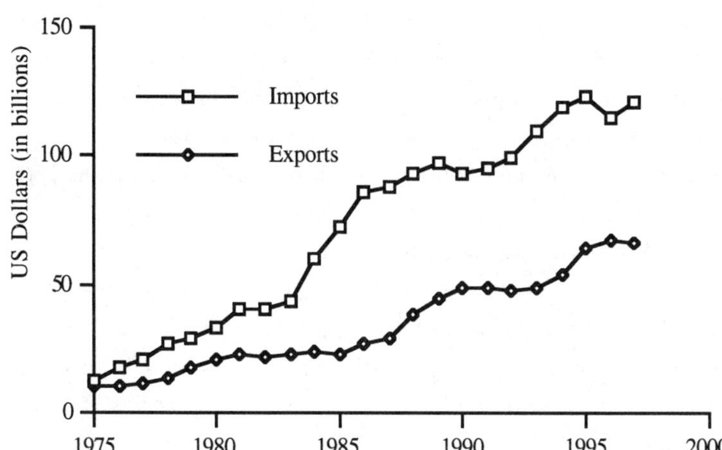

Source: Bureau of Economic Analysis, July, 1998.

Japan's fault. Between 1980 and 1994, US exports to Japan grew by US$31 billion, or 149 percent. Imports, meanwhile, grew by US$86 billion, or 260 percent (Bureau of Economic Analysis, 1994). In other words, US firms had very good success selling in Japan, but the low savings rate and high consumption in the US economy pulled in Japanese goods at an enormous rate. It should be noted, however, that the success of some US firms does not imply that the Japanese market is completely open. The United States has a particular affinity for Japanese goods because they fill the demand for high quality, cutting edge, consumer goods. Given Japan's high saving rates together with its comparative advantage in high-technology consumer goods, it is not surprising that the US runs a bilateral deficit with Japan.

There is a widespread but often unanalyzed belief that the Japanese market is relatively closed to foreign goods. This is a complex issue involving the industrial organization of the Japanese economy and is far beyond the scope of this chapter. Suffice it to say that regardless of whether or not the market is as open as it could be, the belief that it is closed has caused an intense amount of political pressure to be placed on the US-Japanese economic relationship. The pressure is somewhat cyclical and depends on the state of the US economy but it is always in the background of US-Japanese relations. The pressure is compounded by the nature of our two economies, both of which have firms that are highly competitive in many sectors of advanced technology. This causes many people to view the trade relation through a lens that interprets events in terms of their contribution to an ill-defined national interest in maintaining a lead in high-technology fields, many of which may have military or strategic implications.

As a consequence, a great deal of energy has been expended through the 1980s and the 1990s in devising strategies to reduce the bilateral trade deficit with Japan. The various strategies have been macroeconomic, microeconomic and structural. Macro strategies have focused on bringing down the value of the dollar *vis-à-vis* the yen. This strategy was first put to the test in 1985 with the Plaza Accord in which the Group of Seven (G-7) agreed to coordinate their efforts to depreciate the value of the dollar.[9] The Plaza Accord succeeded in reducing the value of the dollar, and in cutting the trade deficit with Japan with the usual lag of about 1.5 years. Subsequent appreciation of the dollar after 1989, however, reversed the effects of this effort.

Microeconomic strategies have included the Market-Oriented-Sector-Specific (MOSS) talks that took place in 1985–87. The MOSS talks dealt with a number of sectors in which the US argued that Japanese red tape and bureaucratic obfuscation made it impossible to enter the market. In addition, bilateral talks have been ongoing in a number of sectors on a case-by-case basis. The outcome of these talks is difficult to assess because it is impossible to say what would have happened without the talks. Nevertheless, agreements have been reached in a number of sectors (semiconductors, for example, is the best known) and while both sides have complained at times about compliance, the general strategy of sector-by-sector negotiations seems to have been an important safety valve to reduce the pressure to take more drastic actions. A combination of macroeconomic and microeconomic strategies, which might be called structural strategies, began with the Structural Im-

[9]The G-7 include the United States, Canada, France, Germany, Italy, Japan and the UK.

pediments Initiative (SII) of 1989–91. These talks dealt with problems related to the differing economic structures of the two countries, including the low savings rate in the US and Japanese protection of small domestic retailers. The SII had some success, but was unrealistic in its expectation that it might increase US savings or alter the organizational structure of Japanese industry. More recently, the US has begun a series of talks called the Framework for a New Economic Partnership, which address specific issues of economic integration. These include each country's competition policies, investment policies and industrial support policies. The long economic downturn that Japan has been in throughout much of the 1990s has probably had a positive effect in the United States by taking some of the pressure off the US-Japan trade relationship. From the United States' perspective, restoring growth in the Japanese economy (and reforming the banking sector) has taken precedence over other objectives. At the same time, the relative health of the US economy after the 1991 recession has also reduced the urgency to take action on the trade front. Nevertheless, the strength of the dollar and the recent health of the US economy has pushed up the bilateral deficit once again, and one can only speculate how long it will be before a new issue pops up that suddenly puts political pressure on US trade policy to 'do something about Japan.'

Pathways to Protection

The US-Japanese trade conflict has been the point of greatest pressure on US trade relations during the last two decades, but it is only one of several changes that have raised the level of political heat that is focused on Congress and the president. Another source of political pressure is the internal Congressional reforms of the mid-1970s which removed much of the insulation from industry group lobbyists that Congress had enjoyed in the 1950s and 1960s (Destler, 1994). A third factor is the end of the Cold War and the decline in the United States' willingness to sacrifice trade gains for political objectives. A fourth factor is the rise of the newly industrializing super-exporters of East Asia and the pressure they have put on US industries. A fifth factor is the rise of the trade deficit in the US and the fear (which probably reached its highest level in the late 1980s) that numerous US industries had lost their ability to compete. Finally, with the signing of NAFTA, there is an old fear that has been made new, that the low wages of our trading partners will cause job losses and declining wages. The later fear is made more palpable by the fact that median average US wages have been stagnant since the early 1970s, and have declined in real terms for those without college degrees. As always, one should be careful in interpreting the precise meaning of this. Individual workers have seen wage increases. What the statistics show is that those workers without a college degree who enter the labor force today will earn less in real terms than the first wages of similarly educated workers who entered the labor force in the early 1970s. Most individual workers gain wage increases over time as they accumulate experience on the job. While there is some indication of a reversal of this trend in the late 1990s, it is too early to say if the decline is over.

This is not to argue that these fears are accurate perceptions of the real forces shaping the US economy. There is little evidence, for example, that trade has had much affect on wages, while the evidence is strong that technological changes have affected wages (Burtless, 1995; Cline, 1997). The point is, however, that each of these fears are sources of pressure on the US political system, and each contributes to the growth of strongly nationalistic views and demands for more inward looking policies.

In the US system, the pressure on Congress and the president to supply special protection to specific industries is channeled through one of two procedures. One procedure is to appeal directly to the president. For example, the US restrictions on Japanese auto imports in the early 1980s occurred through presidential action. A more common method for obtaining protection is through one of four different administrative procedures. First, there are countervailing duties that are in retaliation for foreign subsidies. Second, there are antidumping duties that are to counteract the selling of goods below 'fair value'. In the United States, the concept of 'fair value' is generally the average price of a good in the exporter's home market, or its average price in a third country market. Selling at a price below the cost of production is selling at below 'fair value', but firms may sell at a price greater than the cost of production and still be below 'fair value'. Firms sometimes use high prices in their home markets to subsidize the selling of goods at a very low price in a foreign market, where they hope to establish themselves and gain a larger share of the market. Antidumping duties are designed to counteract this tactic. Third is the escape clause relief, a temporary tariff in response to a sudden surge of imports which threaten to destroy a domestic industry; and fourth, the so-called 'Section 301' retaliation, a tariff imposed in response to some other unfair trade practice. In each case, a firm, an industry trade association, a labor union, or some other interest group petitions the federal government to investigate specific trade practices of a foreign firm or its home country. If the investigation results in the determination of unfair foreign trade practices, then a second investigation is conducted to ascertain if the unfair trade practice has actually harmed the US industry. If the second investigation results in a positive finding, then a temporary tariff is imposed. It is not uncommon for the first investigation to determine that a foreign practice is unfair, and for the second investigation to find that it has had no harmful effect on US industry.

In practice, antidumping duties are by far the most common form of special protection granted, although Section 301 duties probably generate the most media attention. Section 301 is named after the section (number 301) in the US Trade Act of 1974 that requires the president's chief trade negotiator (the United States Trade Representative, or USTR) to retaliate with import tariffs against any nation that persistently engages in unfair trade practices. In virtually all cases, there is a lengthy investigation and a series of negotiations before retaliation is contemplated. Note, however, that it is left to the United States to determine the meaning of 'unfair'. The Uruguay Round of GATT made some progress in defining a common way to measure whether dumping is occurring or not. Nevertheless, the US and many other countries continue to apply their own procedures and definitions. If the targets of these actions are dissatisfied with the outcome, they can appeal to the WTO and initiate a complaint there. The potential conflict between the WTO and individual nations over the application of antidumping or other duties is a potential crack in the integrity of the WTO as a credible international organization. Application of Section 301 against US trading partners is widely regarded outside the US as arbitrary, one-sided and harmful to multilateral agreements such as WTO.

To make matters worse, growing Congressional anger at the failure of President Reagan to conduct Section 301 investigations in the 1980s (primarily because he favored foreign policy objectives far more than trade) led to the passage of a trade bill in 1988 which contained a so-called Super 301. Super 301 requires the USTR to produce a list each year that contains the names of countries that systematically engage in unfair trading practices and to open negotiations with them. If the negotiations are unsuccessful in resolving the problem the bill requires the president to retaliate. Presidents Reagan, Bush and Clinton, each of whom have held office under this bill, have worked hard to avoid complying with the bill, but in some years Congressional pressure has prevailed and the USTR has produced the required list. Generally, the effects have been limited because the list is manipulated to contain relatively insignificant trading partners. Nevertheless, it is important because it illustrates the sub-current of nationalistic opinions that lie beneath the surface of US policy and that threaten to erupt whenever isolationist and nationalistic movements gain strength, as they have recently.

Bilateral Alternatives

Perhaps the most important lesson of US commercial policy in the 1970s, 1980s and 1990s is its tendency to seek bilateral solutions rather than multilateral ones. This is not to say that the US does not favor GATT or the new WTO as a forum for achieving solutions. However, the pressure of issues which have a visible and immediate effect on US industries generally results in a bilateral response.

There are several reasons for the US preference for bilateral responses to trade problems. First, it is a much faster way to deal with a problem than taking it before GATT or the WTO. Second, the US has more power in a bilateral negotiation and in many cases is more likely to prevail. The US market is critically important to a very large number of countries, both rich and poor. The threat of losing the market, even on a temporary basis, is a powerful incentive for many countries to reach agreement. It is usually not clear to what extent the loss of access to the US market is an empty threat. For example, numerous recent cases that sought to punish Japanese industries for what the US labeled as unfair practices have been unable to find a set of Japanese products that could be excluded from the US market without harming US firms that depended on them. One of the lessons of globalization is that retaliation often backfires. In a multilateral context, the threat of reducing access to the US market is a much riskier gamble, and undermines the fundamental US policy objective of liberalizing world markets.

A third reason for bilateral approaches to trade problems is that they permit the US to experiment with new solutions which may ultimately be brought to the WTO if they prove successful. The attempt to include labor and environmental agreements in the Uruguay Round negotiations of GATT was partly related to their inclusion in the NAFTA agreement. Fourth, and related to the previous reason, they enable negotiations in areas not covered by the WTO. For example, the 1995 US dispute with Japan over autos and auto parts was partly a dispute over competition policies and Japanese industrial organization. Competition policies (called antitrust policies in the US) are national policies that determine the limits of fair competition. They include rules regarding mergers, collusion between firms and regulation of monopolies. Neither the Japanese, nor the US, nor independent observers could say whether the issue of national industrial organization is included within the WTO's areas of coverage.

A fifth and final reason for favoring bilateral approaches is that they are a powerful force in shaping multilateral talks. For the United States this was a major reason for favoring the Canada-United States Free Trade Agreement (CUSFTA) of 1989, and its extension to Mexico in 1994. Recall that the multilateral GATT talks of the Uruguay Round began in 1986, and that they immediately ran into difficulties so that by 1988 many commentators were arguing that GATT was dead. At the time, the US and Canada were concluding their free trade negotiations and the prospect of these two countries going their own way was an added incentive for other nations to struggle to complete GATT talks. The enlargement of CUSFTA to include Mexico intensified the perception that the US, in particular, was capable of pursuing its goal of liberalizing world markets outside the GATT process. From the United States' viewpoint, this prospect was instrumental in helping to create a successful conclusion to the Uruguay Round.

NAFTA AND THE NAFTA DEBATES

NAFTA represents the strongest expression of the bilateral tendencies in the commercial policy of the United States. In one sense, NAFTA is a completely parallel but alternative set of rules to the WTO for conducting trade relations with sovereign nations. Nevertheless, as pointed out above, the motivating factor for the United States is not to undermine the WTO but to push it forward by posing an alternative that can be interpreted as a challenge.

Beyond the desire to spur the Uruguay Round, there were several additional US motives for wanting a free trade agreement with Mexico. First, Mexican trade barriers were much higher than US barriers so it was perceived that there would be net gains for firms in the United States. Second, among policy makers in the United States there was a genuine ideological commitment to open markets. Again, this should not be interpreted as implying that the US was seeking absolutely free trade. Rather, in accordance with standard neoclassical economic theory, US policy makers believed that more open and liberal markets would benefit each country through the creation of a more efficient allocation of resources. This translates directly into material wealth and higher growth rates. Hence, opening of the Mexican market was deemed necessary for the restoration of economic stability after the long period of stagnation during the debt crisis of the 1980s.

Economic stability in Mexico has a security dimension for the United States given the long and porous border between the two countries. Prosperity in Mexico is clearly in the national interest of the United States since the alternative of stagnation might eventually lead to political chaos. Internal Mexican political struggles could not help but spillover into the United States given the long history of the movement of people back and forth between the two nations. Political and strategic concerns have a long-run economic component as well since Mexico is a large country of more than 90 million inhabitants and a growing middle class. While more sober analysts recognized that deeper integration with the Mexican economy was not likely to bring large immediate benefits to US firms since Mexico's GDP is only about 5 percent of the size of the United States' GDP, the long run benefits of a deepening relationship with a heavily populated and growing country on the southern border are likely to be considerable. For example, the US car industry was quick to perceive that the rationalization of its production between three countries, one of which is a developing economy, would give it strategic advantages that would be harder to obtain without the agreement.

The debates in the United States over NAFTA were loud and strong. To a large degree they gave voice to the fears of globalization that are relatively common among workers in advanced industrial economies. The pace of change seems to have sped up everywhere and appears to be leaving behind those without skills and without a college degree. While studies of the relationship between trade and wages show that trade cannot be responsible for more than a very small part of the growth in wage inequality in the United States (Burtless, 1995; Cline, 1997), technical economic analysis is of little consolation to individuals facing economic disruption of their lives; common sense seems to tell them that competition with workers in low wage firms is a losing proposition. Perhaps the greatest challenge from globalization is for governments to figure out how to manage their domestic economies in ways that reduce the fears that so many people have about the future.

In the United States the overt expression of fears about NAFTA focused on three areas: labor standards, environmental standards and democracy. These issues put the agreement in the forefront of the changes happening in the world trading system. Prior to the Uruguay Round of GATT, there was a denial of any attempt to link nontrade issues (labor, environment, democracy, and so on) to trade. The Uruguay

Round, which was concluded after NAFTA, altered this by permitting countries to use trade sanctions against other nations when they fail to comply with a newly established accord on intellectual property rights. For the first time, the world body has legitimized the linking of trade with a nontrade issue.

NAFTA was somewhat ahead of the Uruguay Round in this respect. The achievement of the linkage of trade and nontrade issues was largely at the insistence of the United States in an attempt to placate domestic US interests that threatened to block the agreement in Congress. In what is perhaps the strangest pairing of bedfellows in twentieth century US history, labor unionists and environmentalists joined ranks to oppose NAFTA on the grounds that it would cause significant job losses and increase environmental pollution. The unions' position was that US producers were likely to move south or source production in Mexico in order to escape US labor laws. Worst-case scenario projections estimated the potential job loss at 400,000. The median estimate of independent economists, on the other hand, was zero. In addition, unions in general worry that NAFTA gives employers another bargaining chip in negotiations with employees since it is easier to make a credible threat to take a business to Mexico if workers refuse to lessen their demands.

Environmentalists worried that growth in Mexico, particularly along the border, will adversely impact the environment. Furthermore, they argue that firms are likely to relocate to Mexico because they can escape US environmental laws and Mexican enforcement of its own environmental laws is lax. Beyond environmentalists and labor unions, another set of opponents to NAFTA argued that the United States should not sign preferential trade agreements with countries that are not open, democratic societies.

By way of response, NAFTA proponents were quick to point out several basic facts about the US and Mexican economies. First, the number of jobs in an economy is determined by fiscal, monetary and labor market policies, not by trade policies. Under most circumstances, if unemployment rises, the Federal Reserve will lower interest rates to counteract it and any impact of trade will be offset. This serves to highlight the primary reason offered by economists for the support for international trade: it improves the allocation of resources. Note that this justification is not based on jobs. Problems of unemployment are far more efficiently handled through macro policies and labor market policies. Second, the size of the Mexican economy is too small to have a significant impact on the United States in the near term. For example, the US averages a net gain in new jobs every month of about 225,000. Even if the worst-case scenario had played itself out and the US lost 400,000 jobs over several years, it is inconsequential compared to the normal job creation power of the economy. In any case, while it is impossible to accurately measure job gains or job losses due to trade, independent analysts put the first few years of NAFTA impacts at close to zero, but possibly a small net gain (Hinojosa Ojeda, et al., 1996).

Third, the proponents argued that NAFTA may actually lead to a cleaner environment since the side agreements created a set of institutions for consulting on these issues and for financing clean-up costs. Most observers recognize, however, that developing economies are generally willing to trade off their environment in favor of more income. That is, they favor economic growth over a cleaner environment when such a tradeoff must be made. At various points in the development process, however, the tables turn and environmental issues rise in importance. It is impossible to say where Mexico is in this schema since it is a large country with income levels and pollution problems that vary by region.

Furthermore, regardless of US, Mexican and Canadian environmental values, most observers point out that the institutions created by the side agreements, both the labor and the environmental ones, have been ineffective so far. This does not necessarily mean that the institutions will never work, but it is not a particularly good beginning and it has continued to provide ammunition to the anti-NAFTA side in the debate.

CONCLUSION: ISSUES FOR DEEPER INTEGRATION

The success of GATT in bringing down tariffs and limiting the use of non-tariff barriers is one of the more remarkable features of the second half of the twentieth century. In the United States, both tariffs and import quotas are extremely limited in their application, in spite of the publicity generated by one or two cases, usually involving Japan. The one important exception is in the area of textiles and apparel, the 'Mount Everest of US protectionism', but even in this case the conclusion of the Uruguay Round of GATT negotiations successfully brought these sectors into the multilateral agreement (Hufbauer and Elliott, 1994).

US commercial policy is unexceptional in the levels of protection it affords. Virtually every industrial nation has low levels of tariffs and/or liberal quotas, usually with one or two exceptions, most often agriculture or textiles and apparel. As a result, the US along with other industrial and many industrializing nations, has begun to address a set of obstacles to deeper economic integration which are more contentious than tariffs and import quotas because they are intertwined with domestic policy. The majority of these issues are in six main areas: (1) environmental policies; (2) labor standard policies; (3) competition policies; (4) industrial support policies; (5) investment policies; and (6) intellectual property rights.

At least three of these areas figured prominently in the NAFTA debates: environmental, labor and investment policies. Two (environment and labor) were far enough outside the current style of trade negotiations that they could not be included directly in the NAFTA treaty. In the future, it is highly likely that the US will look for ways to directly include these issues in its negotiations over trade.

5. Canada's Economic Development and Integration

The theme of this book is North American economic integration. As economists have long known, the advantages of international trade and integration stem largely from the differences amongst the parties involved. This chapter deals with the dual issues of economic differences and economic integration as viewed from a Canadian perspective. There are two fundamental aspects of the Canadian situation which differentiate it from the United States and Mexico: Canada's geographical setting, and the importance of regionalism in Canada. After a discussion of these two defining characteristics of the Canadian reality this chapter covers:

1. a brief history of Canada's economic development prior to World War II (1939), with special emphasis on a specific theory of economic development (the 'staples' theory) and on policies of that era relating to international trade and integration;

2. a review of the Canadian economy since World War II, with particular attention paid to evolving trading relationships and the question of whether these have affected the performance of the economy or the ability to exercise independent economic policies;

3. a brief survey of Canada's economic resources in the 1990s with special emphasis upon its people ('human capital'); and

4. a discussion of a number of recent trade-related policy issues in Canada including Canada's social and regional development programs, the place of 'cultural' industries, foreign ownership, inter-

provincial trade barriers as indicated by the recent 'beer wars', separation in Quebec and government for indigenous peoples.

GEOGRAPHY AND ALL THAT

With an area of 10 million square kilometers (over 3.8 million square miles), Canada is the second largest country in the world, but given its population of only about 30 million, it is one of the least densely populated. In 1993, Canada had under three persons per square kilometer as compared to about twenty-eight persons in the United States and forty-seven in Mexico. It has been argued that Canadians, more than most people, tend to define the world and their place in it in terms of geography. In part, this may reflect the feeling of space and unlimited resources which result from the low population density. In part, it may stem from the very uneven population distribution occasioned by Canada's northern climate: some 80 percent of Canadians are estimated to live within 320 kilometers (200 miles) of the southern border with the United States. This, in turn, generates the strong feelings felt by a small population living immediately adjacent to a very large and powerful one; 'like a mouse living with an elephant' as former Canadian Prime Minister Pierre Trudeau liked to put it.

Also of significance are key natural features of the Canadian landscape which, it has often been remarked, tend to push commercial trade into north-south flows within North America. Movement is easier by sea than land along the Atlantic and Pacific coasts, and unrestricted movement east and west is inhibited by great natural barriers, the barren, exposed Precambrian rock of the Canadian Shield as it dips down to the Great Lakes separating heavily populated southern Ontario from the western prairies and two great mountain chains, the ancient Laurentian-Appalachian chain in the East and the newer Rockies in the West.

Thus the dictates of geography generate a uniquely Canadian situation. A thin ribbon of population stretches east-west along the American-Canadian border, bound together by the, perhaps fragile, threads of national identity, while commercial attraction pulls toward the ease of north-south trade with the much larger neighbor. In light of this it is not surprising that Canada is an example of what economists call a 'small, open economy'. Canada's GDP is the smallest of the G-7 group of industrial countries and trade is extremely important. As pointed out in Chapter 4, in the mid 1990s exports of goods and services amounted to about 33.2 percent of Canadian GDP, as compared to 10.4 percent for the United States, and 17.0 percent for Mexico (International Monetary Fund, 1995). By 1996 Canadian exports reached 39.1 percent of GDP. Mexican exports had also been rising rapidly and by 1996 amounted to 31.5 percent of GDP as compared to 11.4 percent for the United States (International Monetary Fund, 1998). Some countries do have higher export dependence than Canada,[1] but none trades as heavily with a single other nation; nearly 80 percent of Canada's exports go to the United States. The dependence of the small Canadian economy upon external trade, and the overriding importance of the United States as a trading partner, help to explain why international economic policies have often been so controversial in Canada.

Regionalism

It is hardly surprising that regional factors are important in a large country such as Canada. The barriers to east-west movement, noted above, tend to reinforce such regionalism. So does Canada's history, beginning as a colonial extension of the two 'founding nations', England and France, and the preservation of a vibrant French-speaking culture centered in Quebec. This, however, offers an insufficient explanation of the importance of regionalism in Canada. For one thing, the English-French separation is far from perfect, with sizeable primarily English-speaking populations in Quebec (for example, in the west of Montreal and southeast of Montreal in the Eastern townships) and with French speaking centers in Acadian New Brunswick in the Maritimes and in towns scattered throughout Ontario and the Prairies. In practice, and to a limited degree officially, Canada is multicultural. Canada has an aboriginal population (Indian and Inuit) of just over one million, as well

[1] At the extreme, Singapore's exports in 1992 were 165 percent of GDP, compared to Canada's 29 percent for the same year.

as many Metis of mixed Indian-European lineage. Early immigrants came from all parts of Europe, and have been joined by others from throughout the world.

The unusual importance of regionalism in Canada stems from the very high degree of decentralization of the Canadian federal system of government, far more so than that of either Mexico or the United States. Canada has ten provinces;[2] the sparsely populated North has been divided into three territories administered by the federal government in Ottawa. We shall not elaborate in detail on reasons for the strength of the provincial governments. One factor may be Canada's relatively peaceful founding which did not involve a central, federal, authority establishing the nation with the use of force (as, for example, in the War of Independence and Civil War in the United States). Moreover, the acceptance of the French fact as a part of the colonies and nation gave explicit recognition to regional differences. For example, the British North America Act (BNA Act), passed by the United Kingdom parliament in 1867, which brought together four British colonies as Canada, formally recognized the French language and special civil law code in Quebec.[3]

However, at another level the strength of the Canadian provincial governments is somewhat puzzling, since the Canadian politicians who negotiated the terms of the BNA Act were at pains to ensure a strong federal government, influenced in part by the example of regional division in the American Civil War. Thus the BNA Act set out a specific list of powers for the provinces (immigration and agriculture shared with the federal government) and reserved any unspecified area for the federal government. The American Constitution, in contrast, gives

[2]The provinces can be divided into several regions. The Maritimes provinces are Nova Scotia, New Brunswick and Prince Edward Island. The Maritimes and Newfoundland are referred to as the Atlantic provinces. Quebec and Ontario are each considered to be separate regions although together they are sometimes referred to as Central Canada. Manitoba, Saskatchewan, and Alberta are the Prairies. The last region is the most westerly province–British Columbia.

[3]Complete independence for Canada awaited the Statute of Westminister of 1931 which transferred control of foreign policy from the United Kingdom. Until the Constitution Act of 1982 the main element in the Canadian Constitution remained the BNA Act, a law of the United Kingdom parliament.

residual powers to the states. In addition, limits were imposed on the power of the provinces to impose taxes (that is, no provincial 'indirect' taxes). Unlike the United States, however, the provinces were not prohibited the use of deficit financing. Why, then, are the Canadian provincial governments so powerful as compared to lower levels of government in most other countries? In part it reflects the fact that many areas of provincial responsibility (for example, education, health, and welfare) became areas of high growth in the twentieth century. Moreover, primary responsibility for natural resources was allocated to the provinces. Offshore fisheries went to federal government and agriculture was shared. In the prairie provinces control over natural resources followed a 1930 amendment to the BNA Act. Further, several areas of provincial responsibility (for example, 'property and civil rights', powers of 'direct' taxation, 'local works' and matters of a 'merely local or private nature in the province') could be interpreted very broadly. The presence of only ten regional governments–in contrast, for example, to 50 states–also made it easier for the provinces to find areas of common interest and for well-established procedures of consultation to evolve between the federal government and the provinces. It is likely that growing provincial powers generated a positive feedback loop in which citizens became increasingly conscious of being citizens of the provinces as well as Canada and looked to the provincial government to express regional interests.

In some respects the Constitution Act of 1982 can be seen as the culmination of Canadian regionalism, as expressed through provincial governments. This act was reached with the agreement of all the provinces except Quebec. It repatriated the BNA Act from the British Parliament and reaffirmed provincial primacy over natural resources, removed limitations on provincial taxation, formally recognized the necessity of provincial approval of amendments to the Constitution, required periodic consultations between the 'First Ministers' (Prime Minister and Provincial Premiers)[4] and brought the concept of equalization into the

[4]Canada has a parliamentary form of government. Voters elect members to a legislative assembly. Federally that legislature is called Parliament. The party with the most members forms the government. The leader of that party becomes the

Constitution. The failed Meech Lake and Charlottetown Accords were largely attempts to bring Quebec into the Constitution. Their failure reflects, in part, disagreement in Canada about Quebec's place in Confederation. In addition, discussion of these proposals raised a large number of other questions about the ideal constitution for Canadians, which did not relate directly to the Quebec question, but which alienated potential supporters of the Accords. The equalization program is a commitment by the federal government to make financial payments to provinces which have below average tax bases, thereby helping to ensure that all provinces can provide roughly the same level of services to their citizens. It is, perhaps, a proto-typical example of Canadian regionalism. It explicitly looks to a regional definition of inequality (rather than, for example, an individual's personal income regardless of location of residence). Some economists have argued that by transferring resources to poorer regions it supports continued regional differences by inhibiting the migration of resources to the better off areas of the country. Finally, while the program is a transfer of funds by the federal government, the transfer is to provincial governments and not to individuals.

To summarize, it is important, when looking at Canada, that the strongly regional nature of Canadian federalism be appreciated. The provinces have primary power over economic matters within their borders, and many changes in Canadian economic policy, even at the federal level, proceed through a process of formal and informal consultation between the federal government and the provinces.

CANADIAN ECONOMIC DEVELOPMENT BEFORE WAR II

By the year 1000 AD what is known as Canada was sparsely populated by a number of traditional aboriginal economies living in close touch with nature. Trade took place amongst these economies but they were largely self-sufficient. The 'discovery' of North America by European

head of government. Federally the leader is the Prime Minister. Provincial leaders are called Premiers.

explorers opened it to flows of goods, services, capital and labor from across the Atlantic. The Vikings arrived around 1000 and maintained a small settlement for several hundred years in Newfoundland. Continuous ties with Europe began when John Cabot, sailing under the English flag, landed in Cape Breton, Nova Scotia and Newfoundland and the adjacent mainland coast of Labrador (1498). Soon thereafter fishermen from Britain, France, Portugal and Spain began to exploit the rich fish stocks off the Atlantic coast. French contact with Quebec began when Jacques Cartier sailed up the St Lawrence (1534–35) and saw establishment of a settlement at Quebec City by Samuel de Champlain (1608). Thus began a process of economic growth in what we now know as Canada.

Economists argue that economic growth can be generated in two ways: by increases in the quantity of inputs in the economy and by increases in the quality (productivity) of those inputs. While both sources of growth were important in Canada in the period we are discussing, the immigration of labor and capital from offshore was particularly important. We shall not provide a comprehensive review of Canadian economic development. Rather, comments will be organized around two general themes: (1) a theory of economic development, called the 'staples' theory, which has been particularly influential amongst Canadian social scientists; and (2) the evolution of Canada's international trade and integration policies.

The Staples Theory

The staples theory was developed primarily by Canadian economists (Innes, 1930; Mackintosh, 1923; Watkins, 1963), though it has been widely applied elsewhere, including in some of the arguments advanced by spokesmen from developing nations in the north-south debates. In this view, economic growth in a small open economy is driven by the external demand for natural resource products ('staples'). The precise way in which growth occurs depends on the economic linkages associated with the particular staple product. Linkages may be backwards, drawing inputs into the economy, or forwards, involving the further processing of the staple. The distribution of the earnings from the staple is also important. The staples theory lends itself readily to a dualistic view of the world as consisting of powerful 'metropolis' areas and powerless 'hinterlands'. The link with the theories of Raul Prebish discussed in Chapter 3 is obvious. Initially France and Britain were the metropolis and the Canadian colonies were the hinterland. What happens in the staples-producing hinterland is largely determined in the external metropolis. This dualistic view (metropolis vs. hinterland) has colored feelings of regionalism within Canada as well. Historically, freight rates have tended to encourage the production of staples in the Atlantic and Prairie provinces (the new hinterland) and manufacturing in central Canada–Ontario and Quebec (the new metropolis).[5]

A brief extension of this discussion may help clarify some of the arguments in Canada over trade policies. The staples theory could be characterized as an argument in political economy, and contrasted with the narrower view prevalent amongst economists and commercial interests. The staples theory can be recast in the narrower view, where forces of supply and demand determine the prices of goods and inputs as well as trade flows and migration patterns; export demands by the metropolis and staples' production technologies are key factors in the operation of the economic markets. However staples-influenced analyses typically go beyond this to emphasize the importance of the power relationships underlying trade and the social and cultural changes which may occur along with economic growth. Traditional economic analysis tends to see trade flows as stemming from more efficient ways to meet the demands of relatively fixed tastes, thereby improving standards of living for both trading partners; issues of culture and social values are a matter of domestic tastes and, possibly, policies for the domestic government. On the other hand, the broader staples view tends to see tastes, culture and social values as malleable, prone to largely hidden processes of change and subject to the influence of external sources. That is to say, the metropolis will determine taste, culture and social

[5]This view of central Canada is typified in the following story. A prairie farmer in the 1930s loses his wheat crop to drought, his topsoil to the winds, his wife in childbirth and his eldest son to influenza. Standing on his front porch he shakes his fist and shouts, 'God damn the CPR'. Events outside his control in the hinterland are blamed on powers in the metropolis–the Canadian Pacific Railway in Montreal.

values in the hinterland. It is not surprising that proponents of these two approaches will often evaluate trade policies differently.

According to the staples approach, Canadian economic development can be understood by tracing through time the influences of a sequence of export staples. The staples were natural resources in demand by foreign markets: fish, followed by furs, followed by timber, followed by wheat, over the 500-year period from 1500 to the early part of the twentieth century. Of course, a new staple product does not completely displace an earlier one. Canada in the 1990s is, in fact, still a net exporter of all four of the staples just mentioned. As noted, each staple had its own demand, production and income distribution characteristics which set the timing and exact nature of its influence.

The first staple, for example, had minimal linkage effects, since cod were caught on the Atlantic Grand Banks fishing grounds by boats which sailed from Europe, fished, and returned to Europe without necessarily landing on North American soil. Linkage effects were more pronounced with the fur trade, as trading routes and posts spread along the inland water system. Obviously a certain number of trappers and traders were required, so there was stimulus to small-scale farming and retailing (for example, along the St Lawrence River) to provide supplies for traders and ships landing to take on beaver and other pelts. Coordinating and financing this activity necessitated some party taking an entrepreneurial role. This was handled largely by French fur traders, the Hudson's Bay Company (organized in England in 1670) and the North West Company (which began in 1775 with a group of Montreal-based fur traders). Conflict between English and French fur traders in the seventeenth and eighteenth centuries mirrored the hostilities between France and England in Europe. In the Treaty of Paris of 1763 the French colonies in North America were ceded to England.[6] Subsequent English rule left a fair degree of autonomy for the French-speaking culture centered in Quebec.

The third great staple product, lumber, rose to prominence early in

[6]The Treaty of Paris left St Pierre and Miquelon, two small islands in the Gulf of St Lawrence, in French hands. The Hudson's Bay Company absorbed the North West Company in 1821.

the nineteenth century. The Napoleonic War disrupted the movement of timber from the Baltic region to England. England turned to British North America instead, imposing high tariffs on Baltic wood as an incentive. Harvesting trees and producing lumber from sawmills required local labor and entrepreneurship. Agriculture and food processing for the local market were also stimulated. In addition, the empty ships coming to Canada to pick up timber were an ideal passage space for people. The importance of timber as a staple product peaked by the mid 1800s, partly because of the common property nature of trees, which were generally cut without replanting. The cleared land served as a further stimulus to farming.

The second half of the nineteenth century is generally seen as a period of relative economic stagnation, followed by a wheat boom at the turn of the century as the Prairies were subject to a flood of settlement. Expansion of grain production generated a demand for agricultural inputs (equipment and rail links) as well as providing a growing market for consumer goods.

Of course, the staples theory provides an oversimplified picture of the increasingly complex Canadian economy. Criticism of a staples-based approach becomes particularly severe following the wheat boom. On the one hand, there were new natural resource exports which arose after World War I, a variety of metals and then petroleum after the Leduc find in Alberta in 1947. However, these were not dominating export products to the same degree as the earlier staples. Moreover, with its growth the Canadian economy became increasingly reliant on its own internal demands, and less so on the external demands emphasized in the staples theory.

Even today, as was noted above, Canada is more export dependent than either the United States or Mexico. Natural resources, exported in a relatively unprocessed form, still form a higher share of Canada's exports than any of the other G-7 countries. In 1995 agriculture and fish, energy, forestry and mineral products (before significant processing) made up about 35 percent of Canadian exports. The share of food and raw materials in total exports was 31 percent for Canada in 1992. For Japan the figure was 2 percent, while it was 13 percent for the European Union and 18 percent for the United States. Still, most analysts concede that Canada moved past the staples economy stage early this century.

Trade Policy

Economic development does not proceed in a policy vacuum, though the discussion up to now may suggest this. We shall now review the major features of government policy regarding international economic relations in Canada prior to World War II.

The colonial period was dominated by the British mercantilistic outlook up to the early 1840s, long after mercantilism had been discredited by economists such as David Hume and Adam Smith. Under mercantilism, colonies would ship raw materials to the home country in return for manufactured products. It was inevitable, then, that Canada would trade primarily with France (before 1763) and Britain, and that the trade would be in staples. However, when the British move to free trade came, it came very quickly. Duties on products entering the United Kingdom were chopped on both timber and grain in the 1840s, thereby removing the protection the colonies had been provided in the British market.

Canadian producers were forced to reevaluate their markets. It was natural that their eyes should turn to the South. By 1850 the population of the United States had passed 23 million, a large proportion living in the Northeast where substantial industrialization had already occurred. After negotiating a free trade agreement amongst themselves, the British colonies had Britain negotiate for them on tariff reductions with the United States. The Americans insisted on gaining access to the coastal fisheries in the Atlantic. With this concession, the Reciprocity Treaty of 1854 was signed, under which a large number of agricultural and primary goods would move free of duty between the United States and the British North American colonies.

The Reciprocity Treaty was short-lived. Either party could, after ten years and with one year's notice, abrogate it. The United States did so and the Treaty ended in 1866. Exports to the United States increased substantially from $8.6 million in 1854 to $34.8 million in 1866.

However, the role of the Reciprocity Treaty in stimulating economic development is controversial. Waite (1987, p. 320), for example, argued that 'Prosperity had come in the wake of the Reciprocity Treaty', but Norrie and Owram (1996, p. 183) have suggested:

> the problem, of course, is that there are many other important developments in this period in Canada, the United States, and abroad that might have affected trade between the two nations at least as much as the Treaty.

If analysts are unable to agree on the significance of the first free trade agreement between the United States and Canada in the 1850s, it should not surprise us that disagreement exists today about CUSFTA and NAFTA.

The BNA Act forming Canada came in 1867 hard on the heels of the end of the Reciprocity Treaty. Creighton (1965) argues that the 'Fathers of Confederation were optimistic that the greatly increased size of the market would ensure prosperity for the four provinces when they united'. Canada was initially made up of four provinces, Nova Scotia, New Brunswick, Quebec and Ontario, the latter two much smaller than they are today. In 1869 Canada bought the western territories of the Hudson's Bay Company. Manitoba entered Confederation in 1870, British Columbia in 1871, Prince Edward Island in 1873, Saskatchewan and Alberta in 1905, and Newfoundland in 1949. Innes and Easterbrook (1950), however, argued that Canada's future prospects looked limited by its huge national debt, its failure to develop US markets and the possibility of US exantion into Western Canada.

Geography and politics were combining to limit Canada's trading options. Free trade in Britain removed the protection Canada required in a distant market, while tariff barriers in the United States limited access there, while exposing Canadian producers (and territory) to expansionist American interests. Over the next decade a policy evolved, largely under the direction of Canada's first Prime Minister, Sir John A. Macdonald, known as the National Policy. Essentially it involved a Dominion (national) land policy designed to encourage settlement of the Prairies, a trans-continental railroad to bring the country together and allow easy export of grain, and the raising of tariff barriers to protect domestic industry. Once again, the effects of the trade policy have been controversial. Some have emphasized the importance of tariffs in stimulating a Canadian manufacturing sector. Others have argued that tariffs inhibited the development of efficient exporting manufacturers; rather they drew foreign capital into Canada to build small inefficient 'branch plants' for the local economy while forcing reliance on staple resources for export earnings.

Controversy about the desirability of high tariffs made itself manifest in policy differences between the two main political parties. Macdonald's Conservative party saw high tariffs as an essential ingredient in maintaining a strong national identity, especially in face of the powerful neighbour to the South. After the mid 1890s, the Liberals, under Wilfred Laurier, who initially favored free trade, saw tariffs as a revenue source, but were skeptical about their protectionist benefits. Canadian policy in the first third of the twentieth century alternated between the poles of higher and lower tariffs. The Liberals came into power in 1896, and by 1900 the average tariff stood at about 17 percent, down from 22 percent in the 1880s. More dramatically, the Liberals negotiated a new free trade agreement with the United States. However, the Liberals lost the 1911 election, fought largely on the free trade issue; the Liberal cause was not helped by President Taft's suggestion that the new Reciprocity Treaty was a practical step toward union between the two countries. The newly elected Conservatives continued the policy of minor tariff reduction until the start of World War I in 1914.

Instabilities in the international economy after the war led most countries to move toward higher tariffs once again, a process which became more pronounced with the depression beginning in 1930 (see Chapter 4). However, an attempt to stimulate your domestic economy by raising tariffs–a 'beggar your neighbour' policy–serves to make everyone poorer if everyone practices it. The election of a Liberal government under Mackenzie King in 1935 marked a shift in trade policies back to a tariff reduction orientation, starting with an agreement with the United States. Since that time Canadian trade policy has been consistently oriented towards multinational negotiations to reduce tariffs as well as periodic negotiations with the United States to reduce them on a bilateral basis.

CANADA'S ECONOMIC PERFORMANCE SINCE 1945

It is clearly not possible to provide a detailed review of Canada's economic policies over the past fifty years. Rather, we shall provide summary comments on two main issues: (1) Canadian policies regarding international trade; and (2) general trends in the macroeconomic performance of the economy, with particular emphasis on how recent years differ from earlier periods.

The stage can be set by reference to a framework for economic policy which the reigning Liberal party adopted in the 1945 election. It was a Keynesian framework (see Chapter 3). Trade liberalization formed part of the approach. It also involved a strongly expanded role for the government (as initially proposed, the federal government); there would be expanded social programs and the government would pursue active fiscal and monetary policies in order to maintain full employment and relatively stable prices. Whether finance ministers always took this prescription seriously is, however, a subject for debate.

Trade Policy

Since 1945 Canada has been supportive of trade liberalization. This is seen in part in its backing for multilateral tariff reductions through GATT. Average Canadian tariff levels, which had risen to 20 percent in the mid 1930s, were down to 8 percent by 1950, varied up and down slightly in the 1950s, then resumed their fall, reaching about 4 percent by 1979, and continue to decline. Small changes in the average tariff, up or down, can be hard to interpret since the average tariff reflects both tariff rates and trade flows. An average tariff value masks a wide range of specific tariff rates. Tariffs on some goods, however, remained high until the signing of CUSFTA.

Somewhat more controversial have been the various bilateral negotiations with the United States. The controversy stems in large part from the ever present fears of some that it is detrimental to Canada's interests to strengthen connections with its giant neighbour. In 1944, Canada removed tariffs on agricultural machinery coming from the United States (31 years after the United States had removed their tariffs against similar Canadian products). The first major move to bilateral tariff reductions between the two countries in the postwar period was in the 1965 Auto Pact. It was, with some safeguards, a free trade agreement between the two countries for automobiles and parts. The Auto Pact had a dramatic effect on the Canadian auto industry and ultimately on the Canadian economy. Prior to the pact the Canadian industry had been protected by a relatively high tariff (17.5 percent). Only 3 percent of the cars purchased in Canada were made in the United States. Most 'American' cars were produced in Canadian factories on short production runs. While American duties on Canadian produced cars were substantially lower, the higher production costs in Canada were sufficient to prevent much exportation to the United States. Prior to the Auto Pact only 7 percent of Canadian production was exported to the United States. Within four years that figure had reached 60 percent. Moreover, the price of cars in Canada dropped significantly and the wages of workers in the auto industry rose to roughly the American level. These gains were possible because of the rationalization of production which the Auto Pact allowed. Canadian plants specialized in a few models or components thereby allowing much longer production runs with substantial economies of scale. Most Canadian production was sold south of the border. Far fewer Canadians drove Canadian-built cars, but Canada built more cars.

The Auto Pact was not the only important bilateral trade agreement of the 1960s. Canada and the United States also signed the Canada-United States Defense Production Sharing Agreement. This agreement allowed Canadian producers to bid on American defense contracts. During the last years of the 1960s Canada had an export surplus on defense materials because of the American involvement in the Vietnam War.

On January 1, 1989 reciprocity was finally back. On that date the new Canada-United States Trade Agreement (CUSFTA) took effect.

This agreement was viewed by many as a dramatic change. In some ways it was. On the other hand it can be seen as the logical conclusion of the process which began in 1935 with the bilateral agreement to reduce tariffs between the two countries. It can even be seen as the conclusion of 120 years of Liberal policy on trying to reinstate the Reciprocity Treaty. Ironically, it was not a Liberal government that negotiated the agreement. The Liberals were in opposition and opposed the Conservatives under Brian Mulroney who negotiated and signed CUSFTA and, later, NAFTA as the free trade agreement was expanded to include Mexico.

North America was not alone in pursuing lower tariffs in the postwar period. Falling tariffs are one of the factors which has stimulated international trade over recent decades. It is, of course, difficult to separate the effects of trade liberalization from other factors contributing to globalization. In Canada, as in most countries, the share of the economy directly involved in international trade increased significantly. Canadian ties to the United States became stronger. Whether these are beneficial changes has been a controversial issue in Canada, one to which we will return later in this chapter.

Macroeconomic Performance

This is not the place for a detailed review of Canadian macroeconomic policies and performance in the postwar decades. Rather, we shall focus on a few key macro issues, those which have proven particularly significant or which relate most immediately to the international economy. A policy issue which develops to become of concern can most readily be illustrated by way of contrast. In what follows we shall often compare the situation in the current decade to that of earlier decades. Occasionally the contrast will be with other trading partners, especially the United States.

The years immediately following the World War II started out as years of extremely strong macroeconomic performance, at least from the perspective of the 1990s. Up to the early 1970s, economic growth was generally high, except for a brief recession in 1954 at the end of the Korean War, and a larger recession from 1957 to 1961 when the employment rate passed 7 percent. Inflation was generally low, apart from a burst in prices when price controls were taken off after the war and in 1951 at the start of the Korean War. With the exceptions noted, both inflation and unemployment were generally below 5 percent, and interest rates also low, right into the 1970s.

Despite the official recognition given to Keynesianism in Canada, this strong performance seems more due to the exceptional economic climate in the world economy than to deliberate government macroeconomic stabilization policies. For example, a tax cut in 1954 which helped stimulate the economy seems to have been motivated largely by the presence of a budget surplus. A more explicitly Keynesian orientation was apparent in the early 1960s, most notably in a conflict between the Governor of the Bank of Canada (the Canadian central bank), who emphasized a tight monetary policy to control prices, and the Minister of Finance, who was concerned with high unemployment rates. An important agreement specified that the Minister would have the final say in macro policy.

One peculiarity of Canadian economic policy in this period was the adoption, for much of the time, of a flexible exchange rate, despite the norm of fixed exchange rates specified in the Bretton Woods Agreement which set up the IMF. The Canadian dollar rose from its fixed value of US$0.9045 during the war to a premium over the American dollar for most of the 1950s. However, in 1962 the dollar began to fall and was fixed at US$0.925 for the rest of the 1960s. In the 1940s Canada showed a surplus on both its goods (that is, trade) and its current (that is, goods and services) accounts with the rest of the world; Canada was a net capital exporter. The 1950s, however, saw the pattern emerge which has been normal since then–a surplus on goods but an overall deficit in the current account. That is, a sizeable deficit in services (including interest and dividend payments on foreign capital) more than offsets the trade surplus. Thus Canada has generally been a net importer of capital. Associated with this was a key economic controversy over foreign investment. Proponents argued that it was quite appropriate for Canada to borrow abroad, using the funds to finance an excess of imports of goods and services over exports. In this way more goods, particularly capital, were made available to the economy and this increased economic growth. Opponents argued that the foreign capital brought with it business and social practices which were undesirable, and increased the vulnerability of Canada to unwelcome external pressures. This was particularly so, it was argued, for the direct ownership investment from the United States had become very important after World War I. Moreover, it was said, excessive reliance on foreign investment tended to be a vicious circle, since more borrowing was needed to cover the interest and dividend charges on past borrowing. The positions in this debate foreshadow the later controversies over CUSFTA–proponents extolling the economic advantages of freely flowing capital versus opponents warning of the loss of Canada's identity.

This relatively satisfactory macroeconomic performance through to the early 1970s serves as a convenient comparison point for a number of the problems which have come to the fore in recent years. Figures 5.1, 5.2 and 5.3 show comparative values for Canada and the United States of three key macroeconomic indicators for years from 1964 through 1995.

Figure 5.1 shows annual percentage increases in real Gross Domestic Product, that is in the real quantity of goods and services produced in the economy. The variability in economic growth over time is apparent, but there seems to have been a reduction in average growth since the late 1960s and early 1970s. (The average annual rate of increase was 5.6 percent for Canada and 3.9 percent for the United States for 1964–73, compared to 2.8 percent for both for 1984–93.)[7] Canada has generally had a higher growth rate than the United States, but this seems to have largely disappeared in the past decade. Readers are reminded that growth reflects increases in the quantity of inputs in the economy as well as their quality, and that Canada's population has grown faster than that of the United States since the 1960s.

Figure 5.2 shows unemployment rates in the two countries. The low rates of the late 1960s have not been matched since, but it is in

[7] These comparisons are indicative only, making no allowance for factors such as phases of the business cycle.

Figure 5.1 Real Rates of Growth in Canada and the US, 1964–97

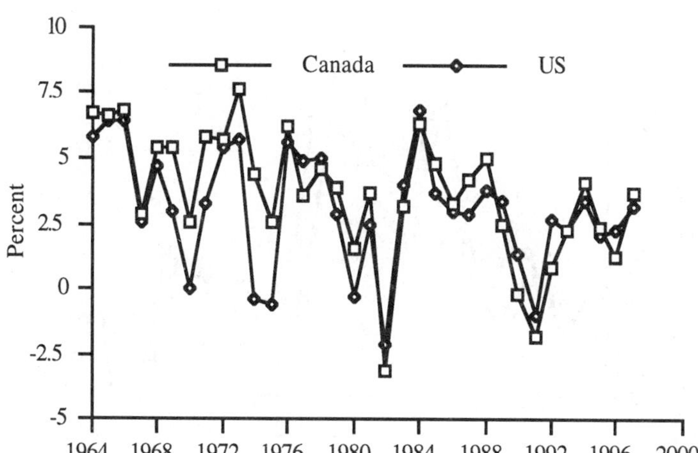

Source: Statistics Canada (1998), *Canadian Economic Observer, Historical Statistical Supplement, 1997/8* (11-210).

Figure 5.2 Unemployment in Canada and the US, 1964–97

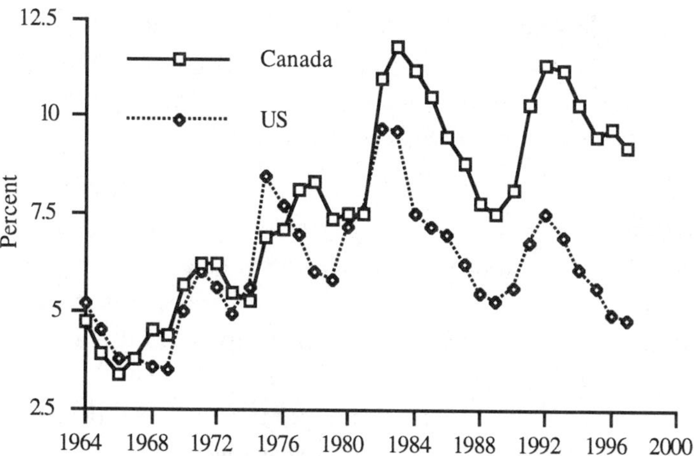

Source: Statistics Canada (1998), *Canadian Economic Observer, Historical Statistical Supplement, 1997/8* (11-210).

Figure 5.3 Inflation in Canada and the US, 1964–97

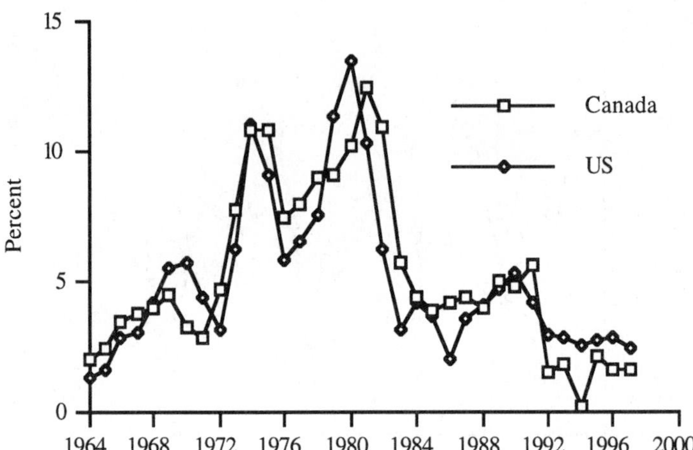

Source: Statistics Canada (1998), *Canadian Economic Observer, Historical Statistical Supplement, 1997/8* (11-210).

Canada that the persistence of high unemployment is particularly apparent. From 1964 to 1973 the Canadian and American unemployment rates were relatively close; the Canadian rate averaged 5.0 percent, 16 percent higher than the American rate of 4.2 percent. However, from 1984 through 1993 the Canadian rate was 50 percent higher (9.6 percent for Canada versus 6.4 percent for the United States).

Inflation rates are shown in Figure 5.3, based on the consumer price index (CPI). The stagflation–high unemployment plus high inflation–of the mid 1970s to early 1980s is apparent from Figures 5.2 and 5.3. During this period Canadian inflation generally exceeded that of the United States, as did the unemployment rate. Inflation has declined sharply since then. In the early 1990s it was at levels roughly comparable to those of the late 1960s in the United States, but considerably lower than that in Canada. If one supposes that there is a tradeoff between employment and inflation, it is noticeable that inflation rates at the level of the late 1960s now seem to go with higher unemployment. The higher recent unemployment rates in Canada than the United States

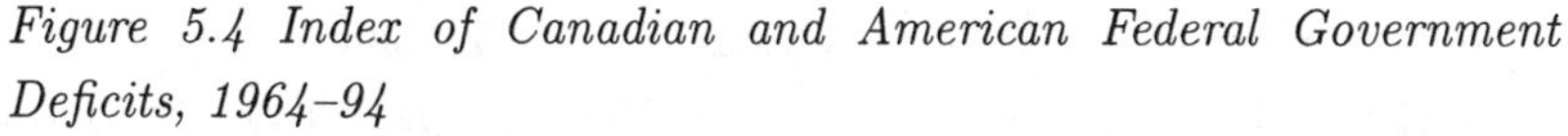

Figure 5.4 Index of Canadian and American Federal Government Deficits, 1964–94

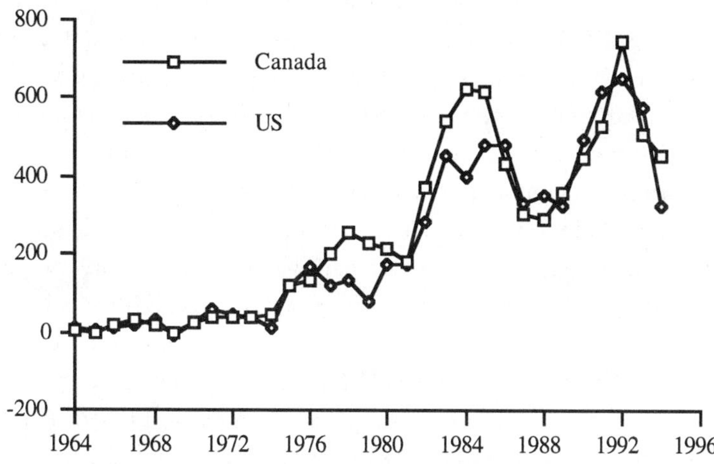

Source: International Monetary Fund (1995), *International Financial Statistical Yearbook*, International Monetary Fund (1998), *International Financial Statistics*, September.

are consistent, in this view, with Canada's lower inflation rate. Note, however, that Canadian unemployment was higher in the mid to late 1980s even when price rises were somewhat higher on average in Canada than in the United States.

Figure 5.4 illustrates another dimension of the Canadian economy which shows appreciably poorer performance in the 1980s and 1990s. Shown are changes in the size of the federal government budget deficit for both the United States and Canada. (Note that this figure compares the deficit in each country with its own in the base period. It does not compare the changes in the deficit in one country with the other country.) Immediately after World War II, government budgets typically moved between positions of surplus and deficit. The 1960s generally saw small deficits but, as the figure shows, the size of the deficit increased sharply thereafter. (It should be noted that part of the increase reflects inflation, as dollars become of less value over time.) To allow comparisons, the Canadian and American federal government deficits have been indexed to a value of 100 for the average of the years 1974–76 (a base period which was chosen arbitrarily). Continual deficits imply a growing government debt. In 1989 the federal government budget deficit was 3.62 percent of GDP for Canada and 4.84 percent for the United States. It is hard to know what meaning to ascribe to continued high government deficits. There is a widely accepted but normative presumption that they imply that the government is spending in an imprudent manner, unless there is clear evidence that it is building up valuable capital assets for the future. Some express fear that high borrowing by the government will squeeze out private investment spending, thereby reducing the growth rate of the economy. If the funds are borrowed abroad, then foreigners have a future claim on the country's output. Interest and debt repayments to domestic citizens are a transfer from one group of taxpayers to another. In 1975 less than one quarter billion Canadian dollars of the Canadian federal debt was owed to foreigners; by early 1996 the figure was over Can$110 billion, almost 25 percent of the total federal debt. Comparable figures for the United States are US$66 billion and almost US$937 billion, the latter is also almost one quarter of the American debt (International Monetary Fund, 1998). Rising debt also makes financing government activities difficult, since a greater sum must be devoted to interest payments. In the 1990s both federal governments have begun to address their large budget deficits, necessitating rather painful decisions about increasing taxes and/or reducing spending. It should be noted that persistent high unemployment, especially in Canada, ties into the budget problems, since it translates into higher welfare payments and reduced tax revenue. Fiscal tightening may, of course, worsen unemployment. Figure 5.4 shows the federal budget deficit. Canadian provinces also saw a tendency to higher budget deficits in the 1980s and early 1990s. In 1995 expenditures by provincial governments were 98 percent as large as federal spending (net of transfers to other levels of government). Local government spending was 40 percent as large as federal spending. Hence the finances of lower levels of government are significant in Canada.

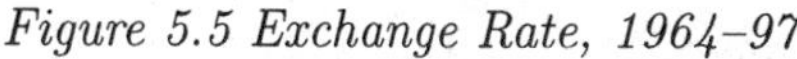

Figure 5.5 Exchange Rate, 1964–97

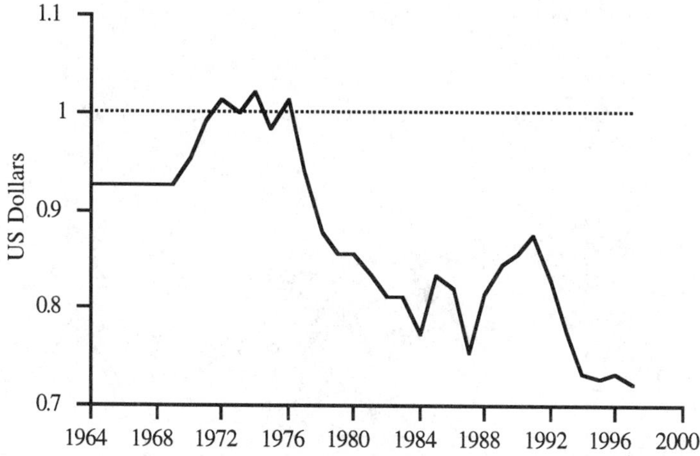

Source: Statistics Canada (1998), *Canadian Economic Observer, Historical Statistical Supplement, 1997/8* (11-210).

Figure 5.5 shows the Canada-American exchange rate (American dollars per Canadian dollar) from 1964–95. During most of the 1960s the Canadian dollar was pegged at US$0.925. As can be seen, the Canadian dollar appreciated in the early 1970s, but then fell considerably in value after 1976, trading up and down since then, but at a substantial discount to the US dollar. The depreciation of the Canadian dollar after 1990 probably contributed to the resumption of economic growth in 1992, which observers have seen as export driven.

Since 1970, Canada has generally shown a positive trade balance, but has had a deficit on the entire current account. Figure 5.6 shows these values for the years since 1977, with the only exceptions apparent (a small current account surplus from 1982–84). The current account deficit worsened sharply after the mid 1980s. For comparative purposes American values are also shown; the United States has shown persistent deficits on both accounts, which become larger after the early 1980s. Unlike Canada the United States has often shown a surplus on the services account, so that the current account deficit was generally smaller

Figure 5.6 Canadian and American Balance of Payments

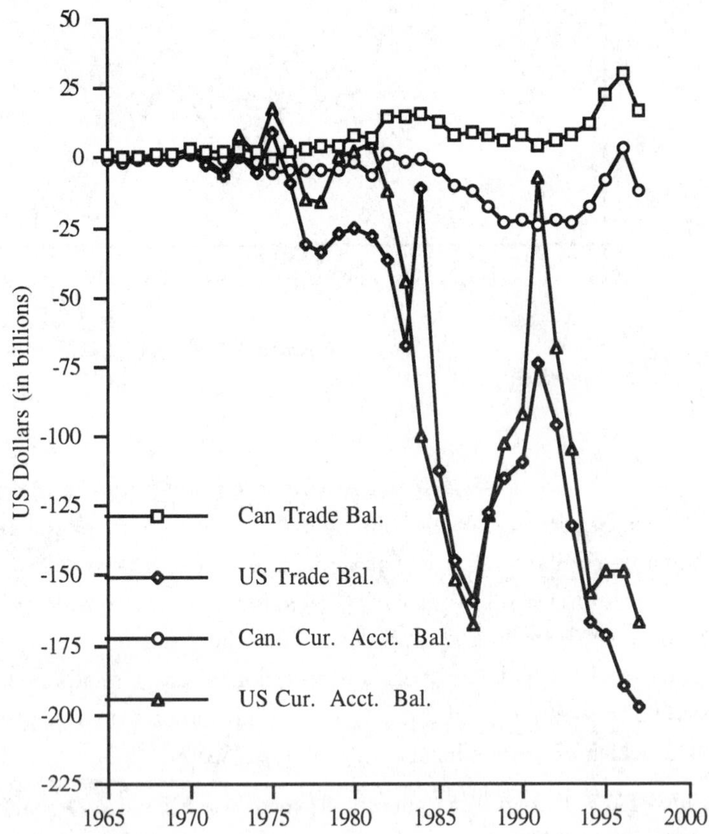

Source: International Monetary Fund (1995), *International Financial Statistics Yearbook, 1995*; International Monetary Fund (1998) *International Financial Statistics,* July and September.

than the trade deficit.

We turn from this brief description of Canadian macroeconomic performance in the postwar period to a discussion of macroeconomic policy. A useful, if somewhat fictitious, starting-point is to assume that Canadian policy in 1946 reflected an early version of Keynesianism, as indicated by the government's 1945 White Paper on employment. In this view active fiscal and monetary policies could be used to keep the economy near full employment with low inflation. From the perspective of the 1990s this Keynesian view seems naive at both the theoretical and empirical levels.

Theoretically, this early Keynesian view now strikes most macroeconomists as far too simple. We shall touch on only two of the many reasons for this. First, it soon became apparent that Keynesian policy prescriptions were more complicated in an open economy such as Canada. Thus, for example, an expansionary fiscal policy will be dampened somewhat by increased imports, and changes in monetary policy, which affect interest rates, might translate most readily into changes in flows of international capital with attendant changes in the exchange rate (or foreign exchange reserves, in the few years the dollar was fixed).

More fundamentally, a number of developments in macroeconomic theory began to cast doubts on the simple Keynesian model. Many of these stemmed from the search for a firm grounding for macroeconomics in models of the behavior of individuals. Economists turned to their usual models, which assumed rational behavior on the part of individuals. A world in which individuals are rational and markets clear readily–as is commonly assumed in microeconomics–provides no obvious basis for extensive involuntary unemployment. Furthermore, it became apparent to some economists that the assumption that people are fundamentally rational should also apply to their use of knowledge, including the formation of expectations. Models of rational expectations yielded surprising conclusions, including the suggestion that the government's macroeconomic policies might prove ineffective because rational economic agents will have anticipated the policy before it occurred. Macroeconomic theory entered an era of considerable disarray. Neo-Keynesians found it important to look at the impacts of less than fully rational behavior and imperfect markets as possible sources of unsatisfactory macroeconomic performance. Neoclassical economists usually argued that the economy adjusted quite quickly to some 'natural' rate of employment, and that government policy impacted almost entirely upon price variables (the inflation rate, interest rates, the exchange rate). Their analysis therefore concentrated upon factors which might affect the natural rate of unemployment. Did increases in welfare and unemployment insurance benefits in Canada make people more willing to accept unemployment? Might technological changes, and resultant modifications in the economy's mix of job skills, raise the natural unemployment rate or induce a cyclical dimension to it? The net effect of these theoretical developments has been that the focus of government fiscal policy has shifted from a Keynesian stabilization emphasis to a 'structural' emphasis upon issues such as industrial policies, research and development, education and training, labor mobility and the like.

It is, therefore, difficult to provide an easy assessment of Canadian fiscal policy in the postwar period. By the early 1990s, it seems fair to suggest that the fiscal policy environment was dominated by two conflicting factors. Unemployment rates seemed to be stuck at unacceptably high levels (around 10 percent) and it was widely accepted that budget deficits were a problem which had to be addressed. Since tax increases were generally perceived as politically unacceptable, governments turned to expenditure cuts. This is the precise opposite of traditional Keynesian expansionist policies. However, in theory at least, there is still room for reevaluation of the pattern of government expenditures with more programs aimed at structural problems in the economy.

Monetary policy in Canada has, for the past several decades, been aimed largely at the stable price objective. This may reflect a predilection of policy makers, but is also consistent with those views which cast doubt on the ability of monetary policy to have much of a real effect on the economy. It has been suggested that authorities in the Bank of Canada may elect one of two main types of variables upon which to focus: interest rates (that is, the price of money) or the size of the

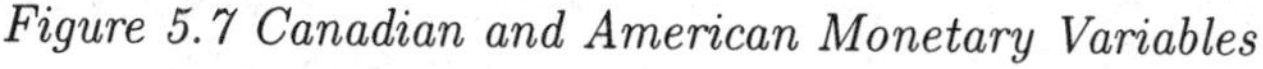

Figure 5.7 Canadian and American Monetary Variables

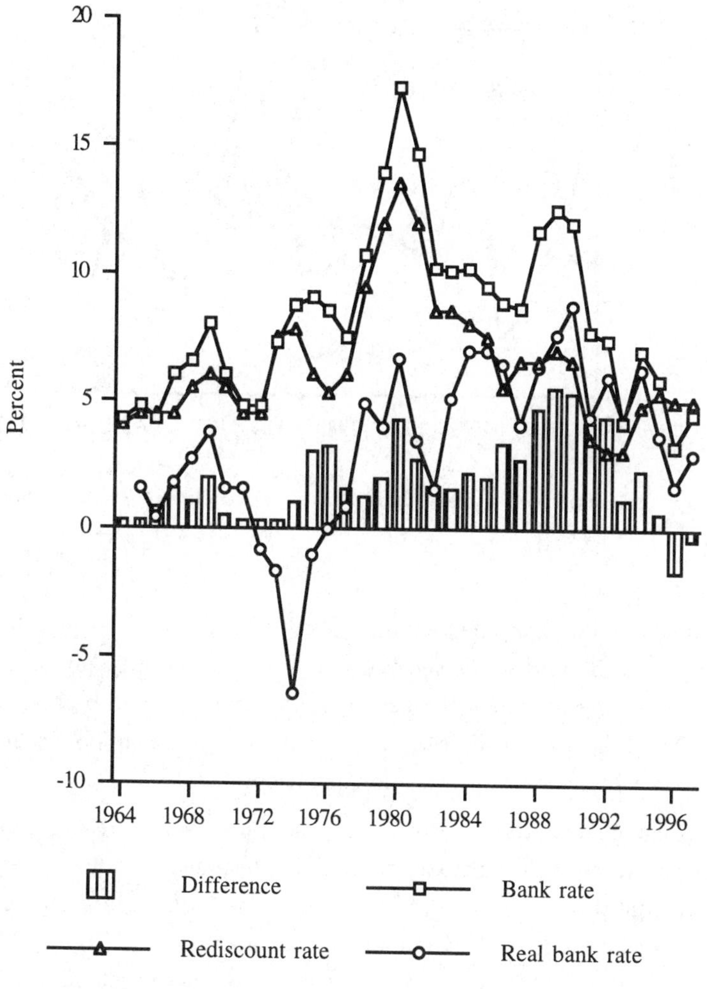

Source: International Monetary Fund (1998), *International Financial Statistics Yearbook.*

Figure 5.8 Canadian and American Money Supply

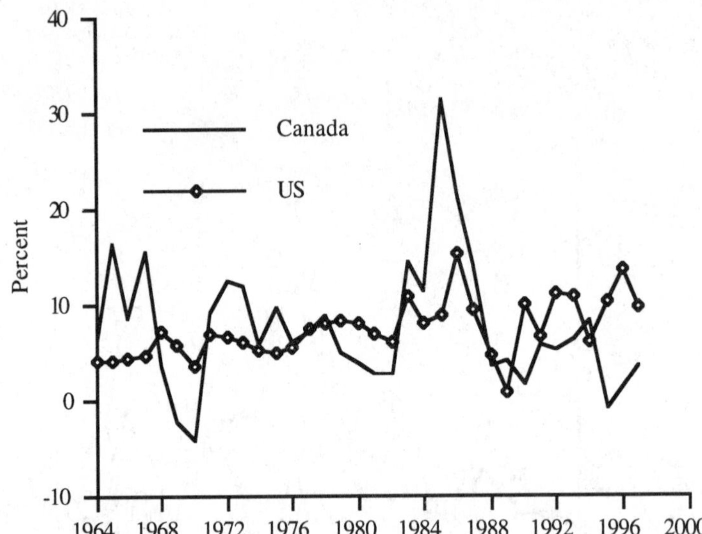

Source: International Monetary Fund (1998), *International Financial Statistics Yearbook.*

money supply. Over the years the Bank's focal point has, apparently, varied. In the mid 1970s the Bank first announced a policy of 'monetary targeting' in which the key decision variable would be the supply of money. A slow, steady rise in money supply would support economic activity while generating very low inflation.

It can be seen from Figure 5.7 that the Canadian interest rate almost always exceeds the American rate. It is presumed that flows of short-term capital are responsive to the size of the interest rate differential; by implication, so is the value of the Canadian dollar. Higher interest rates could reflect one or more of at least three factors: (1) higher interest rates designed to fight inflation; (2) higher interest rates designed to maintain the value of the Canadian dollar; (3) higher interest rates as a by-product of the combination of a monetary targeting policy and current economic conditions (in Canada and abroad). Figure 5.7 also shows the difference between the bank rate and the annual inflation rate; this provides an indication of the real rate of interest and, therefore, the tightness of monetary policy. It can be seen that the real bank rate has been much higher after the late 1970s than before. If monetary policies do have real economic effects, this would help explain the higher unemployment in recent years.

Figure 5.8 shows the annual percentage change in the supply of money (narrowly defined–M1). Once again, there is great variability in the Canadian data, more so than is generally seen in the United States. The data suggests those periods in which the Bank of Canada has followed monetary targeting (maintaining relatively slow and stable increases in the money supply). Such targeting began in the mid 1970s and held to the early 1980s, beginning again in the late 1980s. Monetary policy since the late 1980s might be referred to as a war on inflation with the goal of unconditional surrender.

In conclusion, what was Canada's economic situation in 1998, the year this chapter was written? Earlier tight monetary controls had brought the rate of inflation to a very low level. In 1998 it continued to be low. The federal budget deficit was eliminated. Provincially deficits were either eliminated or at least substantially reduced. Unemployment, which ran in the low and mid 8 percent range, while down from recent years continued to be high compared to the 1960s. Regional variations in unemployment rate also continued to be high. In June, 1998 rates ranged from 16.6 percent in Newfoundland to 5.5 percent in Alberta. The Canadian dollar which had traded at between 70 and 73 cents US during 1997, dropped to below 64 cents US, significantly lower than it had been 20 years earlier, and also somewhat lower than suggested by the relative value of goods in the two countries. On a purchasing power parity basis, many observers suggest that the Canadian dollar should be trading at about 80 cents US (see Introduction to Part II). This relatively low value for the Canadian currency might reflect the assessment of currency traders. There has been much debate about whether the low value of the Canadian dollar is desirable. It is generally agreed that the fall in the value of the dollar reflects, at least in part, the low level of short-term interest rates in Canada and the resultant loss of appeal of Canada as a place to hold short-term capital.

It is possible that short-term capital flows have overreacted to a falling dollar increasing the downward pressure on it. Some have argued that the Bank of Canada should tighten monetary policy to support the value of the dollar, while others believe that a lower dollar is one of the results of a monetary policy which is loose enough to address the continuing high unemployment in the economy. There is also disagreement about whether the falling dollar is entirely a result of the relatively low interest rates in Canada or whether it also reflects more fundamental factors. These factors might be cyclical or longer term. For instance, falling international prices for many natural resources which have resulted in part from the economic problems in the Far East which began in 1997.

Some critics, usually from a conservative perspective, suggested that the fall in the value of the Canadian dollars in 1998 is simply the continuation of the fall which began in the mid 1970s and reflects an increasing weakness in the Canadian economy relative to the American. This weakness is usually tied to the growing government debt in Canada and the larger (relative) size of the Canadian government. They often suggest that tax cuts and debt reduction would lead to a higher Canadian dollar. This prescription ignores the possibility that lower taxes would lead to greater imports which in turn would increase the pressure on the Canadian dollar. Even debt repayment could lead to an increase in the supply of Canadian dollars (and therefore a further drop in its value) as foreign creditors were repaid and domestic creditors used the repayments to buy foreign assets which paid greater yields. These critics do not explain why they believe that a larger government role should necessarily lead to a lower value for the Canadian dollar. Given the improving employment situation in Canada and the prospects for continued economic growth in the last years of the 1990s, it seems likely that the fall in the value of the Canadian dollar in 1998 will be temporary.

Despite the evidence of unused productive capacity, Canada continued to borrow significantly from abroad–more than $130 billion in the first five years of the decade; that is, Canada continued to run a sizeable current account deficit. It was more than 12 percent of current account credits in all the years in the 1990s except 1996. This deficit continued to reflect the investment income and services portion of the balance of payments. The balance of trade was still largely positive, although the surplus would likely have been lower had Canada's unemployment been less. That is, higher output and incomes as unemployed workers are drawn into production would induce higher imports.

In much of Canada the most hotly disputed economic issue in the first half of the 1990s has probably been the size of government deficits. Most provinces have moved to reduce or eliminate these deficits, emphasizing expenditure cuts, usually with an objective of no deficit, or even surpluses to allow retirement of the provincial debt. In its 1996–97 budget the federal government announced a substantial reduction in its deficit, with a balanced budget in sight before the year 2000. In fact, if the government's employment insurance fund is included, the federal government was in a surplus position in 1998. Major questions remain. The cutbacks by government seem likely to exacerbate, rather than help, the unemployment problem. It is obvious that improving the financial position of the government by cutting expenditures raises very difficult questions about where cuts are to take place, and whether such cuts will endanger the various educational, social, health and cultural programs to which Canadians have become accustomed. A related issue, with a somewhat longer-term horizon, is the fate of the government-run Canada Pension Plan, which has been underfunded in actuarial terms. As the Canadian population ages, it will be necessary to increase contribution rates and/or reduce benefits and/or fund pension payments out of general tax revenue; none of these options is politically attractive.

Finally, many suggest that considerable structural change in the Canadian economy may be necessary both to address the problems just described, as well as to position the economy in increasingly global markets. The role of the government in structural adjustments is subject to much debate. Does the government have an essential role to play in initiating and coordinating the changes necessary in the Canadian economy? Will the changes require an active government role to ensure that the benefits of wider participation in the world economy are shared equally? Or are taxes and existing government programs one of the main factors inhibiting the structural adjustments needed? These questions set the agenda for one of the most critical public policy debates of the 1990s–the free trade debate, to which we will turn after a brief discussion of the resources, especially human resources, available to the Canadian economy.

CANADA'S RESOURCES

The economic strength of a country derives from the quantity and quality of its resources. It is useful to consider three broad groups of these resources: human resources, natural resources and accumulated capital resources which can be used in the production of other goods and services. It is not the purely physical dimension of these resources which counts, but their 'knowledge-augmented' value. Vast resources of petroleum lie under the Canadian Prairies, but the exploitation awaited the necessary geological knowledge and drilling technologies. Capital equipment ranges from the simple hammer through to the most sophisticated computer chip, from a small warehouse to a large robotic factory. Many economists insist that it is essential to view people as 'human capital', that is, as individuals with a wide range of acquired skills and talents. It is evident that the knowledge-augmented natural and capital resources represent the effects of past investment in human capital which generated that knowledge. Some analysts suggest that another important resource group is also essential for a nation's productive activity. This group might be called 'coordinating resources'. They consist of the management skills necessary for production and a wide range of institutional features, often regulated by the government, including definitions of property rights and the scope of market exchange mechanisms. In Canada, there are large numbers of people with good management skills, and economic exchange takes place to a significant extent through well-established markets under generally stable government regulations. As suggested in Chapter 4, the transaction costs associated with doing business should be low in these circumstances.

A nation's economic productivity is the result of all these resources.

There is no single formula for success. Countries like Canada, the United States, Australia and Saudia Arabia boast natural-resource wealth and high incomes. However, many other countries are endowed with natural resources but are still poor. Switzerland and Japan have limited natural resources but are very productive. Similarly, large populations do not guarantee high per capita production nor do small populations necessarily generate low production per person. The key element seems to be what we have called human capital, in the form of a highly-skilled population and a significant stock of knowledge-augmented capital. Even this combination need not generate success, as illustrated by the former Soviet Union which had a well-educated labor force and a large stock of capital equipment, much of it quite sophisticated, but which lacked effective coordination resources. We shall comment briefly on Canada's natural and capital resources, and then focus in on its human resources with particular emphasis on education and training.

Canada is natural-resource wealthy. As discussed earlier, the staples view of Canadian economic development stresses natural resources as the engine of growth. Canada still relies heavily upon primary production of natural resources and secondary processing of resource products for a significant share of its output and trade. In economic terms, Canada has a comparative advantage in the production of many natural resources. Some attempts have been made to provide meaningful measures of Canada's natural resource wealth, but inherent uncertainties make the task difficult. For example, what value would one have ascribed to Alberta's petroleum resources in 1947, before the key Leduc discovery? It is clear that fisheries and forests, temperate agriculture and minerals will continue to be major contributors to the economy into the indefinite future.

The stock of physical capital in Canada is also large. The capital resource base has been measured, generally, in terms of the cumulative undepreciated expenditures on capital equipment. However, this quantitative measure fails to capture the qualitative, knowledge-augmented dimension of the capital stock.

Canada has a relatively well-educated labor force. According to a recent Statistics Canada study (Statistics Canada, 1991), only 7 percent of the adult population is completely illiterate. However, this figure is based on the lowest definition of literacy, of four levels of reading ability. The highest level required the ability to read at a fairly advanced level, for example, to read a long newspaper article and evaluate the arguments and evidence in that article. Only 62 percent were judged literate by that standard. Similarly 86 percent were numerically literate at the lowest level, but only 62 percent met the highest standard.

Compared to the United States, Canada has a somewhat higher proportion of individuals that have not graduated from high school and a somewhat lower proportion of individuals that have graduated from university. While these gaps are narrowing they are still significant. The last census reported that the median years of formal schooling for Canadian adults (whether male or female) was 12.5 years. This was up slightly from 1986 when the corresponding figure was 12.2 years, while in 1976 the median level of formal schooling was only 11.2 years (Statistics Canada, 1993). The median level of schooling is remarkably uniform across Canada. Except for Newfoundland and the Northwest Territories, all provinces and the Yukon Territory had medians in 1991 between 12.2 and 12.8 years. The Newfoundland median was 11.4 and the Northwest Territories were low at 11.2 years. The median age of schooling decreases with age. In 1991 the median for those aged 25–44 was 13.2, while for those aged 45–64 it was 11.7 years, and for those 65 years or older it was only 10 years.

In 1992 about 43 percent of the adult population had some postsecondary education. Specifically, 11.8 percent had a university degree and another 22.3 percent had postsecondary certificates or diplomas (including trade certificates). The remaining 8.8 percent had attended a postsecondary institution but had not graduated. For the 1990–91 school year there were 532,000 full time university students enrolled, up 39 percent from the 1980–81 year. There were 249,000 enrolled in trade and vocational programs, about the same as in 1985–86 but down from 1983–84 (Statistics Canada, 1994).

Total government spending on all levels of education for fiscal 1991–

92 was a little over $53 billion or about 7.8 percent of 1991 GDP. Since the early 1980s funding in real terms for education has increased relatively little. With the recent deficit reduction policies, several provinces have actually cut education spending. Alberta, for example, has proceeded with cuts of 20 percent which were completely phased in by 1997. However, in 1998, in response to many complaints by citizens, the Alberta government has 'reinvested' some funds although not nearly enough to restore precuts levels. The federal government funds a portion of higher education through transfers to the provinces. These transfers have been cut. Such cuts in education raise concerns about the future rate of increase in the quality of the Canadian labor force. Governments introducing the budget cuts argue that existing resources can be used much more effectively and that an increasing share of the costs of advanced education would fall on the students themselves. Critics feel that the government undervalues the social benefits of education and failed to realize the access problems created for students from disadvantaged backgrounds. They find it strange that governments which speak of the extreme importance of a flexible and well-trained population should use expenditure cuts in education funding to address their budget problems.

The above discussion refers to general educational expenditures. While there has been some political rhetoric, there really have been no significant special training or retraining programs to meet any restructuring made necessary by CUSFTA and NAFTA.

There is another important element to the development of Canadian human resources. Canada has traditionally received a significant number of net immigrants each year. In 1993, 255,042 individuals immigrated to Canada. While in absolute terms the United States receives more immigrants, Canada receives a substantially higher number in proportion to its population. Recent changes in Canada's immigration laws have resulted in a shift in the type of immigrants that are landing. Essentially, there are three categories of immigrants–family, refugee and independent. Families and refugees are accepted on humanitarian grounds and may or may not bring needed jobs skills or strong educational backgrounds. Independent immigrants are admit-

Table 5.1 1994 Wages for Selected Occupational Groups

Industry	Wage rate	In US Dollars
Mining, oil wells	22.44	16.20
Manufacturing	16.85	12.17
Services	13.32	9.62

Source: Canadian Economics Observer, Historical Statistical Supplement 1997/98.

ted on a points basis, with points assigned for education and valuable job skills. In 1981, 35 percent of those landed were independent immigrants. By 1991 that proportion had fallen to 28.9 percent. Another change in immigration law essentially allowed immigrants to substitute financial capital for human capital. This allows individuals who invested the required amount in Canada to be eligible to immigrate. These changes mean that Canada may be less able to supplement its indigenous human capital than has been the case in the past.

It is difficult to compare labor legislation between the United States and Canada because both have a federal form of government and therefore there are 51 sets of laws in the United States and 14 (including 1 federal, 10 provincial and 3 territorial) sets in Canada. However, in general Canada's labor laws might be described as more 'pro-labor' than American legislation. Certainly workers are more unionized in Canada. However, this may not be as an important difference as it would seem because most of the difference in unionization rates can be explained by the strength of public sector (government employees) unions in Canada.

Economists will tell anyone who will listen that absolute labor costs do not determine trade. Trade depends upon all costs, not just labor costs, and reflects comparative, not absolute advantage. However it is certain that there will be those who wish to compare wage rates between countries. Table 5.1 gives average hourly wages rates for Canada for selected major employment categories for 1997. The value in American dollars at the 1997 exchange rate is also given.

THE CANADIAN FREE TRADE DEBATE

This section examines a number of issues which emerged in the debate over the free trade agreements. Most of the issues to be discussed surfaced during the CUSFTA negotiations, although in some cases they re-emerged during the later trilateral NAFTA talks. In general, Canadians were less concerned with the addition of Mexico to create a trilateral agreement than they had been about the initial bilateral negotiations with the United States. In part, this may have been because some of those opposed to a bilateral agreement had argued that Canada should not be tied to a trade agreement with just the United States, but should be seeking a multinational agreement. It was difficult for them to oppose the addition of a third nation to the CUSFTA agreement. More importantly, the volume of Mexico-Canada trade is relatively small so the addition of Mexico was not likely to have significant effects one way or the other, although some expressed fear that it might divert United States trade away from Canada to Mexico. Still, it was generally the opinion of those who studied the issue that if there were to be a Mexico-United States trade agreement, it was in Canada's interest to be part of it to reduce the chances of Mexico gaining trade advantages with the United States which might allow it to displace Canadian exports (Cadsby and Woodside, 1993).

In the limited space available no attempt will be made to determine, in any comprehensive way, the validity or lack of validity of all claims made by various groups who opposed the two trade agreements. It is important to realize that it is not the validity of these objections that makes them relevant politically, it is the tenacity of belief of those who hold them. Therefore the purpose of this discussion is to briefly outline the arguments that emerged in the free trade debate. Since the economic arguments in favour of free trade are discussed elsewhere in this book, we shall put more emphasis upon the opinions of those opposed to CUSFTA.

Opponents of CUSFTA

A number of Canadians expressed the fear that free trade with the United States would result in Canadians becoming 'hewers of wood and drawers of water'. Of course, this objection runs counter to the experience over the last 50 years during which tariffs have been coming down. During that period the proportion of Canadian exports which are manufactured goods has been rising. However, it is not a surprising position, given Canada's historic dependence on staples, as outlined above. Moreover, for more than a century Sir John A. Macdonald and his Conservative political successors had preached a national policy which argued that tariffs were necessary if Canada was to develop a large domestic manufacturing sector. A related objection argued that CUSFTA was a sell-out of Canadian natural resources. Again there is some historical basis for the argument. The Reciprocity Treaty of 1854 was approved by the Americans only after they gained access to the fisheries on the Grand Banks. A later free trade proposal would have granted Americans fishing rights off the west coast of Canada. The image of Canadian water and oil flowing uncontrollably south is sufficient to arouse strong opposition in many. It seemingly reinforces the view that free trade will leave Canada as an exporter of raw materials to the United States and an importer of manufactured goods. Ironically, such critics see CUSFTA as a new mercantilist policy.

It is not only the sellout of resources that opponents of free trade fear. They have also predicted the sellout of the Canadian manufacturing industry. Foreign ownership remains a matter of concern for many of those opposed to free trade. The foreign ownership issue is not a simple one. Until the First World War most of foreign investment in Canada was British. As the British divested their Canadian holdings to finance two world wars, the balance shifted and the Americans became the dominant source of foreign investment. The form also shifted from portfolio to direct investment.[8] By the 1960s a significant proportion of Canadian industry was American controlled and nationalists of all political backgrounds became concerned. Legislation was passed

[8]Portfolio investment does not imply control whereas direct investment does imply control.

which required the screening of foreign takeovers. By the 1980s the furore was dying down, and this legislation was watered down. However, some, particularly those on the political left, continued to voice concerns. They view CUSFTA as providing American multinationals the opportunity to buy up what was left of Canadian-owned industry. Paradoxically, the reduction of trade barriers also reduced one of the motives for foreign ownership. In the days of high tariffs, American firms often established Canadian branch plants to avoid the tariff wall. Thus free trade could mean less foreign ownership. The opponents find little solace in this possible turn of events. They see no reason why removing tariffs should lead foreigners to sell back to Canadians. Even worse, perhaps, if a branch plant was established simply to avoid a tariff wall, there might be no reason at all to maintain the plant with free trade. Such plants might simply be closed or, with the advent of NAFTA, moved to Mexico to take advantage of the lower wages. Either way, CUSFTA would generate undesirable effects. Some manufacturing plants would be closed and the jobs shifted to the South, and whatever manufacturing was still economic would be run by Americans.

It has also been argued that cultural industries are threatened by CUSFTA. Cultural industries can be viewed as 'strategic goods' industries which are vital to a nation's independent existence. The Canadian negotiators of CUSFTA recognized this and created a specific exemption for the cultural industries. The critics argue that the exemption may well be of limited usefulness, for there is also a provision which allows retaliation if the exemption is exercised. The recent controversy over the New Country Network tends to reinforce this view. When the Canadian Radio-Television and Telecommunications Commission ordered cable companies to replace the American country music station with a Canadian country station, the American station retaliated by ceasing to play most Canadian artists. The final result was a compromise under which the American station bought a minority position in the Canadian station. Canada is not alone in its fear of American 'cultural imperialism'. Several other countries have legislated national content rules for radio, television, movies and other cultural industries. In the meantime, Canada is beginning to export another music channel to Mexico. As of June 1, 1995 the Canadian MuchMusic signal began to be available in Mexico. The whole debate as it relates to television may become moot because of technology changes such as direct view satellites. However, it is likely to remain important for books, movies and the recording industry.

One controversial issue has been Canada's denial of the tax deductions for Canadian advertisers who purchase space in Canadian editions of American magazines for example, *Sports Illustrated.* This measure was introduced by the Canadian government to offer protection to small-run Canadian magazines who have higher costs because they lack the economies of scale of the American competitors. Recently the Americans successfully challenged these measures at the WTO and the Canadian government is planning to counter with a new, revised version.

Perhaps of greatest concern to those who oppose CUSFTA and NAFTA is the future of Canada's social programs. Many of Canada's social programs are not that different from their American counterparts. The federal government in Canada provides a payment called Old Age Security, for most Canadians over 65. For those with little or no other income it is augmented by a program called Guaranteed Income Supplement. A third program provides pensions to retired Canadians, the Canada Pension Plan (or the Quebec Pension Plan). Payments under this plan are based on the contributions made by employees and employers during the individual's working life. Self-employed workers are also covered, but they must make both the employee and employer contributions. While the exact nature and level of support in these programs is not the same as under American Social Security and welfare programs, the differences are not so great as to cast doubt on the ability of free trade to function.

Canada also has a federal operated employment insurance (EI) program.[9] It has recently been changed. Some have suggested that the changes are a consequence of CUSFTA. Canadian employment insurance has been raised by the United States in trade disputes (Bowker, 1988), the argument being that the government program gives an un-

[9]Until 1996 EI was called unemployment insurance (UI).

fair advantage to Canadian businesses. However, the changes in the Canadian program probably would have been made in any case, since it had evolved into much more than employment insurance. In areas of chronically high unemployment it had become a welfare scheme. It was also used as a job retraining program. A recent study (Sargent, 1995, p.47) concluded that the Canadian program was significantly more generous than the program in a 'typical' American state. Using the 1970 Canadian system as a base, the Canadian program, as of September 1994, scored a generosity index of 114 compared to the 'typical' state score of 81, with the United States Federal Extended Benefits (FEB) included. However, the state of New York's program scored 128 with FEB included. It is hard for the United States to argue that Canada's program is incompatible with free trade when New York has an even more generous unemployment insurance program.

It was noted above that employment insurance has become a form of welfare in areas of chronically high unemployment. Canada has a serious problem of regional disparities. Certain areas–Newfoundland, the Maritimes and parts of Quebec, Manitoba, and Saskatchewan–have substantially lower per capita incomes than the country as a whole. For some regions this problem has existed for generations. Unemployment rates in many of these areas are well above the national average. The federal government has tried a variety of programs including subsidies to firms that will locate in these areas. Those opposed to free trade argue that Canada may be forced to reduce or eliminate many of these programs. Some of these who supported freer trade have stated–possibly cynically–that it might be for the best if the programs were successfully challenged, since they inhibit relocation of Canadian resources.

Canada's government-funded medicare system, however, has drawn most attention. Americans often refer to the Canadian plan as socialized medicine. In point of fact it is not the practice of medicine, but the medical insurance, which is socialized. Technically each province has its own program, so there are minor differences between provinces. The federal government does provide part of the funding for the provincial programs. As the federal government subsidizes the programs, the federal government is able to maintain national standards. It requires that all provincial plans be universal and prohibits extra billing. The provincial government and the provincial medical associations negotiate a fee schedule. Individual doctors bill the province according to that schedule. They are not allowed to bill the patient. Originally, the federal government provided 50 percent of the funding; however, the federal share has dropped and will continue to do so. As the federal share decreases so does its ability to enforce national standards.

Canada spends a significantly smaller proportion of its GDP on health care than the United States does, but has lower death rates and longer life expectancies. In 1990 Canada spent $1,837 Canadian per capita, or 9.2 percent of GDP, on health care. The United States spent $2,566 Canadian per capita or 12.2 percent of GDP. Moreover the rate of increase in costs in the United States has been higher than in Canada (Nair et al., 1992). A Canadian female's life expectancy at birth is 80.6 compared to 78.6 in the United States. The figures for males are 73.7 and 71.6 respectively. The age standardized mortality rates are 727 per 100,000 in Canada compared to 820 per 100,000 in the United States. The infant mortality rate in Canada is about 7 per 1,000. In the United States it is nearly 50 percent higher at 10 per 1,000 (Nair et al., 1992, p.181). The greater efficiency of the Canadian health care system comes about in part because the proportion spent on administration is smaller.

Some American interests view medicare as a subsidy to business. Most of the cost of the Canadian health care system comes out of general revenue, whereas many American employers pay substantial premiums for their workers' insurance. For this reason it may seem to American employers that their Canadian competitors have an advantage. However, it should be noted that Canadians pay higher taxes than do Americans. The higher taxes sometimes lead Canadian businesses to claim that they are the ones at a disadvantage. Opponents of free trade may use both of these arguments. Challenges by the United States, it is argued, could force Canada to abandon medicare and to open up medical services to competition from private American insurance companies and medical clinics. In addition, Canadian businesses in competition with American firms will force reductions in Canadian taxes to the lower levels assessed in the United States; therefore depriving Canadian governments of the financing required to fund Canadian social programs.

Those who fear that free trade is a threat to Canadian social programs are not all on the 'anti-American left'. They have some evidence to support their position. The recent debate over health in the American Congress demonstrated that there are those who are strongly opposed to a Canadian-style health care system. Recent changes in Canadian drug patent laws were in part the result of American political pressure and multinational drug companies lobbying in Canada. American medical insurance companies are ready and able to move into Canada should the institutional framework change to allow them (Pedersen, 1995). Moreover, American legislation relating to trade with Cuba indicates the willingness of some American legislators to use commercial policy to gain domestic political ends, even if the policy dictates actions by individuals and firms under the jurisdiction of another government.

Proponents of CUSFTA

It is less necessary, in this chapter, to set out the arguments of those who supported CUSFTA and NAFTA. In essence, their argument is the classic economic defense of free trade discussed in Chapter 2. If individuals can trade freely, then producers can specialize in those activities in which they have a comparative advantage, the value of total output in the free trade area can be increased, and the free exchange of goods and services makes everyone better off. There are areas of special concern, such as the export of fresh water resources, the protection of cultural industries and the maintenance of social programs. While disagreements may arise in these areas, CUSFTA generally recognized them as special areas in which existing programs could be maintained, and which would not be subject to unrestricted free trade. As mentioned in Chapter 4, CUFTA and NAFTA represent managed trade, not free trade despite the claims implicit in their names. Moreover, there was no guarantee before CUSFTA that the United States might not object to a variety of Canadian policies, including these in the areas just mentioned, and CUSFTA has the advantage of setting up a formal dispute resolution mechanism. It is important to note that the United States, even in the absence of NAFTA, could appeal to the WTO against Canadian policies to protect social programs which they regard as discriminatory.

Given the increasing globalization of the world economy and increasing worldwide competition, the Canadian government would have been under pressure to reduce taxes and streamline many social and cultural programs. Free trade, because it increases the wealth of the country, actually enhances the ability to maintain such policies. The fear that NAFTA will see a flood of Canadian businesses to Mexico, where wages are low and environmental standards less stringent than in Canada, is unfounded, and implies that the opponents have failed to grasp the key argument in favor of international trade, that it hinges on comparative advantage, not absolute advantage. Of course, CUSFTA and NAFTA will mean that Canadians must make adjustments, but even without the free trade agreements changes in the world economy would necessitate adjustments in Canada. The point is that the adjustments required by CUSFTA and NAFTA are ones which increase the well-being of the Canadian economy.

Other Issues

Several unique aspects of the Canadian economy deserve brief comment. The regional disparities issue has an interesting sideline. Canada itself is not a completely free trade zone. Some barriers to interprovincial trade still exist. The 'beer war' is illustrative of such barriers. The 'beer war' resulted from the Province of Ontario's efforts to place barriers on the importation of foreign beer, but it may have had its roots in the fact that until recently each province was able to prevent the importation of beer from other provinces. While interprovincial barriers are coming down, they still do exist. In fact, some observers have suggested that under free trade the barriers to trade between Canada and the United States and Mexico will be less in some respects than the barriers to trade between provinces. It is partly for this reason that the government of Canada, under the terms of NAFTA, must provide compensation for provincial programs which violate the free trade agreement.

The position of Canadian aboriginal peoples is a hotly debated topic in Canada. There are unresolved land disputes, and a feeling in many quarters that earlier agreements were not fair. Moreover, the aboriginal people exhibit economic, health and social indicators at levels far below the average Canadian. Native groups currently have some special commercial rights on their reserves. Many of the native groups are seeking 'self-rule'. It is not clear what such self-rule would involve. It seems likely that it will involve some degree of what might be called home rule–the ability of natives to administer their own system of justice, to control natural resources and economic development on their reservations and similar matters. It is not likely that self-rule would extend to issues of foreign or trade policy. Some indications of what might be involved in self-rule may be seen in the 1998 agreement between the Nisga'a band and the federal and British Columbia governments. As of the fall of 1998 the agreement had yet to be ratified by any of the three parties. The band currently occupies a 62 square kilometer reservation in northwestern British Columbia. In the agreement the aboriginal band would be given $300 million and nearly 2,000 square kilometers of land including forestry and mineral resources and a share of the salmon fishery. The band would have governmental powers in this region over land use and health, education, culture and social services and would have taxation powers within the area. The band would be subject to the same laws and regulation as other Canadians with respect to commercial and trade policy, criminal law, national defense, foreign affairs and sales and income taxes. The payment of these taxes would be phased in over a period of time. Therefore it is no more likely that Canada's aboriginal peoples will develop their own commercial policy than it is that aboriginal people in the United States will. The residents of transborder Indian reservations claim the right to transport goods across the border without restriction. While this is a possible source of complications, such as the black market cigarette trade which forced Canada to lower its tobacco excise tax, it is not a major or uniquely Canadian problem.

Finally, Quebec separatism remains a continuing possibility. The 1995 referendum was won by the side supporting continuing union with Canada, but the 'Yes' and 'No' sides were almost evenly divided. While it remains clear that not all those voting to secede wished complete independence for Quebec, it is also clear that many within Quebec would like to see greater recognition of Quebec's unique Francophone culture and, perhaps, greater powers for the Quebec provincial government. It also seems clear that the issue of separatism will not disappear. Quebec has, and likely will always have, a substantial group of people who feel that their potential and their cultural objectives can be realized only in an independent Quebec nation. Many of these people will be unpersuaded by arguments that Quebec already has large powers over social and economic matters, that independence would generate economic costs, or that preservation of the francophone culture can be better maintained within a bilingual Canada, than in an independent Quebec alone in a largely English speaking North America. Therefore, the threat of Quebec separatism is unlikely to disappear. At the same time, this seems to be a problem which is largely internal to Canada, at least up to the point at which separatism actually has to be negotiated. It is noteworthy that despite the tone of xenophobia which many observers have noted in parts of francophone Quebec, the assumption of Quebec separatists has generally been that free trade within North America could continue even with Quebec's independence. It is also noteworthy that many Canadians outside Quebec have expressed doubts about such a future arrangement.

CONCLUSIONS

This section is called conclusions mainly because it comes at the end. NAFTA is still very new. It is not possible to reach conclusions. Rather it is time to look into the future to see what is likely to develop.

While the implementation of CUSFTA and NAFTA in Canada was controversial, it is here and it is likely here to stay. That is not to say that the opposition is dead. It is not dead and it will continue to be vocal. The opposition has strong historical roots which go back well before Canadian Confederation. The British mercantilist policies of the Canadian colonial period and the role of staples in Canadian economic development have left an image of Canadians as 'hewers of wood and drawers of water'. The United States has insisted on access to Canadian resources as a condition for freer access to American markets ever since the original 1854 Reciprocity Treaty. This insistence has, in the eyes of many Canadians, created the fear that the United States is only interested in Canadian resources. In the nineteenth century the Canadian colonies formed a nation. This nation building was in part a defensive act against perceived American expansionism. The American concept of manifest destiny, a land claim dispute over the Pacific Northwest, and the unfortunate tactics of the campaign by the Taft administration to secure Senate approval of a trade agreement with Canada, all tended to support the view that Americans wished to absorb Canada. In the twentieth century the rise of American multinational corporations has only served to shift the fear of American political domination to a fear of American economic domination. Even the obvious benefits to Canada of the Auto Pact have not convinced doubters who feel that it only benefits the United States and the American big three auto manufacturers.

In spite of the continuing opposition, it is unlikely that any future government will abrogate either accord. Continuing argument about CUSFTA and NAFTA also reflects the fact that far more has happened in Canada and the world since December 31, 1988 than the implementation of the free trade agreements. It can never be possible to sort out completely the effects of North American economic integration and the effects of all the other changes.

The 'danger to social programs argument' is a difficult one. Clearly there is pressure on Canada's social programs. However, it is likely that pressure would have developed without NAFTA. The federal government and the various provincial governments have been running large deficits. There have been threats of downgrades by the bond rating services, and some provincial bonds and federal foreign currency denominated bonds have actually been downgraded. It has become widely accepted that governments must reduce spending (or raise taxes) to reduce if not eliminate their deficits. The phrase 'we can't afford it' is increasingly common. Except in the province of Saskatchewan, tax increases seem to have been regarded as politically unacceptable, although many governments feel that the introduction of 'user fees' is a different matter. Therefore many politicians and voters see a need to cut social programs. In the long run the problem is made worse by an aging population that will put heavier demands on old age support plans and health care. Moreover, as the federal government moves to reduce its deficit, it has announced that it will reduce transfer payments to the provinces. These reductions mean that the provinces will have less money to fund social programs, but also that the federal government has less leverage to force national standards on the provinces.

Thus it is likely that Canadian social programs will be weakened not by free trade but by an internal shift to the political right. However, those opposed to NAFTA will see any reduction of social programs as a result of NAFTA even if it is in fact the consequence of internal politics. The situation will be further complicated by the fact that those wishing to cut social programs may claim that such cuts and the resultant tax savings were made necessary to meet international competition. While both claims are doubtful, it does indicate that the controversy will continue. Moreover, it points out that the frames of reference for those engaged in the debate are often quite different. Proponents of free trade see it as an economic issue, with the gains from trade increasing the ability of Canadian governments to develop and fund Canadian social programs. Opponents of free trade tend to see the agreement in terms of economic and political power, with free trade transferring significant control over developments in Canada to the American government and to foreign corporations who have little if any familiarity with Canadian values, and no incentive to gain such familiarity. In fact, they believe it is in their interest to promote American values. In this way Canada will be changed forever and Canadians will not even know it is happening. To the extent that this characterization of the free trade dispute in Canada is accurate, it is necessary that the terms of the debate be considerably broadened beyond the 'bread-and-butter' issues on which economists usually focus.

The fact that both CUSFTA and NAFTA are in place does not mean that all issues between the countries are settled. There are a number of bilateral and possibly trilateral issues to be resolved. Each of the three countries could doubtless supply its own list of ongoing issues. High on Canada's list would be the West Coast Salmon dispute, the repeated reopening of the softwood lumber countervail cases, the protection of Canadian magazines and the issue of trade with Cuba. The future of NAFTA will to some considerable degree depend upon the ability of the member countries to resolve these differences.

The last issue relates to the possible expansion of NAFTA. Canada is likely to strongly support such expansion and has already signed a free trade agreement with Chile. From a Canadian perspective a multinational trade area is superior to a bilateral or trilateral area. It would reduce American political and economic influence, and it is in Canada's interest to develop new trading links. A strong multinational trade area would reduce Canada's dependence on the American economy and bring the benefits of diversity.

6. Mexico's Economic Development

The Mexican economy has been at the forefront of North American economic news since 1982. On many occasions, this prominence was due to the fact that the country's policy makers were being castigated for gross mismanagement of the economy. On other occasions, it was because Mexico was being held up as a showcase of International Monetary Fund and World Bank stabilization and structural adjustment policies. What has remained unchanged throughout these contrasting scenarios is Mexico's inability to recover the historical growth rates that it enjoyed during the 1950s and 1960s. As outlined in Chapter 3 and confirmed in Chapters 4 and 5 is that this scenario is also consistent with the experience of Mexico's two NAFTA partners. Economic development has been postponed repeatedly as a vicious policy cycle heaped hardship on the population. A chronology of key post-World War II events in Mexico illustrates this point well:

- 1950s–1960s Sustained economic growth with low inflation and a stable peso.
- 1970–77 Rising inflation and external debt culminating in a major peso devaluation in 1976.
- 1978–81 Rapid economic growth based on oil exports.
- 1982 External debt crisis triggered by external shocks and economic mismanagement.
- 1983–85 Refusal to participate in a Third World debtors' cartel. Adoption of strong stabilization policies to become the IMF model 'adjusting country'.

- 1985 Major currency devaluation. Earthquakes in Mexico City, causing massive destruction of infrastructure. Mexico found to be out of compliance with IMF agreements.
- 1986–87 Mexico becomes first 'Baker Plan' country to receive short run relief from its international obligations to enable its economy to grow in order to repay its external debt over the long run.
- 1987 Stock market crisis, another devaluation.
- 1988 Presidential elections, in which strong claims were made that the official PRI party has been defeated for the first time in sixty years.
- 1988–89 Successful heterodox stabilization.
- 1989–94 'Impressive' trade liberalization and privatization of government enterprises.
- 1993 Slow growth and high external financing.
- 1994 Elections and high spending stimulating rapid growth in the economy.
- 1994 (December) Abrupt devaluation triggers the deepest recession since the 1930s.
- 1995 IMF and World Bank claims of exchange rate mismanagement and insufficient structural adjustment.
- 1995–96 Deep economic and political crises.
- 1997 Gradual economic recovery and political reforms.
- 1998 Low oil prices and Asian crisis reduce economic growth.

Since 1982, the Mexican economy has been characterized by stagnation, with worsening poverty and an increasingly uneven distribution of income. Surprisingly, there was little evidence of social tensions or political turmoil throughout this period. However, in 1994 a series of events shocked the country–a revolt in the state of Chiapas, political assassinations, and a sharp devaluation at year's end–and gave clear evidence that serious social and political problems were accumulating.

In less than twenty years, Mexico had moved from a relatively stable situation to a major development crisis, even though this period saw challenges in the second half of the 1970s and encompassed the 1982 debt crisis. The difference between the situation today and that faced by Mexico in the aftermath of the 1982 debt crisis is that it would be exceedingly difficult now to implement the same kind of policies adopted in the early 1980s–mainly because they require a high degree of credibility, something that has been undermined by the poor performance of the economy in the last fifteen years and today's level of social and political dissatisfaction.

This chapter will first provide a brief historical background, a condensed review of Mexican history from colonial times to the land reforms of President Cárdenas in the late 1930s. It then turns to the import-substitution industrialization period, whose decline set in motion the search for alternative development strategies in the 1970s. It next addresses the 1982 debt crisis, the 1982–88 period of stabilization, and the 1989–94 neo-liberal experiment, underlining the latter's major successes and failures. The chapter ends with a description of the 1995 crisis and some thoughts about the problems of long-term economic development in Mexico. Throughout the chapter the relationship between the nation's trade and development policies is emphasized.

FROM COLONIZATION TO MODERNIZATION

Soon after the discovery of America in 1492, Spaniards arrived on Mexico's Gulf Coast with plans to conquer native civilizations and establish a colonial power under the Spanish Crown. Tinted by strong feudal characteristics, dominance in the territories of New Spain depended on a complex web of local and regional groups that derived their power from ownership of extensive tracts of land (haciendas). The economic, social and political system rested on a comprehensive set of detailed rules. The class hierarchy had Spaniards at the top, followed by Criollos (individuals descended from Spanish parents but born in New Spain), Mestizos (descendants of Spaniards and natives), and natives, Africans and Zambos (descendants of natives and Africans). There was no judicial system; social order was based on the protection that the powerful granted to those at the bottom of the hierarchy who sought their support. Production was largely organized around meeting the needs of the haciendas and exporting natural resources (mainly gold and silver). There were no incentives for establishing industries since it was more difficult to produce than to trade for finished goods.

Early in the nineteenth century, Criollos, who far outnumbered Spaniards in the new territories, revolted against the Spanish Crown, winning independence in 1817. As Mexico's economic and political links with Spain loosened, new economic and social opportunities appeared, but most of the local and regional structure of power remained untouched. In the 1850s pressure was building to modernize the country along the lines of the then influential liberal ideology. Presidents Benito Juárez (1858–72) and Lerdo de Tejada (1872–76) clashed with powerful local and regional groups in an attempt to build a nation-state that would provide the framework for the development of a national economy. There were several attempts to lower interregional and international barriers to trade, though the latter was pursued with less enthusiasm than the former. Mexico's first rail line (thirty years in the making) was completed, and entrepreneurship and private investment were promoted during these administrations.

However, despite enormous efforts by the central government, little progress was made toward building a national economy. La Reforma, as this period was known, encountered many obstacles to modernization, including the 1862 French invasion and the temporary imposition of Maximiliano of Austria as Emperor of Mexico. Although liberal ideology proclaimed the need to develop entrepreneurship within society, modernizing Mexico also needed a strong state, something not in existence at the time. In addition, flawed agricultural policies weakened the system of communal property and further strengthened the power of owners of large landholdings known as latifundios.

The presidency of Porfirio Díaz (1876–1911) set the stage for the

Mexican Revolution which began in 1910, but Díaz also created the conditions for Mexico's modernization. Relying on centralized dictatorial powers organized around privileges and political favors, Díaz garnered sufficient political strength to implement the reforms that Juárez and Lerdo de Tejada had so ineffectively initiated. For the first time in Mexican history, national economic development was a stated goal of government programs. Díaz's strategy was a simple one: attract as much foreign direct investment as possible, doing whatever was necessary to that end. Foreign investors received unlimited facilities, and Mexico was soon dependent on external capital to an extreme degree. Díaz and the group of intellectuals that supported him–'*los científicos*'– believed that foreign investors were better businessmen than Mexican entrepreneurs in most respects. Excluding agriculture and craft production, about two-thirds of Mexican production was given over to the control of foreign capital. During this period, called the 'Porfiriato', the economy grew at unprecedented rates led by light manufactures, mainly for domestic consumption, and primary commodities, exclusively for export. Most resources were channeled to the construction of infrastructure, led by railroads. Although rail links were developed mainly to connect major cities to ports to facilitate exports, the construction of a national rail system also created the conditions for the integration of the domestic market. Large flows of foreign capital entered the country, mainly into the government securities that financed the construction of infrastructure.

Along with economic dominance comes political power, and foreign capital soon held leverage in Mexico's domestic politics. However, the political alliance that sustained Díaz was sufficiently strong that foreign interests remained second in terms of political importance. The real threat to the Porfiriato would come from within–in the form of growing social unrest and disputes among economic groups. The Porfiriato was a period of extensive social exclusion. In a still dominantly rural economy, about four-fifths of households owned no land, and about half the population lived in serf-like conditions in rural areas dominated by haciendas. When the Mexican Revolution (which ended the Porfiriato) began in 1910, under the leadership of a growing but politically excluded middle class and nationalistic intellectuals, large segments of the rural population joined the movement, organizing around their own rural leaders. Thus it was that land redistribution and democratization of political life in Mexico became the two central demands of the revolution.

The armed phase of the revolution ended in 1917, although political turmoil continued, including armed revolts in several regions. During the revolution, political power was fragmented among a number of local and regional forces under the leadership of different *caudillos*. These leaders vied for position in the postrevolutionary period, making for a national government that was fragile and unable to articulate a national development program. In 1929, a new political party (the PNR, Revolutionary National Party) was created in order to unify what came to be known as the 'revolutionary family'–the multiplicity of leaders who had played key roles in the revolution, and their followers. The PNR provided a forum for the internal resolution of disputes among the regional groups, and it succeeded in ending the series of political assassinations of the 1920s.

Trapped in attempts to resolve their own political conflicts, postrevolutionary governments postponed addressing one of the core demands of the revolution: land reform. During the 1920s and early 1930s the promise of land redistribution was used as a political tool to quiet discontent in the countryside, but the government did not modify the structure of property ownership in any substantial way. Land remained in the hands of large *latifundistas*, and this situation remained a persistent source of conflict.

Backed by a strong coalition of grassroots organizations and defying the most powerful groups within the party, Lázaro Cárdenas won the presidential nomination of the PNR in the mid 1930s. Based on his experience as governor of Michoacán, one of the poorest states in Mexico, President Cárdenas encouraged the organization of poor peasants in groups of 'petitioners', which in turn pressed the federal government to redistribute land. Within four years, Cárdenas had radically modified Mexico's structure of land ownership. In order to avoid future reconcentration, land was not allocated as private property. Rather, peasants–transformed into *ejidatarios*–were given the right to cultivate *ejido* land, but they could not sell it. In the 1990s Mexican law was substantially modified to allow *ejidatarios* to rent/lease their lands in order to facilitate the operation of the market in the agricultural sector.

The Cardenista land reform was more than a means to quiet social unrest in rural areas. It was conceived as part of a comprehensive development strategy. Reallocating land into smaller units would supposedly increase agricultural production–by bringing formerly idle land under cultivation and by intensifying cultivation on all land as peasants applied their intensive cultivation practices. An increase in agricultural production, in turn, would support the industrialization process in a number of ways: (1) it would increase the supply of foodstuffs for the growing urban population; (2) it would provide raw inputs for industrialization; and (3) by increasing exports of primary commodities, it would provide foreign currency to support the import of intermediate and capital goods required by the industrial sector.

The land reform of the 1930s was not limited to land redistribution. As the agricultural sector was to play a central role in Mexico's development strategy, Cárdenas created new institutions to provide *ejidos* with credit, technical assistance, and infrastructure. Results were impressive. Agricultural production increased at a rapid rate.

President Cárdenas introduced other reforms as well. He nationalized Mexico's oil industry in 1938, which had previously been in the hands of foreign firms. This nationalization proved to be a key step in the country's industrialization. In addition, land reform and the mobilization of petroleum-sector workers facilitated workers' and peasants' organization and their incorporation into the official party. When the PNR became the PRM (Party of the Mexican Revolution) at the end of Cárdenas's presidency, the terms were set for Mexico's rapid industrialization: social and political stability was guaranteed through the incorporation of all sectors of Mexican society within the official party; a strong national state had emerged, with control over key national resources; and the agricultural sector was showing impressive growth rates.

During the 1940s the Mexican government was in a strong position to take advantage of favorable international conditions to support rapid industrialization and accelerated growth. With Mexico's access to manufactured imports cut off (as most world economic powers became involved in World War II), local producers were poised to benefit from a captive domestic market and from an increasing demand for raw materials and basic manufactures for export. Favorable domestic and international conditions brought about a period of rapid growth and economic prosperity, but they also determined the strategy of industrialization that the Mexican government would pursue in the following years: the substitution of domestically produced goods for imported manufactures, or import-substitution industrialization (ISI).

INDUSTRIALIZATION AND IMPORT SUBSTITUTION

ISI has been criticized from a number of theoretical perspectives. One of the strongest criticisms is that ISI introduces major distortions in the allocation of resources throughout an economy, promoting the growth of an inefficient industrial sector. Although there may be elements of truth in this observation, in order to understand ISI's virtues and its flaws one must also consider the historical context in which this strategy has been implemented by developing countries.

The Mexican economy presents a classic case of import-substitution industrialization. During the 1950s and 1960s, ISI spurred high economic growth and rapid industrialization. However, in the 1970s accumulating problems signaled that import substitution had reached its limit as a useful development strategy.

The Success of Import Substitution

In the early ISI period in Mexico, vigorous industrialization provided the foundation for strong economic growth. Between 1950 and 1970, manufacturing output grew at an average 8 percent per year, leading rapid economic expansion. Gross domestic product grew at an average rate of 6 percent a year, and GDP per capita rose at an average of 3–4 percent annually.

Not only was the economy growing, but profound structural changes were taking place as well. Industrial and manufacturing activities increased in importance relative to total output and employment. Manufacturing's share in GDP increased from 17–23 percent between 1950 and 1970, while primary activities decreased from 19–9 percent of GDP in the same period. The distribution of employment shifted from primary (agricultural) activities toward industry and services. Mexico was clearly becoming an industrializing country.

BACKGROUNDER: MEXICO'S ECONOMIC GROWTH

Figure 6.1 shows the wide fluctuations characteristic of Mexico's economic growth over the last four decades. Despite such marked fluctuations, one can clearly identify two distinct periods. The 30 years between 1951 and 1981 were times of rapid economic expansion. For all but three of these years (1953, 1976 and 1977) GNP grew at more than (and usually much more than) 3.5 percent a year. Beginning in 1982, however, the Mexican economy has been unable to achieve grow rates above 3.5 percent a year (except in 1990, 1991, 1996 and 1997).

Within these two periods we can also identify several sub-periods. From 1951 to 1970 the average growth rate was 6.6 percent a year. This is the same average growth rate for the 1971–81 decade, but the annual rate slowed to 4.8 percent between 1971 and 1977 and then soared to 8.4 percent from 1978 to 1981. Within the second period of slow economic growth, we find very low rates in 1982–86 (–0.5 percent a year) and more moderate though low rates in 1987–94, averaging 2.7 percent a year. The peso devaluation in December 1994 triggered the worst economic recession in modern Mexican history. GDP declined by about 7 percent in 1995. Although the economy improved in 1996, because of the extensive contraction of the economy during 1995, the Mexican economy is still far from fully recovering its pre-crisis production level.

Another distinctive feature of Mexico's economic performance in these years was the macroeconomic stability that accompanied industrialization, particularly during the 1960s. In 1954 and 1958 the country, facing a crisis in its balance of payments, had devalued the peso

Figure 6.1 Mexico's Economic Growth (GDP), 1951–95

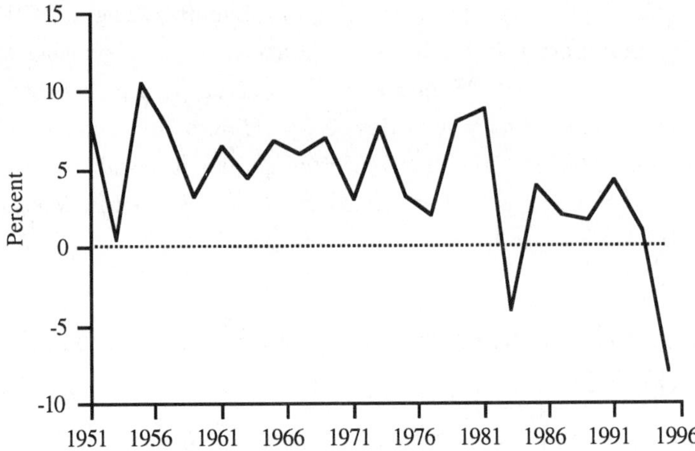

Source: INEGI (1996) *Estadisticas Historicas de Mexico.*

sharply. Since then, a more conservative approach to fiscal and monetary policies had led the way to several years of relative price stability. Price increases measured about 3 percent a year, a remarkable achievement by Latin American standards and one that gave this period its name: the period of stabilizing development.

Industrialization Policy

Industrialization was supported by a wide range of policies designed to promote industry and transfer resources to industrial activities, particularly manufacturing. Industrial policy targeted specific sectors to benefit from strong incentives and protection. The Ministry of Trade issued a list of products that qualified for government support programs; selected industries benefited from tax reductions, credit allocations, preferential interest rates, rebates on import duties and access to import quotas.

Mexico's trade policy was characterized by high levels of protection for industrial activities. Import licenses were required for more than two-thirds of total imports. Import duties ran as high as 100 percent, with the higher rates imposed on final products and the relatively lower rates imposed on selected intermediate and capital goods. In general, import duties were higher for consumer durables and lower for intermediate and nondurable consumer goods. This taxation structure translated into high levels of protection for domestic producers of consumer durables, who enjoyed high profit rates based on import restrictions on competing products.

The ISI strategy relied on private investment in most activities. However, the state played an important role in promoting industrialization, not only through indirect regulation of the economy but also through direct investment in selected sectors. In those activities where national private investors were hesitant and foreign direct investment was not desirable–for national security reasons–the state intervened directly in the ownership, organization and management of industrial and manufacturing enterprises. In the early stages of industrialization in the 1940s, public investment accounted for as much as half of total capital formation, although its importance declined to about one-third in the 1950s and 1960s.

Examples of the role of the government in promoting development in Mexico include the provision of basic utilities such as water, gas, electricity and telephone services. The government also provided physical infrastructure such as roads, railroads, ports and transportation, as well as managing the extraction, refining and marketing of petroleum. The state operated important companies in sectors like transportation equipment and steel. Direct management of key enterprises was an integral part of a strategy aimed at promoting industrialization. By setting prices low for key inputs, the government was actually subsidizing industrial production and the process of urbanization.

The government provided particularly strong industrialization support to the automobile sector. High duties on imported cars–along with fiscal incentives to transnational corporations from the United States, Germany, Japan and France to produce in Mexico–nurtured the development of a fast-growing auto sector in Mexico that soon accounted for a large share of employment and of manufacturing value added. Given the automobile firms' high level of protection, their output was oriented almost exclusively to the domestic market. Large inefficiencies accumulated in the sector's structure of production, ultimately undermining its ability to develop into an international competitor.

Industrial development was also supported by a policy of wage restraint. Government control over the largest labor unions helped to keep real wages below productivity growth. Wage policy was implemented through two main mechanisms. First, there was a centralized process of wage bargaining that set regional and job-specific minimum wages. Minimum wages, in turn, served as the reference point for individual firms and sectoral wage negotiations. Second, the ability of workers to organize and demand wage increases was, and still is, severely curtailed by the existence of tripartite organizations comprising representatives of workers, employers and government officials, which limit union actions. As a result, wages increased very slowly in real terms, below the rate of productivity growth. There were a few exceptions; in such fast-growing sectors as automobiles and steel, real wages were relatively higher and wage increases were closely tied to productivity gains.

Regarding resource allocation, there were explicit mechanisms for transferring resources to the manufacturing sector. First, price increases for primary products–mainly agricultural commodities–lagged behind prices for industrial products. In addition, manufacturing producers were the main beneficiaries of the cheap electricity, fuel and railroad transportation provided by state-owned enterprises. Second, the government channeled resources directly into the development of urban areas through public investment in infrastructure and the allocation of preferential credit to manufacturing activities. Third, to the extent that Mexico's exports were dominated by primary products and the country's imports consisted mainly of intermediate and capital goods, exchange rate management, which led to overvaluation of the peso, amounted to a tax on primary products and a subsidy to manufacturing activities. Thus, exchange rate policies also contributed to the transfer of resources from primary activities to manufacturing and industrial activities.

Macroeconomic Policy

Macroeconomic stability was achieved through a mix of conservative fiscal and monetary policies. Public deficits were kept below 1.5 percent of GDP, and the government maintained tight control over the money supply. The most important tool of monetary policy was the high level of reserves that commercial banks were required to deposit with the Central Bank. Thus interest rates were also determined by policy design. Every year, government officials would set the desired level of public expenditures and the mix of deficit financing from domestic banks and external borrowing. The private sector would then borrow the remaining funds from domestic banks and obtain any additional funds from external sources.

The Exhaustion of ISI

The strategy of import substitution was very successful in promoting rapid economic growth led by an unprecedented expansion of the industrial sector. Eventually, however, ISI succumbed to its own internal contradictions. Toward the end of the 1960s the momentum for industrialization was slowing. Once the relatively 'easy stage' of import substitution–the production of nondurable consumer goods for the domestic market–was completed, it was difficult to advance into the production of more complex industrial products, including capital and intermediate goods. This was due to a variety of factors including: risk aversion by Mexican entrepreneurs, lack of human capital and lack of research and development capacity.

BACKGROUNDER: THE AGRARIAN REFORM

Although the demand for land was the central issue that mobilized peasants during the Mexican Revolution, post revolutionary governments did little to modify the structure of land tenure. In the first fourteen years (1920–34) land redistribution proceeded at a very slow pace; under pressure from local communities, about 7 million hectares had been distributed, mainly as a way to quiet social unrest. The presidency of Lázaro Cárdenas (1934–40) brought a different orientation to the rural question. Cárdenas radically modified the

Table 6.1 Agrarian Reform

Year	Number of hectares distributed	Number of beneficiaries
1920–34	7,534,241	738,521
1934–40	17,889,792	810,473
1940–46	5,518,970	152,220
1946–52	3,501,835	72,901
1952–58	3,188,778	65,337
1958–62	4,318,528	61,899
1964–69	8,030	73,338

Source: Eckstein, (1966); Vernon, (1974); de la Peña, (1964).

Table 6.2 Rates of Growth in GDP and Output in Agriculture (in percent)

Year	GDP	Agriculture & Livestock
1940–45	7.6	3.6
1945–50	6.3	9.1
1950–55	6.9	8.1
1955–60	4.7	2.7
Avg. 1940–60	6.4	5.9

Source: Eckstein, (1966); Vernon, (1974); de la Peña, (1964).

structure of land tenure with the redistribution of almost 18 million hectares among 800,000 peasants.

President Cárdenas perceived land redistribution not only as a legitimate demand of poor peasants but as an effective way to expand agricultural production by increasing the cultivated area and improving its productivity. Within this context, land reform was expected to play a central role in Mexico's economic development. The growth in agricultural production was very dynamic in the years that followed the land reform. Table 6.1 shows that average growth rates in agriculture between 1940 and 1960 nearly matched the rapid growth rate of the economy overall in that period. The growth of production in agriculture actually exceeded GDP growth in 1945–55 (see Table 6.2).

The high priority given to industrialization and the systematic transfer of resources from primary activities and rural areas toward industry distorted development in both rural and urban sectors. Huge disparities between expected income in the cities and average income in rural areas caused massive rural-to-urban migration, reinforcing the urban bias of development. The rapidly growing urban areas absorbed increasing amounts of resources for productive and social infrastructure. The incentives to the industrial sector–low interest rates, subsidies, high rates of protection–were very successful in accelerating industrialization, but they discriminated against primary activities and precluded the possibility of a more balanced pattern of growth. These incentives to the industrial sector also resulted in an artificially low price of capital, with perverse consequences for employment and the distribution of income, for two reasons. First, they created a highly concentrated structure of industrial production with correspondingly large profit margins, which contributed to widening income inequality. Second, they generated a very capital-intensive structure of production, with low capacity to create employment. Further, as the size of the industrial sector expanded, so did the subsidies and other distortions needed to sustain it. Thus, it became more and more difficult for the government to foster further growth. As the number of industries supported increased, the patchwork of policies became confusingly complex and sometimes conflicting and counterproductive. Success in business often depended more on the ability of management to maximize government support than producing a viable product.

Balance-of-payments problems became increasingly severe. The level of protectionism that characterized industrial development in Mexico created an industrial sector that was unable to compete in international markets. Moreover, fixed exchange rates eventually led to overvaluation, further discouraging export growth. Although protectionist measures prevented a massive influx of imports, the structure of production was highly dependent on imported capital. Thus, any increase in the pace of economic activity led unerringly to a corresponding increase in imports. In 1970, for example, more than 90 percent of total imports were intermediate and capital goods. On the other hand, years of policy neglect in agriculture and primary activities decreased the exporting capacity of those sectors. By the late 1960s, historical surpluses of primary products gave way to shortfalls. The rural sector was no longer able to provide adequate supplies of agricultural products for domestic consumption, and living conditions in rural areas deteriorated, not only in relation to urban residents but also in absolute terms.

Two problems were slowly eroding the foundations of macroeconomic stability in Mexico. The first was the reluctance to adjust the exchange rate, which eventually led to overvaluation. Rooted in the political and economic turmoil generated by devaluations in the 1950s, political leaders were hesitant to adjust the exchange rate to hold inflation in check, fearing that any devaluation would be interpreted as a sign that their policy choices were flawed. Although a 3 percent annual inflation rate was low by Latin American standards, it was higher than the rate prevailing in the United States, Mexico's major trading partner. Toward the late 1960s the exchange rate became slightly overvalued, and it was clearly out of line by the mid-1970s.

The second problem was an unsustainably narrow tax base for public revenue. The proportion that taxes represented in GDP was low in Mexico compared to developed countries, but it was also low in relation to other developing countries at similar levels of industrialization. If the government was to continue playing an active role in development, additional sources of domestic funds had to be found.

Thus the country's development strategy was facing increasing difficulties in several domains: (1) the sources of foreign exchange that had supported import-substitution industrialization were drying up; (2) the easy stage of import substitution was over, making it more difficult to sustain fast rates of industrialization and economic growth; (3) macroeconomic stability was under strain; and (4) social problems were arising due to persistent inequalities in the distribution of income, as well as inequalities in the access to opportunities for social advancement.

THE 1970s: COPING WITH THE LEGACY OF ISI

During the 1970s and up to 1981, the goal of economic policy was to try to resolve some of the most severe problems generated by ISI policies. Traditional policies to support industrialization were supplemented by programs designed to promote manufactured exports. Several programs were designed to boost agricultural production. Policies of wage restraint were modified to allow some improvement in real wages. Specific policies were formulated to alleviate rural poverty as well as marginalization among the urban population.

Although some aspects of economic policy represented important departures from traditional import-substitution policies, it is safe to say that the main thrust of fundamental policy decisions remained the same. Protection of the domestic market was kept high through the imposition of import tariffs and an extensive use of quotas. The structure of protection remained unchanged–that is, higher duties for manufactured products in relation to primary goods, and higher duties for consumer durables among manufactured products. Overvaluation of the exchange rate increased throughout most of the period. To a large extent, however, the urban bias of economic policy did not waver: the structure of relative prices, the allocation of credit, and the deployment of infrastructure continued to favor industrial and urban activities over agricultural and rural development.

Emphasis in particular policies varied over time and especially between the two presidential administrations of this period–those of Luis Echeverría (1970–76) and José López Portillo (1976–82). More important, however, was the change in Mexico's macroeconomic framework toward the end of the 1970s. A sharp rise in Mexico's oil exports increased the availability of foreign exchange. Up to the mid 1970s, the government had followed a policy of self-sufficiency with respect to natural resources, deeply rooted in the historical events that led to the nationalization of the oil industry in 1938. Oil extraction was basically limited to domestic consumption. Indeed, during years of peak demand or supply shortages, Mexico had imported oil. In the late 1970s, however, after the US government publicly announced the existence of large and long-known oil reserves in Mexican territory, that policy was reversed. Taking advantage of high prices in international oil markets, the Mexican government designed a strategy to increase petroleum extraction and oil exports in a very short period, and the oil industry became a central piece in the design of economic policy.

At this point Mexico also left behind the policies that had marked its period of 'stabilizing development'. Public deficits of more than 3 percent of GDP–after inflation–became common, and in some years they exceeded 5 percent. This new level of expenditures, coupled with rising international prices, pushed domestic inflation to average rates of 12 percent a year between 1971 and 1975 and 22 percent on average from 1976 to 1981.

The 1971–76 Period

Policies implemented in the early 1970s were a first attempt to tackle some of the challenges posed by the decline of import substitution and the contradictions that surfaced in the late 1960s. Industrialization proceeded very much along the same lines as before. Unlike Southeast Asian countries once their easy stages of import substitution were completed, Mexico did not attempt to transform domestic manufacturers into successful exporters. Mexico also did not pursue more aggressive programs of import substitution that would have carried it toward the second stage of import-substitution industrialization–nurturing the development of a strong capital goods sector–as did Brazil.

Mexico adopted a more moderate approach to promoting manufactured exports. In a few industries, the government granted special tariff exemptions for the import of intermediate and capital goods tied to specific export targets. A public agency, the Mexican Foreign Trade Institute (IMCE), was created to facilitate export activities. Drawback provisions for import duties on exported goods were also designed to stimulate exports. Following the example of some Asian countries, Mexico facilitated the establishment of export-processing zones (EPZs) along its border with the United States. However, industries that flourished under these programs were isolated from the rest of the economy, and there was no clear medium-term strategy to integrate them with the domestic industrial sector. As noted in Chapter 3, EPZ *maquiladoras* import up to 98 percent of their inputs, purchasing only 2 percent from domestic producers. These industries, located under the export-processing umbrella, were basically conceived as a means to obtain foreign exchange and create employment on a regional basis, rather than as a component of an overall strategy of industrialization.

To the extent that the industrialization approach to development remained unchanged, the nature of social policy did not differ substantially from previous years. Nevertheless, there was some effort to improve social conditions among large segments of the population. Indeed, public expenditures on social programs increased relative to GDP and resulted in a substantial improvement in socioeconomic indicators–most noticeably in literacy, infant mortality and life expectancy. Some analysts have also found a more egalitarian distribution of income toward the late 1970s, when several programs were implemented to reduce the concentration of resources in Mexico City, mainly by decentralizing federal offices and a few industries. However, the system of relative prices continued to favor urban areas. Although substantial gains in real wages improved the distribution of income in urban areas, the gap between urban and rural areas widened.

One of the weakest areas in overall economic performance during these years was the external sector. The manufacturing sector did respond to export incentives by doubling foreign sales between 1971 and 1976. Although exports were increasing at an average rate of 19 percent annually, most industries remained normally oriented toward the domestic market, with exports representing only a small fraction of their total sales. On the other hand, the industrial sector's dependency on imported intermediate and capital goods did not improve, and an increasing import bill was the cost of moving ahead with the process of industrialization. As a result, and despite the rapid rise of manufactured exports, the external trade balance continued to deteriorate. Mexico's trade deficit increased from 2.3 percent of GDP in 1971 to 4.6 percent in 1974, to fall slightly to 4.1 percent in 1975.

Growing trade deficits must either be resolved through a devaluation, be financed with external resources or be halted through contractionary policies. Taking advantage of international conditions, Mexico chose the option of financing its growing deficit with foreign debt. Since the mid 1960s Mexico had enjoyed relatively easy access to international capital markets. In the 1970s the government was able to borrow from the large pool of international loan funds made available due to international financial innovation, liability management, and the recycling of OPEC oil surpluses. A substantial proportion of Mexico's public and trade deficits were financed in this way, although debt ratios started to show some warning signs as debt grew faster than GDP and interest payments came to represent a large proportion of export revenues.

A substantial slowing of private investment became one of the most critical problems in these years. In the context of increasing imbalances generated by the industrialization process and of political actions taken by the government to lessen social tensions, harsh recriminations surfaced between government officials and segments of the private sector, and this contributed to a major retrenchment of private investment. Not only were new investments postponed, but the private sector also 'lost' underinvested plants to the government. Private businesses took the back seat, and the state was forced to take up the slack. One way the government averted economic recession, growing unemployment, and greater social tensions was by taking over bankrupt businesses and undertaking major investment projects in such diverse industries as steel, electricity, automobiles, and even tourism. Although representatives of the business community blamed the government for the slowing of private investment, these years clearly represent a foreshadowing of what would later come to be recognized as a major economic problem: the chronic risk-averse behavior of Mexican entrepreneurs. It is of note that, despite its increasing role, the government did not seriously challenge the dominant position of the private sector in the economy. In fact, the government protected the private sector's short-term interests through major concessions in key decisions. At one point, for example, the government abandoned a fully designed fiscal reform that would have caused the private sector to experience a shortfall in revenue. The interest of private national investors were further protected by the adoption of restrictive legislation on foreign investment.

Mexico's overall economic performance continued to deteriorate. Economic growth slowed from an average annual increase in GDP of 7 percent between 1960 and 1970 to 6.5 percent a year from 1971 to 1976. Manufacturing output, which had been increasing by 8 percent a year between 1960 and 1970, rose by only about 4 percent during the later period. A fundamental cause of concern was the slowdown in productivity experienced during this period. Given the reluctance of private investors to expand production, economic growth was financed largely by a substantial increase in public investment, which contributed to drive up public investment as a portion of GDP by several percentage points. This public investment was not always guided by economic efficiency, but rather by multiple–often contradictory–criteria: to save jobs, bail out private companies, develop certain sectors of the economy, and so on. This governmental approach, together with a retrenchment of private investment at a time when import-substitution industrialization had entered its critical phase and there was no apparent reorientation of production toward exports, explain the period's sharp slowdown in productivity.

President Echeverría's first attempt to reestablish conditions for strong growth, based on the old principles of import-substitution industrialization, terminated in a severe balance-of-payments crisis, a major devaluation, and economic recession. Heavy public-sector investment, combined with meager tax revenues, increased fiscal deficits. These deficits, when coupled with high rates of inflation in the world economy, fueled double-digit inflation in Mexico. Rising prices, in the context of a fixed exchange rate regime, led to real appreciation of the peso, which added pressure to the already high deficits in the country's trade and current accounts. External borrowing to finance those deficits would only work for a limited time, and in 1976 the government was forced to implement a recessionary economic policy–including a major devaluation–in an effort to improve its trade and public deficits. By then, an adjustment in the exchange rate was long overdue. The economic and political situation had become so volatile that the government's efforts to stabilize the economy sent panic through exchange markets and ultimately provoked a drastic devaluation of the peso by approximately 100 percent. The government's intention in undertaking a devaluation was to correct macroeconomic imbalances, revitalize the economy, reduce external borrowing, and improve export performance. The announcement of major oil reserves at about this time, in a context of rising international petroleum prices, took the economy in a very different direction.

The Oil-Export-Platform Experiment

The 1976 devaluation and a strict policy of stabilization implemented in 1977 reestablished basic macroeconomic equilibrium by reducing inflation and decreasing trade deficits as imports contracted. These policies carried a high cost: no economic growth.

Soon, however, Mexico changed tack and undertook a rapid increase in its oil exports. Oil revenues soon substituted for foreign borrowing. Since the country was no longer dependent on foreign debt, this also removed all foreign constraints on Mexico's growth. The country repaid its IMF loans and, using public investment, set the pace for rapid economic expansion. Between 1978 and 1981, GDP increased at an average rate of 9.2 percent a year, and inflation held to a relatively moderate 25–30 percent. Massive public investment was funded primarily through heavy taxes levied on petroleum-related activities, so deficits remained small. Mexico's ambitious oil-exporting program required large amounts of investment, beyond the capacity of either public resources or domestic savings. As had happened in earlier eras, international funds began to pour into the country to meet this need. Given the high price of oil in international markets, foreign borrowing did not appear to be a risky policy; borrowing would finance a large increase in oil exports, and the oil revenues would provide the resources to service the debt. In strictly financial terms, this strategy was perceived as sound, especially since real interest rates in international financial markets were negative. The expected rate of return on the investment financed with foreign debt easily exceeded the rates of interest on external credits.

The trade regime that prevailed in Mexico during this period was basically a holdover from before. More attention was given to programs to stimulate exports, and the structure of protection was made somewhat more efficient by replacing quotas with tariffs. From 1977 to 1980, manufactured exports more than doubled, but the rapid acceleration of economic activity, partial trade liberalization, and real exchange rate appreciation increased the value of imports three times over. By 1979–80, Mexico's trade deficits, excluding oil exports, had reached an historic peak.

Oil revenues made it possible to allocate more resources for social programs. While President Echeverría had used a policy of real wage increases to check social unrest, President López Portillo did not support such a policy. Real minimum wages, including the wages of low-skilled government employees, fell below their 1976 level. It was only within the industrial sector that real wages increased.

Although the economy was booming in the late 1970s, this did not translate into strong industrialization efforts. Also it did not reverse the downward trend in productivity. The capital goods sector remained small, even when compared with other import-substituting countries, and Mexico's production of intermediate goods was also lagging. In spite of a rapid increase in manufactured exports, export volumes were an insignificant share of total production for most firms. Aggregate rates of investment reached levels that exceeded even those of the 1971–76 period. Again, productivity did not show any signs of improvement. Lacking specific policies to deepen the process of industrialization, and facing an increasingly overvalued currency and a persisting high level of protectionism, Mexico allocated its resources to finance marginal investment projects with low rates of return.

The argument can be made that, since investments mature over a long period, any investments undertaken in the late 1970s would not show results until much later. Thus, any assessment of productivity performance during these years would have to be qualified to take into account the period over which investment projects mature. Moreover, one could argue that the investments made in the late 1970s sustained the economy during the stagnation of the 1980s. However, even if we adopt this longer-term perspective, there is no evidence that investments made during the oil boom were actually profitable. In fact, the economy became increasingly unstable.

A Debt-Ridden Economy

The rapid expansion of the Mexican economy in the late 1970s weakened its financial resilience against external shocks. The high rates of investment of the period were largely financed by oil exports: at the end of the 1970s oil exports represented about two-thirds of total exports and one-third of all federal government revenue. The remaining revenue came from foreign loans. Thus the economy was exceedingly vulnerable to changes in oil prices and in international lending rates. Complicating things further, toward the end of the decade, dollarization and capital flight began to plague the economy. High inflation in Mexico fed the expectation of a sudden devaluation of the peso, and wary domestic investors began converting their savings from peso-denominated to dollar-denominated assets. By 1981, dollar-denominated assets accounted for about one-third of domestic institutions' financial assets. Capital flight also ran high as Mexicans moved their deposits to foreign banks.

BACKGROUNDER: EXTERNAL DEBT

Mexico is one of the few developing countries that has enjoyed relatively easy access to international capital markets–a privilege that has brought consequences both good and bad.

After international capital markets were reestablished following World War II, Mexico began borrowing heavily, and it continued to do so until the 1970s, primarily to foster national development. Between 1946 and 1955 the value of Mexico's international loans increased at an average annual rate of 27 percent; and from 1955 to the early 1970s, although foreign public borrowing slowed, it remained an important source of funds to finance the country's fast economic growth.

Importantly, Mexico's external debt was well under control up to the early 1970s (see Figure 6.2). Then Mexico's stable pattern of foreign borrowing gave way to a spurt in international borrowing that began in 1973. Taking advantage of highly liquid international markets and very low, often negative, real rates of interest, the Mexican government accelerated its for-

Figure 6.2 Mexico's Public External Debt, 1964–98

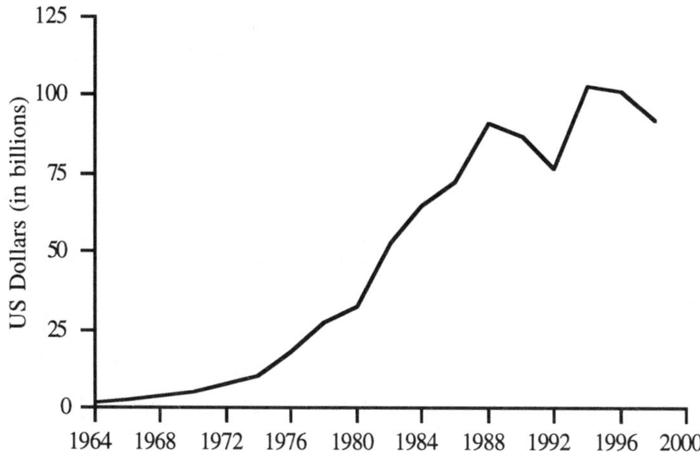

Source: Banco de Mexico (1999).

eign borrowing from 1973 to 1976 in order to finance large public investment programs. Total external debt nearly tripled between 1972 and 1976.

The 1976 peso devaluation and Mexico's agreement to abide by an IMF stabilization package put a temporary cap on the country's foreign borrowing, but when Mexico announced the discovery of huge oil reserves, the cap was quickly forgotten. Expectations of sizable earnings from oil extraction and a developing petroleum industry led to an important increase in foreign public borrowing, with external debt rising from US$23 billion in 1977 to about US$34 billion in 1980. Government officials justified such high levels of indebtedness by pointing to the country's rising earnings through expanding exports and overall economic growth. The external debt situation still appeared to be quite manageable.

Then in 1981–82, the international oil price collapsed. Both Mexican government officials and commercial bankers believed that the price drop was temporary and attempted to cover the revenue shortfall with even more debt. Their failure to correctly interpret the situation did much to undercut Mexico's economic strength. In just one year (1981) the country's external debt increased by more than US$20 billion. By March 1982, when foreign banks refused to continue lending to Mexico, the country's public external liabilities exceeded US$50 billion. Moreover, Mexican businessmen, caught up in the euphoria of the oil boom years, had also accumulated large foreign liabilities. Total external private debt (from financial and nonfinancial borrowers) had risen from $7 billion dollars in 1977 to US$17 billion in 1980. By 1982, without new loans to refinance existing ones, Mexico was bankrupt.

Throughout the 1980s the Mexican government pursued a debt management strategy that resulted in the bulking of foreign debt. Between 1983 and 1988 Mexico added some US$20 billion to its foreign liabilities. Meanwhile, Mexico, along with other Latin American countries, was suffering through in a deep economic recession, with negative per-capita GDP growth rates and rapidly deteriorating social conditions. It was not until the end of the decade, under the Brady Plan, that Mexico was finally able to reduce its foreign debt. By 1994 foreign debt had been brought down to less than 30 percent of GDP, from more than 70 percent in 1986 and 1987. Once the drag of debt payments had been eased, growth mildly recovered.

THE DEBT CRISIS

Two external shocks hit Mexico in the early 1980s. First, rising international interest rates more than doubled the cost of servicing Mexico's debt. Second, international oil prices plummeted, causing a drastic reduction in Mexico's revenues from exports. As suggested above dominant perception at the time was that these events were temporary, and so the Mexican government decided to continue current policies of economic expansion, for which additional borrowing was needed. International banks agreed with Mexico's prognosis, and in 1981 alone, they advanced Mexico an additional US$20 billion in loans. Interest rates did not drop, however, and oil prices remained low. Not only did Mexico's oil-export strategy become unsustainable, but the government's strategies for managing the two external shocks had actually made the situation worse, prompting a severe financial crisis.

In March 1982, under strong political pressure from organized workers, the Mexican government approved a wage increase beyond that negotiated in the stabilization package that Mexico had signed with the IMF. In reprisal, angered financial institutions reportedly decided not to roll over (extend the term on) Mexico's foreign debt. By August of that year, the Mexican government announced that it was unable to meet its international financial obligations. The peso was devalued again, by nearly 200 percent in the government-controlled market and by even more in the free market. Seeking a resolution to this latest crisis, the government reduced public expenditures to a minimum and initiated negotiations with private international banks and the IMF.

Turning Stabilization into a Development Strategy

Mexico's announced inability to service its external debt in August 1982 signalled the beginning of an international debt crisis that put the burden of adjustment almost entirely on developing countries. International financial institutions cancelled all new loans to developing countries, and debt forgiveness was not even on the negotiating agenda. Even though its economy was not growing, Mexico (along with other heavily indebted countries) had to take on additional external debt just to service past borrowing. This strategy had severe repercussions. As indicated above, between March and December 1982, the peso devalued by more than 200 percent. In 1982 GDP decreased by 0.6 percent; in 1983 it declined dramatically by –4.2 percent. This contraction of the economy translated into a decrease in imports of about 60 percent from 1982 to 1983, which produced a large surplus in the trade account. In one year, the Mexican government's strategy for debt management engineered a major reversal of financial flows. From a net inflow of resources that represented as much as 6 percent of GDP before 1982, Mexico started to transfer net resources abroad that were equivalent to 6 percent of GDP.

Implicit at the center of this strategy was the need to preserve the integrity of the international banking and financial systems. The debt crisis was considered to be one of illiquidity, not insolvency, so debtor countries were supposed to pursue policies to reestablish their basic macroeconomic stability, and this would allow them to return to international capital markets. Although not so openly publicized, capital repatriation was also an important target. Between 1979 and 1982, estimates of capital flight from Mexico ranged from US$20 billion to US$70 billion. According to this general approach, capital repatriation and reestablishing voluntary lending to Mexico would ensure the country's return to economic growth. These two objectives, however, were highly dependent on private investors' confidence in the policies of stabilization, and these depended, in turn, on how closely Mexico followed the orthodox policy advice of the IMF. Operating under these constraints, the government emphasized scrupulous compliance with its international financial obligations. This policy effectively eliminated any possibility for collective action with other debtor countries, which reduced Mexico's potential for political initiative and leadership in international negotiations.

The stabilization policies hinged on drastically cutting demand by reducing public expenditures, credit, and real wages. However, so severe were these adjustment policies that the Mexican government resorted to other, less 'orthodox' policies to reduce the deficit in the current account, such as imposing quotas on all imports and increasing import tariffs. This completely reversed the trade liberalization that Mexican had initiated in 1978, and exchange rate policies went well beyond restoring a balanced exchange rate–by 1983 the peso was clearly undervalued by as much as 30 percent.

By 1983 Mexico had cut its budget deficit to 8 percent of GDP (down from 16 percent in 1982). Once the rate of inflation is taken into account, adjustment policies produced a major reduction in the government's operating budget. Inflation can distort budget accounts in several ways. Nominal deficits tend to be higher because interest payments on the public debt increase nominally to compensate for inflation. Similarly, as tax collections accrue to the government with delays, the real value of revenue is lower at the effective time of collection. In the opposite direction, government benefits from issuing money when prices rise, collecting the so-called inflation tax. Taking account of some of these effects leads to estimates of what the budget deficit would be if inflation were zero. One of these estimates is the operational deficit. From 8.8 percent of GDP in 1981 and 5.2 percent in 1982, the deficit was reduced to 1.9 percent of GDP in 1983. Real wages were drastically reduced, cut by 50 percent from their 1982 level. Further, credit collapsed relative to its level in 1982. Although Mexico met and maintained its stabilization goals according to schedule, and the international banking and financial systems escaped breakdown,

Mexico (along with many other debtor countries) did not return to international voluntary capital markets.

Short-term stabilization had become Mexico's *de facto* development strategy. Budget deficits, wages and credit remained under strict control for most of the 1980s to ensure that there would be no demand pressures that could threaten prices or the trade balance. Inflation remained high, and there was no economic growth. One can hardly expect a country to regain credibility and return to international voluntary markets when inflation systematically outruns projections, investment is halted, and the economy stagnates.

By 1983 the net transfer of resources abroad was equivalent to six percent of GDP. The debt-stabilization strategy required a large surplus in the balance of trade. Although Mexico's manufacturing exports increased, import coefficients remained high so that the needed trade surpluses could only be sustained if the economy was repressed. Servicing the public debt–and, to a lesser extent, the private debt–also created conditions of recession and a drastic reduction in overall investment rates.

In order to service its external public debt, the Mexican government turned to domestic borrowing. Increasing government borrowing in the domestic market in a context of persistent inflation and financial vulnerability had the effect of driving up domestic interest rates, which further aggravated the economic situation. Not surprisingly, inflation continued to afflict the economy. More important than the persistence of inflationary pressures was the high cost associated with this set of policies: consumption, investment and overall economic activity were drastically curtailed.

The most notable exception in the recession-prone Mexican economy was the financial sector. The stock market boomed in 1984–85 and again in 1987. Revenue from the holding of financial assets increased as a share of total income in the wealthiest households. Exporting sectors were also performing well. Intra-firm trade with the United States rose rapidly in the automobile and machinery sectors. Helped by an undervalued exchange rate, a few other manufacturing sectors, including cement and beer producers, also increased their exports. And *maquiladora* plants mushroomed along Mexico's northern border. By 1998 they employed about one million workers (approximately 20 percent of the labor force in manufacturing) in more than 4,000 plants.

Managing and negotiating Mexico's external debt, together with a series of external shocks (including the 1985 earthquakes in Mexico City), set the pace for economic performance in these years. Most notably, in 1986 there was a combination of external shocks and negotiation entanglements: the price of oil collapsed, and it took the entire year to renegotiate and implement a package of debt restructuring. Economic activity was severely depressed. Gross domestic product decreased by 3.6 percent relative to 1985. In September 1987–when what was defined as an 'historic' debt agreement was finally in place, and economic policy was geared for stabilization–a worldwide stock market crisis hit the vulnerable Mexican market. The price index for traded shares plummeted, dragging the peso to a 240 percent devaluation in the exchange market.

Following the 1982 debt crisis, economic policy had been continuously reformulated under conditions of instability, external shocks, program inconsistencies and debt burden. Although international organizations made every effort to label the strategy a success, as a stabilization strategy it was clearly a failure. It increased the vulnerability of the Mexican economy to external shocks, and it could not provide the framework for a more sustainable restructuring of the economy. The 'lost decade', as the 1980s have come to be known, was in part policy induced, and its social and political costs remained to be paid.

The social costs of stabilization were high. Real wages were below their 1976 level, employment was stagnant, informal activities (unregistered and illegal transactions) proliferated but income from these activities decreased, and social programs were curtailed precisely when they were most needed. Poverty increased in absolute and relative terms, and inequality in income distribution worsened. Clearly, development had been postponed, often forgotten in the whirlpool of debt negotiations.

A new external debt agreement was needed, but it would be months before negotiations could begin. Something had to be done. Elections were scheduled in eight months, and the economy was again in recession, with rising inflationary pressures. As elections got closer, the popularity of the government faded.

The Neo-Liberal Experiment

By the end of 1987 the Mexican government abandoned the most orthodox principles of stabilization and adopted a heterodox program which, again, included an important reduction in government expenditures in order to decrease the budget deficit. This time, however, prices were not allowed to move freely. They were frozen for a few months at a time, and any subsequent changes were negotiated and closely supervised by an institutional tripartite body led by the government and including representatives of the business sector and labor. Through this mechanism, economic policy determined key prices: for energy, basic foodstuffs, and, more importantly, the exchange rate. After the peso had suffered years of instability in the foreign exchange market, the government's economic advisers concluded that a fixed exchange rate was a key tool for regaining macroeconomic stability. The exchange rate was frozen for a few months and gradually adjusted thereafter according to target inflation rates.

BACKGROUNDER: MEXICO'S RECORD ON INFLATION

Compared to other countries in Latin America, Mexico has been relatively successful in keeping inflationary pressures down. A number of factors have been suggested to explain this behavior: a more orthodox approach to monetary policy, relatively easy access to international financing, and the fact that Mexico is a diversified economy and well-endowed with natural resources. From the late 1950s to early 1970s, Mexico enjoyed rapid economic growth accompanied by price stability (see Figure 6.3). In 1973, however, prices started to move in an upward direction: from 1973 to 1982 annual inflation rates increased to around 20 percent a year. Inflation accelerated even further in 1983 in response to the heavy burden imposed by the external debt, internal inflation, and a succession of external shocks. Then in 1989 inflation started to ease, falling below 20 percent a year. This declining trend was

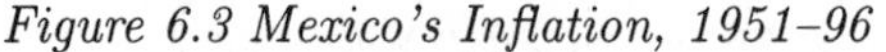

Figure 6.3 Mexico's Inflation, 1951–96

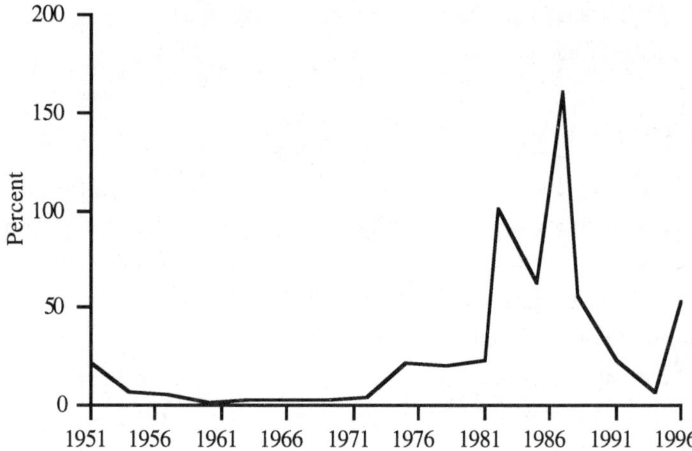

Source: INEGI (1996) *Estadisticas Historicas de Mexico.*

interrupted by large price hikes in 1995 and 1996 as a result of the sharp devaluation of the peso in December 1994.

This time around, stabilization policies were accompanied by more comprehensive structural adjustments in an attempt to reestablish the conditions for long-term economic growth. Almost 1,000 public corporations were sold to private businesses; others were simply closed. The government withdrew from the steel, automobile and sugar sectors, among others. Most notably, the government sold the highly profitable telephone company, and it returned the recently nationalized banks to private hands.[1] The government unilaterally implemented a comprehensive policy of trade liberalization. Import licenses were lifted for almost all goods, and import tariffs were simplified and reduced. With these changes, the average rate of protection in Mexico was lower than that in the United States. Breaking away from a long nationalistic tradition of keeping a certain distance from the US government–a tradition based on fears of political and economic domination–the Mexican government in 1991 saw the imperative need to establish an economic relationship with the US which would diminish further the uncertainties of

[1]Banks had been nationalized in 1982.

trading with a economic superpower. This new economic relationship would have to be qualitatively different than the various agreements signed with the US during the decade of the 1980s such as the one on subsidies and countervailing duties (1982) and the Framework Agreement (1987). The former became the basis for Mexican participation in GATT, while the 1987 agreement was a prelude for the decision to enter into a free trade agreement with the US. Accompanying the liberalization of trade which had been occurring at a rapid pace since 1982, the Mexican government also sought a substantial reduction in its debt burden, with mixed results. Its objective was to stem the outflow of financial transfers abroad, which at that time represented 6 percent of GDP. In 1989, under the auspices of the Brady Plan, a three-item menu was offered to Mexico's creditor banks: (1) they could lend fresh money to indebted countries to allow them to reestablish regular debt service; (2) they could reduce outstanding debt; or (3) they could decrease interest rates on outstanding loans. Most banks opted for the third alternative. After implementation, these interest payments translated into net financial transfers from Mexico equivalent to about 2–3 percent of GDP. The plan was presented officially as a successful negotiation to reduce Mexico's external debt, and domestic markets reacted favorably by cutting interest rates. Attracted by more favorable expectations, portfolio investment started pouring into the country.

Popular discontent with economic circumstances, and the underlying social and political tensions, turned Mexico's 1988 elections into a clear message for the government and for the dominant PRI party. Many observers believe that Carlos Salinas de Gortari actually lost the election to nationalist and socially sensitive Cuauhtémoc Cárdenas and assumed the presidency through fraud; in the best of cases, Salinas won by a hair. Entering office under a cloud, the Salinas administration understood that social policies had to be rebuilt. Public expenditures on social programs soon rose as a proportion of GDP, and a coordinating unit (Solidarity, or PRONASOL) directly linked to the president was created. Solidarity's stated objective was to alleviate poverty by implementing a nationwide program of public expenditures in various areas. Solidarity's supporters claimed to have initiated a new age of social policies guided by the principle of maximum efficiency in the alleviation of poverty. Programs sought better targeting in order to reach the poorest sectors of the population in a way that would avoid encouraging unproductive behavior.

INTEGRATING INTO NORTH AMERICA AND DEVELOPMENT

Rooted in old suspicions about US expansionist intentions, Mexico's relations with the United States have always been controversial, and Mexico has placed high value on asserting its independence based on noninterventionist principles. As long as Mexico pursued an inwardly-oriented development strategy, international economic integration was not an issue (although, for diplomatic reasons more than anything else, Mexico did participate in several initiatives to integrate markets in Latin America).

Yet, despite its independent diplomatic stance on international issues, Mexico's economic relations with the United States were close. Most foreign investment in Mexico originated in the US and, Mexican trade with other Latin American countries was small compared to Mexico's trade flow with the US. Businesses in Mexico and the US built a complex web of economic relations. Banks in the US had been key lenders to Mexico since the mid-1960s. This is the process that has been referred to as Mexico's silent integration with the United States.

BACKGROUNDER: ECONOMIC INTEGRATION

Mexico's economic relations with the rest of the world traditionally have been dominated by its close ties with the United States. Export figures by country show that during the 1940s about 80 percent of Mexico's exports were sold to the United States. During the 1950s and 1960s that proportion decreased, but it oscillated around a still high 60 percent level. Since then the share of trade with the United States has further increased, to represent about 75 percent of total exports in the 1990s.

The picture is very similar if one looks at the origin of foreign direct investment in Mexico. Historically, investments by US corporations account for the bulk of foreign investment in Mexico. Looking at Table 6.3, which presents the annual flow of monies into Mexico from investors in other countries, we find that investments from the United States historically represented about two-thirds or more of the total value. Other important sources, though on a much lower scale, are the United Kingdom, Canada, Germany and Japan. The large proportion of foreign investment flows represented by the United States in the first half of the century became even larger during the years of high growth, to represent about four-fifths in the 1960s, but this decreased somewhat in the troubled decade of the 1970s.

As Mexico's economic strategy switched toward a more open policy in the mid 1980s, the importance of US foreign direct investment recovered ground. Between 1989 and 1994 the United States accounted for 63.2 percent of the total accumulated flow of foreign direct investment (excluding reinvested earnings) in Mexico, which is consistent with its past share of 60.2 percent (SECOFI, 1995).

Table 6.3 Annual Flow of Foreign Direct Investment in Mexico (in percentages for selected years)

Year	US	UK	Germany	Canada	Japan	Other
1940	61.4	8.1	0.0	24.5	0.0	6.0
1950	68.9	5.3	0.0	15.2	0.0	10.7
1960	83.2	5.1	0.6	2.3	0.5	8.4
1970	79.4	3.3	3.4	1.6	0.8	11.5
1979	68.0	6.7	5.2	3.0	2.6	14.5

Source: Authors calculations based on Banco de México (1980), p. 297.

Events in the 1980s modified Mexico's diplomatic stance on international issues. As its economic activity became increasingly dependent on external forces, Mexico's separation between diplomacy and economic relations tended toward a reconciliation with the United States and a greater distancing from other Latin American countries. For example, after Mexico had decided not to join GATT in 1981 (Mexico's adherence had long been a goal of US diplomacy in Mexico), the country reversed itself in 1986, three years after the eruption of the debt crisis, and joined GATT. In Latin America, Mexico lost the directorship of Sistema Economico de America Latina (SELA), a regional economic forum for Latin America. This was a clear sign of its rapidly failing leadership position in the region.

An important ingredient in Mexico's 1988–94 neo-liberal strategy was the reversal of the country's traditional foreign policy, historically defined along nationalistic lines. Mexico abandoned its efforts to gain treatment as a developing country in international organizations. One clear example can be found in a policy decision made after Mexico joined GATT in 1986: Mexico cut its tariffs much further and much faster than it had agreed to do, the general idea being to put in place a structure of market incentives similar to that of a developed country (using the United States as a model). Another example is Mexico's request to join the Organization for Economic Cooperation and Development (OECD), which includes most of the world's industrial countries. Even more puzzling than its request was Mexico's acceptance into that organization in 1994.

By far the most significant initiative in this regard was Mexico's economic integration with the US and Canadian economies through NAFTA. Many analysts saw this trade agreement as healthy recognition of the deeply rooted tendencies shaping the silent integration of the Mexican and US economies over decades. Importantly, neither the NAFTA negotiations nor the actual text of the agreement include any consideration of the obvious differences in development level and economic structures between the United States and Canada, on the one hand, and Mexico on the other. Basically, the reference point for redefining trade and investment relations was the US code and, to a much lesser extent, Canada. Mexico's strategy has been to emulate industrial countries, especially the US.

THE TWENTY-FIRST CENTURY: THE LESSONS OF CRISIS

After 1989, Mexico had once again become a showcase of the International Monetary Fund and World Bank, the US government and international investors. Mexico's access to international capital markets had been reestablished, money flowed into the country and non-traditional manufacturing exports increased rapidly. Trade within North America is composed mainly of trade between the subsidies of multinational corporations and is referred to as intrafirm trade. The foreign exchange constraint that inhibited economic growth for almost ten years was relaxed. Despite the fast growth in exports, Mexico's trade deficit continued to widen since imports increase at an even faster pace. The availability of international finance and the alleged efficiency gains from privatization and liberalization were all overshadowed by a suspicious lack of growth in the economy. The carefully nurtured popularity of Solidarity was not sufficient to alleviate social tensions in a number of regions. Indeed, serious questions about the effectiveness of this program were raised in January 1994 after an indigenous rebellion in Chiapas (one of the regions most favored by Solidarity) exposed the area's lacerating poverty and oppression and the inefficacy of Solidarity as a poverty-alleviation program.

By December 1994, the tensions building in the economy led to turmoil in the exchange market, and a 100 percent devaluation of the peso ensued. The trade deficit had skyrocketed to levels similar to the oil-financed imbalances of 1980 and 1981. Amidst a climate of political assassinations and incessant cries for democracy, capital became nervous, either exiting the country or seeking refuge in dollar-denominated government bonds. With its economic policy hinging on its credibility, the government refused to adjust the exchange rate. A devaluation was equivalent to admitting the complete failure of the administration's strategy of economic restructuring, since neither economic growth nor the trade deficit could make the record look any better. Probably most importantly, the strategic interests of the group in power were at stake, including the signing of NAFTA, forthcoming national elections, and President Carlos Salinas's campaign for the directorship of the World Trade Organization. Risking a speculative attack on the peso, the administration allowed the exchange rate to become overvalued. The inept management of exchange rate policy by the new administration of President Ernesto Zedillo (1994–2000), which precipitated a major exchange rate crisis in December 1994, was just the trigger in an unavoidable devaluation.

The 1994 devaluation was like opening Pandora's box. In the six months following the devaluation, the government had to negotiate an emergency financial package for US$50 billion, with unpalatable conditions attached. Although there is no record of a similar deal having been negotiated previously, no one dared to call this one 'historical' in the way governments had referred to prior large debt negotiations. The package's restrictive policies and exorbitantly high interest rates halted economic activity in Mexico. Gross domestic product growth was negative in 1995, and open unemployment increased from 5 to 8 percent. A very worrisome sign of the severity of the recession was the fact that the traditional mechanism used to cope with unemployment–the informal sector–was not sufficient to absorb the large number of newly unemployed workers. Medium-sized and small businesses were crushed by recession and debts incurred during the 1994 'easy-money' electoral run-up. A serious banking crisis became a real possibility.

The 1994 devaluation and subsequent crisis clearly revealed that Mexico's recent economic achievements had been exaggerated and that deep economic, social and political problems were building. Trade liberalization led to significant adjustment costs as protected firms were forced to compete with imports. Many businesses failed, and employment did not increase sufficiently despite the rapid increase in exports. Privatization and deregulation did not follow a careful plan and were plagued by favoritism and anomalies. Important businesses were turned over without due attention being given to the previous experience of the new owners. One exception, again, was the domestic banking sector, whose recently privatized banks received ample protection from foreign competition. The result in the banking sector was inefficiency, high cost, lack of financing and an increase in foreign private indebtedness.

BACKGROUNDER: INCOME DISTRIBUTION

Comparatively[2] high levels of income inequality have characterized economic development in Mexico. Although the information about household income and expenditures is limited and what data exist were collected with varying methodologies, making comparison difficult, several authors have attempted to trace the evolution of income distribution in Mexico. Using only the income/expenditure surveys that are methodologically comparable, Hernández and Córdoba (1982), found that income distribution became more unequal between 1958 and 1970. The Gini coefficient (which ranges from zero to one and takes a higher value as inequality worsens) increased from 0.45 in 1958 to 0.496 in 1970, suggesting that there was a tendency toward a greater concentration of income during Mexico's years of rapid industrialization (see Table 6.4). Especially relevant was the impact on the poorest 10 percent of households; their share of income fell dramatically from 2.3 percent of total income in 1958 to a mere 1.4 percent in 1970.

During the 1970s, explicit efforts were made to reverse the increase in income inequality engendered by the industrialization process, with an emphasis on improving real wages, especially among unionized workers. Wages as a share of GDP increased from 35.8 percent in 1971 to its peak value of 40.5 percent in 1976. Some analysts have identified a more egalitarian distribution of income toward the late 1970s. However, social programs and the resulting improvement in living conditions were generally restricted to urban areas and mainly benefited the most organized sectors of workers, leaving the income gap between urban and rural areas to widen further. While the share of wages in national income increased and the share of the richest households appeared to decline, the share accruing to the poorest families (where rural households predominate) continued–a revolt in Chiapas, political assassinations, and a sharp devaluation at year's end gave clear evidence that serious social and political problems were accumulating. In less than twenty years, Mexico had moved from a relatively stable situation to a major development

[2]This backgrounder draws on Alarcón Gónzalez (1994). Tijuana: El Colegio de la Frontera Norte.

Table 6.4 Income Distribution 1984–94

Deciles	1984	1989	1992	1994
I–III	9.0	8.1	8.0	8.0
IV–VI	19.6	17.9	17.5	17.4
VII–IX	38.6	36.0	36.3	36.2
X	32.8	37.9	38.2	38.4
Gini	0.429	0.469	0.475	0.477

Source: INEGI (1984–94).

crisis. Clearly, a new development strategy needs to be formulated, one that gives special emphasis to the basic needs of the population.

Although opinions differ about whether or not poverty decreased between 1988 and 1992, Solidarity did little to improve living conditions among the poorest of the poor. Most often, Solidarity funds were used to gain political support, diverting funds away from sectors that were most in need of aid. In addition, the published figures on the program's funding were misleading: it is not difficult to demonstrate that monies from the regular government budget found a place under the PRONASOL rubric.

While the social programs of the 1970s and 1980s had the structural limitation of having been designed within the ISI development approach and were skewed to the urban, industrial sectors, the social programs of the 1990s suffered from the assumption that it was just a matter time before marginal sectors of the population would be incorporated into the market and thereby improve their living standards through their participation in an expanding market economy. There was no effort whatsoever to integrate a vision of economic performance with social improvement in a country where nearly half of the population lives in poverty, and one-quarter in extreme poverty.

During the Salinas presidency, the priority was economic reform, with political reform postponed indefinitely. The December 1994 crisis, however, shook the foundations of Salinas's neo-liberal strategy of development or its remnants as inherited by the new Zedillo administration which had just taken office.

Whatever social or political priorities might have existed in the new Zedillo government, the first order of business after the collapse of the Mexican peso was to set up the conditions for macroeconomic stabilization and recovery, repeating similar cycles that had occurred in 1982 and 1987. There were a number of macroeconomic conditions which were to be addressed first. (1.) Stabilize the value of the Mexican currency which had lost 50 percent of its value from 3.39 pesos per dollar to 6.26 per dollar in the middle of 1995. (2.) Contain inflation which had risen from 7 percent at the end of 1994 to 51.97 percent by mid 1995. (3.) Reduce interest rates which had risen from 17.84 percent in December of 1994 to 54.09 percent at the end of 1995. (4.) Increase international reserves which had accumulated over the 1989–94 period to 14 billion dollars only to fall to 6 billion by the end of 1994. These policy measures lead to a sharp drop in the real gross domestic product. In the third quarter of 1994 GDP decreased by 8 percent. In the fourth quarter it declined another 7 percent. However, all of these negative indicators turned positive in 1996 and 1997, so that GDP growth changed from –0.4 percent at the beginning to 7.6 percent in the fourth quarter. Positive rates of growth continued during all of 1997.

After the collapse of the peso in 1994, it is not surprising that Mexico's trade balance improved dramatically. During 1994 the balance of trade became increasingly negative. The balance of trade improved and became positive between 1995 and the middle of 1997. From August to December 1997, the trade balance once again became negative. In November it was –US$386 million. December's balance deteriorated to –US$733 million. Negative trade balance continued into 1998. This trend is not surprising as macroeconomic conditions stabilize and economic growth takes place. Mexico has always been (or becomes) an importer of goods used in the process of growth and consumer demand also increases for imported items. Finally, foreign direct investment fell from US$11 billion in 1994 to US$7.5 in 1996. As macroeconomic conditions stabilized investment reentered Mexico reaching US$12.1 billion in 1997.

While the exact nature and extent of the role maybe uncertain, NAFTA certainly played a role in the Mexican economic recovery in

1997. The Clinton rescue package of 1995 might not have occurred–or occurred too late–if Mexico had not been sold to the American public as a necessary trade ally during the early part of the decade. Also, the disinvestment which took place (discussed in detail in the next two chapters) would certainly have been greater had not investors of foreign capital had the assurance which NAFTA provided. Yet, what the 1994 crisis and subsequent recovery uncovered was the severe inefficiencies, misconceptions, technical incapacity, authoritarianism and corruption that prevailed in the high spheres of the Mexican government. The lesson left by the devastating experiment of reforming the economy is that balanced and sustainable economic growth can only be achieved if it comes accompanied by parallel social improvement, democracy and rational economic policy that serve the interests of the majority of the population, not just the few in power.

PART III

Introduction

North American economic integration has, since January 1, 1994, focused on NAFTA itself and the three supplementary agreements. As noted in earlier chapters, these agreements now provide the formal 'rules of the game' for further integration and for the resolution of disputes regarding trade and investment issues that inevitably will arise over the course of time. The NAFTA document also provides procedures for expanding the three-country agreement by 'widening' (that is, adding new countries) and/or 'deepening' (that is, adding new concepts like labor mobility or consultation on macroeconomic policies) to the process.

It is important to remember here that it is private firms that trade and invest, not governments. Governments negotiate (possibly in consultation with private firms and their trade associations) international economic treaties which, in turn, create new ongoing institutions (that is, the NAFTA Free Trade Commission) which administer the implementation and operation of the (transnational) treaty under which firms must operate as they buy from, sell to and invest in other countries. Additionally, it must be remembered that in the case of NAFTA each of the three countries embraced the principles of the multilateral GATT/WTO, which implies that their (trilateral) institutions and actions grew out of and must be consistent with those of a larger framework. Finally, implementation of an international economic treaty such as NAFTA requires a higher level of harmonization of a myriad of customs procedures as well as business and legal practices as the economic borders between countries are gradually dismantled–a practical, nuts and bolts process that requires a great deal of energy, patience and good will on the part of representatives from business, government and academia.

In this third and final part of the book we first (in Chapter 7) examine the international environment that led to NAFTA's birth. Then we turn to the content of the agreement itself, NAFTA's main provisions for freeing up trade and investment relations between the three countries during specified time periods. In Chapter 8, we examine the major deficiencies of NAFTA itself, which mainly revolve around Mexico's asymmetric level of development in comparison with the US and Canada. Then we present the main aspects of NAFTA's implementation during the first few years focusing on the institutional structure that will be responsible for its ongoing operations and NAFTA's accomplishments in the areas of trade, investment and dispute resolution. Finally, we look 'beyond NAFTA' to provide the reader with a view of the various options that exist, especially in the Western Hemisphere, for expanding the integration process.

One implicit theme runs throughout this part of the book; that in order to understand NAFTA one must adopt a multidisciplinary perspective. Economics alone is not sufficient. Politics too played an important role in the negotiation of the agreement and those politics were intimately intertwined with the strategies of special interests (for example, businesses which would be hurt or favored) by the outcomes. Again, NAFTA represents managed trade, not free trade. Managed trade will always reflect both economic and political realities. Lastly, it is important to note that NAFTA and its side agreements are legal documents that were negotiated and written by lawyers from the three countries who will interpret the document and its side agreements. In closing, we wish to remind the reader that NAFTA did not initiate the process of North American economic integration. Instead it attempted to provide explicit rules for the process which began decades ago.

7. North American Economic Integration: Trial by Fire

When the North American Free Trade Agreement went into effect on January 1, 1994, it raised the hopes of millions of people in Mexico, Canada and the United States that the agreement would enhance production efficiency, create jobs and increase investment within the North American continent. Its chances for success–for a successful conclusion to the negotiating process, for ratification by the respective legislative bodies of the three signatory countries, and for achieving its objectives–had been enhanced by the global economic context, by economic opening already well under way in Mexico, and by the demonstration effects of a prior bilateral trade agreement between Canada and the United States, CUSFTA.

However, despite high expectations for a wide range of benefits to accrue through North American economic integration, NAFTA was flawed. Its imperfections did not go unnoticed, but for a variety of reasons they were allowed to remain as part of the final document. These weaknesses will plague North America in the future and hinder the operation of institutional instruments as the region attempts to integrate vastly asymmetrical economic systems. In this respect, NAFTA is predestined to undergo a difficult implementation process–and ultimately to emerge as a working agreement born not out of cool mediation, but by trial by the fires of political, economic and social interests.

Preceding chapters have dealt with the processes of economic integration in North America: exchanges of exports and imports, trade in services and so on. There were also chapters on the individual economies of the three countries of North America, outlining in detail their developmental histories and the problems that these histories imply for the process of continental integration.

This chapter's objective is to place NAFTA in context. While a point-by-point examination of NAFTA might suggest that it is a purely economic agreement, its evolution was guided as much by political considerations as by economic ones. Thus any review of NAFTA's origins and early implementation will necessarily lead us into both the economic and the political realms of analysis.

Regarding the economic dimension: in the early days of NAFTA negotiations, many observers suggested that the high degree of economic interdependence (that is, the mutual trade in goods and services) already established between the United States, Mexico and Canada made it 'natural' and 'inevitable' for these countries to pursue additional instruments of economic integration. Bilateral trade between Canada and the United States and between Mexico and the United States is extensive. That between Mexico and Canada still lags far behind, although it is growing at a very rapid rate. Besides being extensive, North American trade is also highly concentrated, involving very few goods and a great deal of intra-firm trade. Up-to-date figures on bilateral and North American trade are available from the US Census Bureau via the internet or on-line services such as CompuServe (look for Reference icon). This argument is only half right; it forgets the dynamic aspects of asymmetry, and the relations in North America were nothing if not asymmetric. Asymmetric interdependence had introduced aberrations into what otherwise would be the everyday exchange of goods and services (Emmanuel, 1972; Sau, 1978). One of the most worrisome of these aberrations in North America was a situation of declining terms of trade, in the goods traditionally exported by developing countries, a disequilibrium that has led many of those countries to run up large trade deficits as they import more than they export, and the resulting currency exchange and payments problems. Before the 1980s, Mexico was largely an exporter of primary products, relying on oil exports to bring in hard currency; and it was dependent on technological and capital imports to make headway against underdevelopment. There was added concern because of Mexico's prior history of protectionism, which made much of the country's productive plant noncompetitive (see Chapter 6). These factors suggest that NAFTA was far from a 'natural' developmental stage within the North American trading regime. Of course, those who support the view of NAFTA being inevitable can point to the earlier efforts of the Mexican and, to some extent, the Canadian governments to isolate their economies from the American economy as proof of how difficult it is to postpone the inevitable.

The second dimension, the political one, is related to the internal and external relations among domestic political actors, and between them and international actors–that is, country-to-country relations. This dimension is just as influential as the economic one. Indeed, the politics of NAFTA were of key importance in Canada, the United States and Mexico (del Castillo and Vega Cónovas, 1996). NAFTA's structure and the process that produced a signable agreement were the result of how the different political actors related to one another. For example, if Mexico had insisted on including the mobility of labor in North America as part of NAFTA negotiating agenda, there would be no agreement today. If Mexico had rejected the side (complementary) agreements on labor, the environment and import surges, there would be no NAFTA. If there had been no Canada-US Free Trade Agreement to serve as a model for NAFTA, it is unlikely that negotiators from the three countries would have been able to come to an agreement within the strict timetable imposed by the fast track negotiating authority granted to the US president by Congress. All of these factors combined to produce a trade agreement that is workable but less than perfect.

If we want to understand how NAFTA came into being we must look to factors in the international arena that facilitated NAFTA's emergence. The following section discusses five key political and economic considerations that largely defined the context within which NAFTA developed.

A later section examines the major components of NAFTA. What is included in this agreement is of particular importance because the accord represents these three countries' attempt to organize under a set of rules designed to govern the trade that already existed between them, as well as to promote trade in other areas where the potential for exchange was emerging. NAFTA is also especially important because of what it does not include; it is illuminating to explore why some topics were deliberately excluded from consideration.

The concluding section returns to NAFTA's shortcomings. It considers why flaws were allowed to remain in the final document and what their likely effects will be on future trade within North America.

THE INTERNATIONAL ENVIRONMENT ON THE EVE OF NAFTA

NAFTA was the product of forces in the global economic environment interacting with the foreign economic policies of the countries of North America. It is important in this regard that there was general concordance in the NAFTA member countries' interpretations of the international economic environment. This 'consensus' among the countries' analyses was not coincidental; it resulted from a common set of ideas, held by economic and political elites, about the place and future of their respective domestic economies in a changing world.

There are three key factors that, in combination, enabled the countries of North America to integrate their trade relations:

- The United States' frustration with the slow progress of multilateral negotiations in the Uruguay Round of the General Agreement on Tariffs and Trade (GATT), together with its freedom to choose the bilateral/trilateral route to advance its foreign economic policies. From 1982 through 1987, the United States had negotiated a series of trade-related agreements with Mexico, including Mexico's entry into GATT, which resulted in Mexico's unilateral establishment of a 20 percent tariff level on its imports (30 points lower than the tariff reductions negotiated in GATT). If the United States entered into negotiations of a North American free trade agreement, it could begin, not from the 50 percent tariff rates of GATT, but from the 20 percent level that Mexico had implemented at the time of its GATT entry.

- Mexico's move toward an open economy. This shift was prompted by the weak state of the Mexican economy in the early 1990s, after a decade of economic downturn that began with the debt crisis of 1982.

- The Canada-US Free Trade Agreement. CUSFTA had produced significant economic gains for sectors participating in bilateral trade. This agreement could serve as a model for bringing Mexico into the North American economic region.

There are several other contributing factors in the formation of NAFTA. At least two of these are sufficiently significant to deserve mention: the trade-diverting impacts that CUSFTA had on Mexico, and the fall of the Berlin Wall which signalled the collapse of the Soviet system. Together, these five factors can reveal much about the complex process involved in the NAFTA negotiations, but they are also useful in determining why certain issues are covered by NAFTA and why they are treated as they are.

The United States and the Uruguay Round

Due to the political and economic reality that the United States is a world superpower, the world's foremost trading nation, and the world's largest market, this country has long been in a position to strongly influence, if not determine, the world's trading agenda. The United States has played a leading role throughout the eight rounds of GATT negotiations (see Schott, 1990), the last of which (the Uruguay Round) began in 1986 and concluded in the fall of 1993. US dominance of trade negotiations generally, and the specific trajectory of the Uruguay Round, catalyzed the push for North American integration and strongly determined the eventual form of NAFTA.

The Uruguay Round was the most prolonged round of GATT trade negotiations. Its slow pace was due to the complexity of the issues under discussion, and also to the vast number of countries taking part. From the end of World War II until the Uruguay Round, trade negotiations had had a very short agenda: how to reduce the protectionist barriers that had been erected with tariff and nontariff instruments, and how to broaden the number of goods covered by tariff reductions. The growing complexity of global production over the past forty years has, however, introduced new trade issues that demand multilateral solutions.

It was in this context that the United States and other developed countries such as the European Union, Japan and Canada, began to promote a New Agenda. This agenda went far beyond questions of tariff reductions to include topics such as increased trade in services, foreign investment, government procurement, agriculture and intellectual property protection (Schott, 1994). Textiles (which had previously been covered by special agreements) were included in the Uruguay Round agenda at the insistence of developing countries. As the 'New Agenda' represented long-standing US concerns which had been at the root of bilateral conflicts between the United States and Canada and between the United States and Mexico since the late 1970s/early 1980s, this was the agenda that was ultimately incorporated into CUSFTA and NAFTA.

In explaining why the United States opted to pursue NAFTA, many analysts have argued that the United States was increasingly frustrated with the lack of progress in the Uruguay Round and determined to develop a strategy that would give faster results. The United States appeared to abandon the multilateral GATT forum and positioned itself to switch to the bilateral route as the basis of its trade policy. Ironically, both CUSFTA and NAFTA originated, not from US overtures, but from requests from the Canadian and Mexican governments, respectively. The relative ease of negotiating a bilateral or trilateral agreement was obvious. The CUSFTA negotiations had begun in 1986, the same year as the Uruguay Round, but were completed by 1989. And NAFTA, initiated in 1991, was also brought to conclusion in advance of the close of the Uruguay Round. There is little doubt that the swift completion of these agreements had an impact on GATT deliberations, forcing this multilateral forum to act expeditiously for fear that the United States would continue to favor bilateral over multilateral actions.

As the United States continued to promote its New Agenda within GATT, US policy makers saw that much was to be gained if a developing country such as Mexico would demonstrate its willingness to adhere to the agenda, with all the new regulations that this implied. If Mexico gave the lead, then other developing countries would have fewer grounds for refusing to follow this path. In this sense, NAFTA was crucial for the United States, because it would set Mexico up as an example to the rest of the developing world. The previous CUSFTA had served as a similar model for developed countries.

MEXICO'S NEW ECONOMIC MODEL

When Mexico entered NAFTA, its domestic and foreign economic policy was markedly different from earlier periods in the country's history. Mexico's new policy orientation was the outcome of a decade of evolution toward new foundations for economic and political understanding between Mexico and the United States (see Chapter 6). It marked a dramatic reversal from Mexico's earlier perception of its neighbor to the north–ever since Mexico had lost half of its territory to the United States in 1848. At that point Mexico had decided that the only way to survive US expansionism was to isolate itself behind a wall just as formidable as any built in China or Berlin but constructed of prejudice about the United States as an alien (Anglo-Saxon, Protestant, greedy) world. These prejudices paralleled those developing in the United States about the 'lazy Mexican' (see del Castillo, 1995).

Mexico's evolution from an inward to an outward orientation is linked with the changes taking place in the country's foreign economic policy (see Chapter 6). Mexico's 'lost decade', beginning with the debt crisis of 1982, had demonstrated that Mexico's hopes for independent development through import-substitution industrialization (ISI) had failed. A new model was needed to spur economic growth and generate the one million new jobs per year that the growing population necessitated (del Castillo, 1993). Thus, Mexico decided to shift strategies; it opted for an open economy beginning in 1982. Economic opening reached its zenith with the implementation of NAFTA in 1994.

Mexico's reorientation toward the outside was not solely of its own making. When Mexico refused to join GATT in 1979, the United States retaliated by revoking Mexico's right to the injury test, a protective measure granted to all countries that have most favored nation (MFN) status. This meant that from 1980 onward, US producers could claim that Mexican imports were hurting their efforts to market their own US products, without having to substantiate their claims with evidence. Any claim of injury would automatically close the US market to that particular Mexican import, and Mexican producers were denied any recourse. This state of affairs compelled Mexico to sign a bilateral Agreement on Subsides and Countervailing Duties with the United States in 1985 in order to protect its exports.

Ultimately, Mexico joined GATT (in 1986), further liberalizing its economy. It shifted away from official pricing and import permits as instruments of protection, choosing instead to adopt import duties in compliance with GATT commitments. Although the latter were negotiated at 50 percent at GATT, as noted above Mexico unilaterally reduced its tariff level to 20 percent. In an effort to improve its trading relations with the United States, its principal trading partner, Mexico signed the Framework Agreement with the United States in 1987, setting up a host of working groups to liberalize trade under the New Agenda.

Mexico took further steps at liberalization in May 1989, when it overhauled its regulations on foreign investment, opening many economic sectors to foreign investors and allowing 100 percent foreign ownership in some cases. To attract foreign direct investment, Mexico also adopted stringent new measures for intellectual property protection; and in 1991 it strengthened protection for process and product patents and boosted its enforcement of trademarks and trade secrets. While Mexico was pursuing this process of liberalization, Canada and the United States signed and implemented the bilateral CUSFTA in 1989.

CUSFTA, Trade Diversion and the Berlin Wall

In its pursuit of economic development during the 1980s, Mexico turned away from protection of domestic industry as an instrument of growth and placed a much heavier emphasis on the country's export potential.

Therefore, CUSFTA posed a danger for Mexican economic growth: it had the potential to divert Mexican exports, having them replaced within US markets with Canadian goods. That is, Canadian industries' preferential access to the US market meant that Canadian suppliers had the potential to replace Mexican suppliers, which could seriously affect key sectors of the Mexican economy. As the various provisions of CUSFTA were phased in, Mexico perceived itself at a disadvantage in areas where it had already gained a market share in the United States, including the machinery, textile, automotive and petrochemical industries. These trade diversion effects were estimated to total about US$662 million in 1988 (del Castillo and Vega Cónovas, 1996).

This impact was not lost on Mexican decision makers. Further, there was the danger that these negative consequences would be compounded if US investments started flowing northward instead of toward Mexico. This was particularly critical because Mexico was already struggling to hold its own as an attractive site for new foreign direct investment after the dismantling of the Berlin Wall and the collapse of the Soviet Union–a time when Europe was redirecting much of its capital resources toward the countries of Eastern Europe.

With its economy open and its economic growth faltering, Mexico saw two principal roles for foreign investment, especially foreign investment from the United States (historically the primary source): first, as a job-creating instrument, and second, as the means to maintain a balanced current account. If foreign investors abandoned their pivotal role in Mexico, the liberalizing trends in the economy would be put at risk, and the job-creating and technology-transfer effects of foreign investment would be lost to the national economy.

When Mexico considered the likelihood that CUSFTA would accelerate growth in both Canada and the United States, it found further evidence that economic liberalization offered a sure road to increased economic payoffs. Hard economic data on the effects of CUSFTA were hard to come by at the time, but an early study by Schwanen (1993) demonstrated that, in the first five years of CUSFTA:

- Canadian exports to the United States grew faster than those to any other market, despite the fact that the US economy experienced much slower growth than other markets importing from Canada;

- in sectors liberalized by CUSFTA, Canadian exports to the United States increased by 33 percent, compared to 2 percent with the rest of the world;
- imports from the United States increased 28 percent in value, compared to 10 percent with the rest of the world;
- Canada made significant gains in the export of services to the United States;
- the evidence did not signal a decline in Canadian economic output; rather it seemed to document growth in industries in which Canada has a comparative advantage; and
- the jobs created and preserved by CUSFTA did not compensate in number for the jobs lost; however, the jobs created were in higher-paying sectors.

Moreover, although CUSFTA had been in operation for only two years before the NAFTA negotiations began in 1991, the earlier agreement demonstrated that–independent of its economic results, which were in dispute–the conflict-resolution mechanisms incorporated into CUSFTA were working as intended. The dispute settlement aspects of the agreement–designed to control the political-administrative interpretation of US trade law and practice–were crucial from a Canadian, and later from a Mexican, perspective. By instituting bilateral panels to resolve trade disputes, CUSFTA curbed the authority of US decision makers in such controversies. Bilateral panels replaced the domestic judicial review of government regulatory bodies' findings concerning anti-dumping and countervailing determinations. Anti-dumping and countervail determinations are the result of research and findings of national bodies (such as the International Trade Administration (ITA), the International Trade Commission (ITC) and the Mexican SECOFI, following national laws and statutes. They fall under what is euphemistically called 'trade remedy laws'. Anti-dumping determinations take place when goods are exported at 'less than fair value', and may cause injury to a domestic industry. Countervailing duties are imposed on goods which may have benefited from direct or indirect subsidies (see Chapter 2). The new panels were considered superior to the pre-Uruguay GATT instruments: they return their decisions more quickly; because they are bilateral, their decision-making process is open to close scrutiny; and their findings are binding. As with Canada, Mexico viewed the dispute settlement mechanism as a means of protecting themselves from the capriciousness of US trade policy.

NAFTA: PROVISIONS

When negotiators from Canada, Mexico and the United States convened in 1991, they agreed that NAFTA should focus on seven substantive areas: market access (through tariff liberalization and new rules of origin), foreign investment, financial and other services, intellectual property, dispute settlement and government procurement.

Further, NAFTA would incorporate one very significant new element absent in all preceding trade accords: NAFTA introduces 'social aspects' into the trade agenda. These are reflected in the complementary or side agreements dealing with workers' rights and environmental issues, to be discussed in a later section.

Market Access

Tariff liberalization A key focus of NAFTA was the elimination of all tariffs on imports among the three countries, with tariffs to be phased out over fifteen years according to four stages of liberalization. These tariff reductions would take place independent of the trade liberalization measures that Mexico had implemented during the 1980s, independent of the terms of CUSFTA, and independent of commitments made in the Uruguay Round related to trade in the global arena.

As originally stipulated in NAFTA, the following tariff reductions would occur. In phase 1, immediately following ratification of NAFTA by the three member countries, Mexico eliminated tariffs on 41 percent of Canadian export product categories and 43 percent of US product categories. Canada, meanwhile, removed tariffs from 79 percent of Mexican export products, and the United States dropped to zero its import tariffs on 84 percent of product categories exported from Mexico.

In phase 2, to end by year five of the agreement, Mexico will drop tariffs on an additional 19 percent of Canadian and 18 percent of US export product categories, respectively.

In phase 3, to be completed by year ten of the agreement, Mexico will reduce tariff barriers to zero on 38 percent of US and Canadian products, while Canada and the United States will drop import tariffs on 7 percent and 12 percent, respectively, of Mexican exports.

During phase 4, to end by the fifteenth year of the phase-in period, all three countries will eliminate any tariffs remaining on imports from their North American partners. Thus, by the year 2009, there will be no tariffs on goods traded among the three countries of North America.

While Mexico would appear to be the prime beneficiary of tariff elimination in the first phase, significantly, some of Mexico's most competitive export products were not included in this initial stage of tariff reduction. These products include glass tableware, ceramic and refractory bricks, specialty steel pipe, live plants, cut roses, tuna and shrimp.

Also, although eliminating tariff barriers is a principal component in NAFTA, this is not to say that the member countries have forfeited all mechanisms for controlling the entry of goods exported by their partners. The three countries can still apply quantitative restrictions on imports from some sectors, such as from other members' agricultural, auto, textile and energy industries. In the agricultural sector, for example, nontariff barriers (NTBs, such as restrictions based on claims of pest infestations) and tariff-rate quotas (TRQs, which impose higher tariffs on a product once imports have exceeded a certain threshold) can still be put into effect. NTBs and TRQs are commonly applied by the US to Mexican sugar, orange juice concentrate, peanuts, corn, beans and winter vegetables. Some of these barriers, however, now contravene Uruguay Round GATT/WTO commitments.

Thus we find additional evidence that NAFTA is managed trade driven by both political and economic considerations. It liberalizes in many areas; but where protection is still thought to be politically or economically necessary, member countries can skirt around adherence to full-fledged free trade practices.

Rules of origin While market access under NAFTA is fostered largely through the phased-in tariff reductions described above, market access is also addressed in the agreement's rules of origin. These rules are designed to keep the benefits and preferential treatment of the free trade area within North America. These rules apply especially to automobiles and auto parts, computers and textiles.

Regarding trade in automobiles, for example, the NAFTA's rules of origin increase the amount of North American components a car must contain in order to be considered 'North American' in origin, and thus be allowed to move free of tariffs within the North American market. The percentage of North American components required for a car to be designated 'North American-made' is now 50 percent; this will increase to 62.5 percent within ten years. Raising the percentage of parts that must be manufactured in North America will discourage US car makers (such as Chrysler and Ford) from sourcing their components from countries outside of North America, such as Korea.

The NAFTA members also agreed to eliminate all quotas and tariffs on textiles and applied two distinct rules of origin in this sector. The 'yarn forward' provision requires North American producers to use North American yarns. The 'fiber forward' provision requires them to use only North American fibers. The 'textile' industry encompasses both the producers of fibers and the manufacturers of textiles and clothing.

Foreign Investment

When market access improves as tariffs are eliminated, other components of trade, the factors that make trade possible, begin to emerge as important issues for negotiation. One such key factor is foreign investment: how foreign investment will be received and treated in the host country, and how investment services can be handled in a transborder fashion. NAFTA addresses both of these concerns.

Prior to the NAFTA negotiations, both Mexican and Canadian law contained provisions that the United States saw as injurious to American investors wanting to invest in those countries. Mexico's history of nationalizations (it nationalized US oil companies in 1938, and it nationalized its banking system in 1982, with the result that many foreign investors lost their dollar accounts) had made US investors very mistrustful of the Mexican investment climate. Moreover, under Mexican law, foreigners could only invest in certain sectors and, within these limited sectors, could hold only up to 49 percent ownership, effectively guaranteeing that control would remain in the hands of the Mexican partners. Canada's investment climate was less hostile to foreign investment. However, in the 1970s, during the administration of Pierre Trudeau, Canada had instituted a review process on foreign investment, which could potentially disallow new US investments in Canada. The goal of NAFTA's investment provisions was to treat foreign investment in a nondiscriminatory fashion. That is, under NAFTA, foreign investors from member countries would have the same rights as national investors in the three countries. In other words, foreign investment would now receive 'national treatment' indistinguishable from the way domestic laws would treat its own citizens..

Regarding the treatment of foreign investment, NAFTA represents an improvement over previous accords, including the bilateral agreement between Canada and the United States. In fact, NAFTA investment provisions represent an entirely new and different approach to the subject. These differences begin with how NAFTA defines 'investment'. Prior accords addressed only foreign direct investment (FDI). NAFTA incorporates a much enhanced definition–expanded to include all financial aspects related to investment in an enterprise: loans to the business, profits, interest, business real estate, equity, any debt the enterprise holds, and so on.

While NAFTA expanded the definition of investment, it also incorporated a new approach to how such investments were to be 'protected'. If there is a dispute over investment issues within the NAFTA region, the companies or individuals involved can take their dispute to binding international arbitration. This protection provision was aimed primarily at Mexico, since Canada and the United States felt that the highly politicized judicial system in Mexico would put them at a disadvantage in any dispute if it were subject to resolution in Mexico. NAFTA's protection of investment also extends to third parties (Japan, for example) if the third party has substantial interests in more than one NAFTA member country.

Investment protection is also covered in NAFTA's provision on 'minimum standards of treatment'. This article of the agreement contains very specific language on how foreign investment is to be treated (especially in Mexico), reducing the risk that countries will attempt to 'interpret' NAFTA's investment protections arbitrarily.

Even so, NAFTA countries can exempt some foreign investments from full protection. That is, while still receiving 'national treatment', some foreign investment can be subject to slightly different, somewhat less advantageous treatment, usually in sectors that are considered less competitive internationally. Therefore, the extent of protection provided to foreign investors in a given country can be determined by looking at how many 'reservations' each country claims in the annexes to NAFTA.

Financial Services

Another key issue is financial services. Over several decades, industrial production has been in a process of reorganization, moving from domestic to global manufacturing; and the movement of investment capital has become internationalized. In part this has been fostered by the revolution in electronic information handling which has facilitated the transfer of financial information internationally. Financial services must now be able to operate across borders. This issue is addressed in a NAFTA chapter on activities such as the securities industry, banking, lending services, insurance, bank deposits and so on.

Any attempt to incorporate financial services within a free trade regime raises two important questions: (1) How many and which financial services can non-nationals provide? (2) What domestic structure will regulate those financial services that are allowed to be provided by non-nationals? When dealing with financial services, the 'right of establishment' (that is, when a foreign company is already established in the host country and is offering a service) will generally give a company preference over cross-border trade in services (a foreign company not established in the country but offering to provide services there).

Liberalizing financial services has been complicated by the fact that each NAFTA country already has a well-developed regulatory system in place, and the systems operating in the respective countries are sufficiently different from one another to make them difficult to harmonize. However, CUSFTA provided guidelines in this area and served to break the ground for the liberalization of financial services under NAFTA.

As finally written, NAFTA gives each country the right to regulate financial services as it sees fit. However, it lays out the conditions under which financial institutions can operate in another country, how financial services are to be supplied from outside a country, and how disputes within this sector are to be handled, that is, NAFTA sets up a dispute settlement mechanism.

NAFTA also address services such as telecommunications, professional services and land transportation, generally providing for cross-border provision of services between the three NAFTA member countries under national treatment protection.

Intellectual Property

Intellectual property rights refer to copyright and related rights, trademark rights, patent rights, rights related to the design and layout of semiconductor integrated circuits, trade secret rights, development rights on new plant varieties, industrial design rights and so on. The application of these rights prohibits someone other than the developer from the use or exploitation of the product or idea without consulting or paying the original developer for the idea, design, title, mark and so on. The main problem in this regard is that local entrepreneurs in many third world countries frequently do not pay the original developer for these rights, in effect 'pirating' the brand name, new process or the actual product itself. Pharmaceutial companies, for example, employ 'reverse engineering' in order to produce a copy of a newly developed drug while illegally reproduced copies of popular videos sell for a few dollars. Protecting intellectual property rights would reduce or eliminate these practices.

Under NAFTA, each member country agrees to protect the intellectual property rights (patents, copyrights, trademarks, trade secrets, sound recordings, films and so on) of the other members within its own national territory–at the same level as that provided to its own nationals. Further, NAFTA dictates that efforts to protect intellectual property rights must not be used as barriers to trade between the three countries.

Dispute Settlement under NAFTA

The Canada-United States Free Trade Agreement was highly innovative, and many of its innovations served as blueprints for the design of the NAFTA agreement. CUSFTA incorporated dispute settlement mechanisms which, although not altogether new, did allow the two countries to settle conflicts in a fair and expeditious manner. These same mechanisms were included in NAFTA. The idea for the creation of bilaterial panels to solve bilateral trade disputes is credited to Representative Sam Gibbons of Florida, a member of the Ways and Means Trade Subcommittee and a specialist in trade matters. Gibbons apparently became involved in the last-minute negotiations in Washington between Canada and the United States when CUSFTA was in danger of collapsing because Canada could not persuade the United States to exempt Canada from American 'unfair trade' laws which Canada regards as biased and as leading to numerous costly nuisance suits (see Doern and Tomlin, 1991).

The trade dispute instruments in NAFTA are directed toward some of the most critical areas of international trade conflicts–specifically anti-dumping measures and countervailing duties. NAFTA provisions allow international (in this case, bilateral) judicial review of actions taken in these areas by domestic agencies.

Under the provisions of NAFTA, each member country has the right to retain its current laws for implementing countervailing duties and anti-dumping measures. However, if a member country wishes to modify its laws in these two areas, it must notify and consult with its trade partners. Finally, if a partner is about to modify these laws, that country can request a review of the proposed changes by a binational advisory panel to determine whether the changes meet the requirements of NAFTA and other international trade law.

The most innovative and functional part of the chapters on dispute settlement is the creation of binational panels that review whether a given country's agencies have administered that country's trade law according to legal procedure and without political intervention. These panels look at the case record and determine whether the final judgment delivered by the country's adjudicative system is supported by the evidence and is in accordance with that country's domestic law. Each country is required to maintain a seventy-five member roster (favoring lawyers) of available panelists. When a case comes up for settlement, each country will choose twenty-five from this list. Within thirty days of a request for a panel, each country will nominate two panelists, who may be challenged by the other country. Within fifty-five days, both countries must agree on a fifth panelist drawn from the rosters. Decisions within a panel are taken by a majority vote, with all five panelists voting. The panel issues an 'initial declaratory opinion', which is open to challenge by the affected party for fourteen days, after which the panel writes its final opinion. Final opinions are subject only to an 'extraordinary challenge', which forwards the case to a panel of three members selected from a fifteen-member roster. After an extraordinary challenge has been raised, the new panel, once instituted, has ninety days to render a decision. Its decision is binding and not subject to challenge. Similar procedures exist to review cases relating to the interpretation of NAFTA itself.

Government Procurement

Governments are major purchasers of goods for both military and civilian applications. Most such purchases have traditionally been reserved for domestic providers and contractors in order to create domestic jobs and incomes. NAFTA opens up government purchases to providers in all NAFTA member countries, specifying threshold levels for different kinds of goods and services. For example, a government agency in a

NAFTA country can contract for up to US$6.5 million in construction services from a firm in another NAFTA country. Suppliers and producers in NAFTA member countries can compete for government contracts under the 'national treatment' clause.

Although NAFTA-country government contracts can no longer be designed or structured to exclude foreign competition, significant levels of protection persist. For instance, all three member countries award research and development contracts to domestic firms only. Further, each country specifies additional areas where it will use only national suppliers. As some liberalization in government procurement had already taken place between Canada and the United States under CUSFTA, Mexico lags behind on this front; for this reason NAFTA agreement specifies that Mexico must establish a specialized publication to announce notices of procurement. This will reduce the transaction costs associated with acquiring information by Canadian and American firms wishing to bid on contracts given their lack of familiarity with the Spanish language and Mexican government procedures–procedures which often lack the transparency which Canadian and American firms enjoy when dealing with their governments.

The Side Agreements

A key innovation in NAFTA is the incorporation of the 'social aspects' of trade, referred to earlier. The side agreements to NAFTA deal specifically with such social concerns. These two agreements (the North American Agreement on Environmental Cooperation and the North American Agreement on Labor Cooperation) reflect popular concerns about the environment and labor rights–especially about how the latter are understood in Mexico–and how these two dimensions could affect trade in North America.

Efforts to integrate these concerns into the trade agreement arose in Washington, when President George Bush asked Congress for authorization to pursue NAFTA under a 'fast track' negotiating authority (see Chapter 4). Had Bush not agreed to incorporate environmental and labor issues into the accord, Congress would have refused to give him fast track authority.

The side agreements turned NAFTA into more than a trade agreement. They set general objectives and require treaty members to carry out continued consultations to assure that these objectives are met. The agreements also define a grievance procedure for resolving any conflict that may arise.

The environmental agreement states that NAFTA countries will work jointly to enhance human, plant and animal life and health and the environment and that no country can lower its environmental, health or safety standards to attract investment. It prohibits 'environmental dumping'–the production of goods in sites where environmental controls are less stringent. And it requires the United States and Mexico to cooperate in improving the border environment through the Border Environmental Cooperation Commission (BECC). It also establishes the North American Development Bank (NAD Bank), funded by the three countries to finance environmental cleanup and enhancement projects.

The side agreement on labor outlines eleven sets of labor rights, ranging from the right to organize to the prohibition of child and forced labor. It calls for equal pay for men and women, injury and illness compensation and the protection of migrant workers. These rights are to be protected through a process of consultation and cooperation, especially through the Commission for Labor Cooperation. This side agreement was included to assure that no party or industry could gain competitive advantage through the exploitation of its labor force.

NAFTA'S SHORTCOMINGS: IMPLICATIONS FOR THE FUTURE

The North American Free Trade Agreement was always posited as being 'a trade agreement, nothing more'. It required no social charter or transfer of economic resources in the form of structural funds, elements that the European Union had developed as part of their integration efforts in order to lessen the effects of economic asymmetry between member countries and regions and mitigate the social effects of rapid social change prompted by the integration process. Mexican President Carlos Salinas de Gortari proclaimed in San Antonio, Texas, at the signing of NAFTA in 1993, that what Mexico wanted was 'trade, not aid', justifying the limited scope of the agreement.

One of the obvious features of the accord is that it contains no remnants of the 'special and differential treatment' that Mexico as a 'developing country' had enjoyed within GATT. Under NAFTA, Mexico would be a co-equal partner with Canada and the United States, and it would receive no special treatment just because it was by far the smallest of the three economies.

However, the Mexican economic crisis of December 1994, when the peso lost approximately half of its value within a matter of days, demonstrated the problems that can arise when trade agreements lack the flexibility (in import and monetary policy) to deal with sudden economic reversals.

Both NAFTA and GATT allow member countries some measure of protection from import surges under emergency action procedures and safeguard measures. However, these protective measures are largely temporary in nature and require some form of restitution to be made to the country being closed out by protection.

Moreover, these protective measures are 'traditional' in the sense that they are oriented toward restricting the flow of goods or services. They offer little protection against surges in the movement of financial resources that are global in nature and can have, for one reason or another, more profound impacts on some countries than others. Mexican policy makers attributed much of the December peso crisis to the uncertainty over the presumed political instability in Chiapas and the murder of the PRI's presidential candidate, Donaldo Colosio, in early 1994 and the later assassination of the PRI's executive secretary, Josè Francisco Ruiz Massieu. Others might suggest that investor nervousness was the result of economic mismanagement. The rapid movement of substantial financial resources can affect currency values and, in so doing, also affect trade flows and the very nature of free trade, since stable currencies are important underpinning in international commercial transactions. The end result of economic miscalculation and freely flowing international capital is that they can lead, as they have done in Mexico since December 1994, to currency devaluations, inflationary spirals, tight fiscal and monetary policies–all of which also put in peril the possibilities for free trade in the future. NAFTA and the now concluded Uruguay Round are inadequate instruments to deal with economic 'near calamities' caused by speculative activities such as those which plagued Mexico since late 1994. NAFTA was not designed as an instrument to stabilize economic activity in the North American market. To do that would require a movement to a much more formal economic union (see Chapter 2) than any of the NAFTA partners desired to accept.

Problems arise for a number of reasons. The first is related to the composition of investment capital. Here one must differentiate between short-term, speculative capital, which was dominant in the new capital flows to Mexico between 1990 and 1994, and long-term foreign direct investment in productive assets. The former can add volatility in periods of economic instability, while the latter type of investment supports steady, productive growth. The second problem relates to capital mobility, which has been greatly accelerated by modern electronic communication. These factors interact as follows: when there is a high risk, whether real or imagined, speculative capital can flow out of a country just as quickly as it flowed in, deeply aggravating the initial conditions of risk. As the affected country loses monetary stability, the prices of goods produced by that country fluctuate, complicating firms' production decisions as well as the country's ability to import and export goods.

Investment measures (regulatory and administrative procedures, legislation and so on) can work to mitigate the impacts that currency speculation and other 'destabilizing' activities have on trade. These measures are well known to trade negotiators; they were the subject of discussions in a North-South context during the Kennedy and Tokyo Rounds of GATT. Both of these multinational trade negotiations built on previous series of negotiations leading toward liberalized worldwide trade and incorporating ever-widening areas of trade, ranging from tariff reductions to trade rules on services, investment, agriculture and government procurement–as occurred in the Uruguay Round. For a detailed explanation of both of these negotiations, see Curtis and Vastine (1991) and Winham (1986). However, they were not incorporated into the WTO or NAFTA (Stewart, 1993). The negotiators of these two accords were concerned with attracting foreign investment, not with holding capital, and therefore they failed to draw on the examples offered by earlier trade agreements. One such measure, discussed in the Uruguay Round negotiations–and included in the 1991 Dunkel Draft of the Uruguay Round–were the TRIMs (trade related investment measures), designed to forestall the exodus of investment capital at critical moments of economic crisis. In the Dunkel Draft, TRIMs would have been tailored to an individual country's level of development (that is, developed, developing or least developed). The negotiators ultimately decided that the issue of whether a government could use investment measures to direct or restrict investments was outside the purview of the WTO, and the Uruguay Round Final Act leaves adoption of TRIMs up to the individual participant countries.

Another aspect of NAFTA that is open to criticism is its incomplete treatment of trade in financial services. Various articles in the agreement are designed to protect countries' rights in the trade in financial services: NAFTA protects a country's right to regulate financial services; accords national treatment to the providers of these services; discusses the issue of supply of financial services; and specifies consultation and resolution procedures for financial services disputes. However, it does not address the issue of how regulated financial institutions may, either on their own or through government action, control the flow of capital on a transborder basis.

NAFTA negotiators were aware of the possible problems associated with market-driven flows of cross-border capital. Their awareness is reflected in the provision that outlines a country's right to ensure the integrity and stability of its financial system, as long as the measures are not discriminatory. Furthermore, NAFTA specifies that nothing in the chapter on financial services 'applies to nondiscriminatory measures of general application by any public entity in pursuit of monetary and related credit policies or exchange rate policies'.

In other words, because NAFTA allows member countries to design their own stabilization policies, if rules could be developed on a continental or multilateral basis to regulate capital mobility and its destabilizing effects, particularly on developing countries such as Mexico, this would go a long way toward underpinning economic stability. At a minimum, these rules might cover the composition of investments in a country's national accounts, specifying optimal ratios of short (or hot) investments versus the direct productive investments that ensure macroeconomic stability. A related issue, which ties back into the Dunkel Draft of the Uruguay Round, is that countries at different stages of development could be made subject to differential investment ratios (referring to the difference in proportions between direct foreign investment and short-term speculative investments). Just as most economic integration efforts permit the parties' exchange rates to fluctuate within certain band limits (15 percent in the European Union until the single currency is established), the same principle (of controlled fluctuations) could be applied to the stock markets of developing nations in order to control widely swinging negative trends. For instance, automatic 'slow-down' procedures could be activated for paper transactions if the aggregate stock began to deteriorate, as happened in the United States on Black Monday (October 19, 1987). In other words, when a situation develops where 'speculative investments' (SI) within the stock market diverge from a prescribed ratio in relation to foreign direct investment (DI) or SI > DI, any undue speculation in stocks will cause financial instability, leading to events similar to those that occurred in Mexico in November and December 1994.

Finally, the Mexican public sector's sale of bonds (*tesobonos*) could be analyzed carefully and regulated to fall within certain ratios (pegged to GNP growth or productivity gains or as a proportion of the budget deficit). This would ensure that the public sector debt would not add to the natural pressures on a country's currency, forestalling the need for emergency actions. Of course, restrictions on the flow of capital will act to limit inbound flows in times of stability and growth. There is a clear tradeoff between the reduction of inbound investment and the risks associated with a speculative outflow. Domestic governments often dismiss the latter, and resent any deterrent to inbound investment. The Mexican crisis of 1994 and the crisis in Asia which began in

1997 are obvious and telling examples of this fact. While international oversight may be able to mitigate to some extent the conditions leading to financial crisis, the effects cannot be fully avoided without improvements in domestic oversight and economic management in the countries in receipt of non-direct foreign investment.

These measures clearly need to be considered as countries throughout the world decide to liberalize their economies, opening them up to the pressures of market forces. Under integrationist schemes like NAFTA, where countries with very different levels of development are brought together and their economic asymmetries put enormous pressures on the least-developed partner, some more formal mechanisms than the *ad hoc* bailout organized by the US in the wake of the 1994 crisis may be desirable. These mechanisms need to be carefully designed to prevent governments from using bailout provisions strategically as a means to forestall difficult decisions or delay essential domestic reforms.

The North American Free Trade Agreement was an incomplete and likely flawed instrument. It must now be deepened in order to take account of these additional dimensions. If steps are not taken, the economic and political pressures to nullify the agreement will increase as further distortions emerge (such as the Clinton emergency rescue package for Mexico in the wake of the December 1994 crisis). Such a situation would augment the costs that any partner withdrawing from the accord would have to pay in a now hostile North America.

8. NAFTA and Beyond

In previous chapters we developed the theory and history underlying NAFTA's creation. Then we examined the content of the agreement itself and its two side agreements. Now we turn to the question of how NAFTA is working in practice since its implementation in January 1994 and speculate on where it might go in the future. Given the complexity of the agreement and its many economic, social and environmental implications, we will limit our discussion to those topics which we believe have most relevance to the readers.

In the first part of the chapter we look at the 'Mexican dilemma'–the special issues presented by Mexico's status as a still developing country (and its consequent macroeconomic instability) and how this status affects NAFTA. Next we look at NAFTA's evolution during the first three years, as a tool for managing the *de facto* integration occurring in the region. In the third section we look 'beyond NAFTA' at the possibility for reforming and/or deepening and widening the current agreement.

THE MEXICAN DILEMMA

We have argued that economic integration in North America was well under way before the signing of NAFTA, as indicated by the flows of goods, services and investments. Given these substantial flows, there was no obvious reason why two developed economies–the United States and Canada–would choose to form a trade alliance with a developing economy like Mexico. Not only was size a problem (the Canadian and US economies in combination are about twenty times larger than the Mexican economy), but there are other problems as well: Mexico's autocratic political system, frequently associated with political violence and disrespect for human rights; and significant differences in legal practices between Canada and the United States, on the one hand, and Mexico, on the other. The differences in legal systems posed problems for Canadian and US trade officials, who were unsure about how Mexico's legal system would treat legal suits related to trade issues. Further, it was unclear what the relationship would be between legal systems and the trade bureaucracy or, worse, a politicized trade bureaucracy.

Thus the North American Free Trade agreement was far from inevitable. In fact, it represents a major accomplishment, a process of successful trade negotiation linking two advanced industrialized nations with a developing economy. Apparently the three member countries were not overly concerned about the asymmetries in the relationship, since they never seriously discussed anything like the transfer of 'structural funds' from developed partners to underdeveloped partner, as was done in the European Union. This apparent lack of concern over the implications of asymmetry could well be the source of problems well into the future.

According to economic theory, there are potential 'gains from trade', and it is in this light that we have to evaluate NAFTA. Does it (or will it) remove obstacles, make trade more efficient, and therefore increase the likelihood for higher living standards in its member countries? Theory also tells us that specialization and competition will produce some winners and some losers. Some industries and firms may not be able to compete under economic liberalization. They may lose market share or even disappear from the economy completely, with clear implications for their workers. Of course, other sectors and workers become winners and losers need not stay losers forever.

There is considerable evidence that pre-NAFTA trade liberalization had produced some very negative effects in Mexico: production and wages became more concentrated, and income distribution became increasingly unequal (Unger and Saldaña 1989). Given that these liberalizing outcomes clash with accepted notions of equity, why did Mexico choose to enter into a trade agreement with two of the most highly developed countries in the world?

The NAFTA as Mexico's Salvation

The following discussion lays out some possible explanations for Mexico's entry into NAFTA and for the dilemma that Mexico's membership presents for this accord. First, from Mexico's perspective the economic opportunities presented by NAFTA seemed to offer the best chance for a 'great leap forward', allowing that country to jump from developing country status to developed country status in a very short time.[1]

Second (and related to the previous point), the corps of new technocrats in the Mexican government, who had just taken over from the corrupt political elites of the old PRI regime, were supremely frustrated with the low economic growth rates that had characterized the Mexican economy since the debt crisis of 1982, despite the technocrats' commendable success in achieving macroeconomic stabilization. Their frustration predisposed them to grasp at the hope for a great leap forward.

Third, the new technocrats saw neoliberal economic theory as Mexico's salvation. Mexico could be saved if it could take its place in the international economy by exporting manufactured goods and services, and by increasing foreign investment in Mexico. This salvation was based, in turn, on two important assumptions: (1) that domestic savings and investment alone were insufficient to grow the economy enough to create an adequate number of jobs for the rapidly growing population, and (2) that exports could be kept internationally competitive thanks to Mexico's low wages and to the acquisition of new technology that would occur when foreign firms began to transfer technological inputs into the Mexican economy. Basically, Mexico was placing its hopes for economic growth on its external sector, and to expand its external sector it needed mechanisms like NAFTA that would promote the foreign investments Mexico so critically needed.

To publicize its new outlook, the Mexican government initiated a worldwide public relations effort, directed especially toward the United States and toward international organizations like the World Bank, the International Monetary Fund, and the Organisation for Economic Cooperation and Development (OECD). The message was as follows:

- Mexico's new politico-economic elites were on par with their counterparts in any developed nation.

[1] In effect, the idea was for Mexico to skip the different processes leading to economic development as put forward in Rostow (1960).

- After a decade of economic adjustment and self-control, Mexico was stable, politically and economically, and foreign investment there was safe.
- Mexico could guarantee this stability if it were admitted into NAFTA and the OECD.
- Mexico's stability was the result of national pacts among key political and economic groups that guaranteed continued peace—even though profits were rising for entrepreneurs and investors where as wages were held low for a docile working class.
- This new economic stability was demonstrated by the relatively minor fluctuations in the value of the Mexican peso.

Although President Carlos Salinas, the architect of this new structure of prosperity, received strong support from the Bush administration, his lofty hopes for Mexico (and for himself, since he was believed to be a front-runner for the directorship of the newly created World Trade Organization) were dashed on the very day that NAFTA went into effect. Mexico's political peace was shattered when, on January 1, 1994, a band of peasants, the Zapatista National Liberation Army (EZLN), emerged from the forests of Chiapas to protest with arms Mexico's involvement in the trade accord. The appearance of the EZLN was followed by the assassination of PRI presidential candidate Luis Donaldo Colosio and the murder of the party's executive secretary, José Francisco Ruiz Massieu, completely destroying any remaining belief in Mexico's political tranquillity. The myth of economic stability went by the wayside as well when newly installed President Ernesto Zedillo devalued the peso by half in December 1994.

One victim of this political and economic turmoil was the widespread popular belief that the country could achieve a great leap forward and reap the desired results, now that macroeconomic stability, the prerequisite for any free trade agreement, had been removed by the course of events. The peso crisis also caused Mexico's NAFTA partners to reconsider the wisdom of their enthusiasm for Mexico's membership. While both Canada and the Clinton administration were prime movers in the organization of the economic package put in place to alleviate Mexico's short-run difficulties, the US Congress used the crisis as a reason to deny 'fast track' authority. This effectively blocked any further expansion of NAFTA to other nations in the Western Hemisphere. The peso devaluation made Mexican exports competitive in price but it reduced the population's ability to purchase imports. The consequent rise in inflation destabilized the pricing structure for goods and services, making economic transactions (at a domestic and foreign level), harder to arrive at because of the uncertainty related to costs of production, transport, an so on. Adding to this uncertainty were soaring interest rates, which surpassed 100 percent, cutting off access to capital for any type of industrial enterprise.

MEXICO'S MACROECONOMIC SITUATION

The political and economic events of 1994 had two principal outcomes. First, the actors to whom the 'marketing of Mexico' had been directed–the US government and financial markets–felt that they had been misled by Mexico's new technocrats. Even so, through the efforts of President Clinton and against widespread popular opposition, Mexico received a pledge of support from the US Treasury Department, the International Monetary Fund, and the Bank for International Settlements in the amount of US$47 billion to help stave off financial collapse. In exchange, Mexico was forced into an austere recovery program with IMF-imposed performance requirements.

Even though Mexico recorded a surplus in its current account (total trade in goods and services) for 1995, the country was in its deepest recession since the Great Depression of the 1930s, with GDP rates in the minus numbers through all four quarters of the year and continuing into the first quarter of 1996. It had become painfully clear that Mexico's pre-1995 pattern of running a current account deficit was not a 'self-financing' strategy, as the country's technocrats had argued to the international community.

Foreign investments in Mexico, whether direct or financial, are highly susceptible to political winds, and this was certainly true in

1994 and 1995. Not only did financial flows react to events within Mexico, but the volatility of capital flows became an important reflection of the instability of economic life in the country. Perhaps more importantly, capital flows themselves became primary determinants of economic events in Mexico (see del Castillo and Vega Cónovas, 1996; del Castillo, 1996).

NAFTA's Shortcomings vis-à-vis the Mexican Dilemma

The economic chaos in Mexico in 1994 and 1995 did not result directly from NAFTA. However, it may have been an indirect result: pressures on the Mexican peso after the country embarked on a NAFTA-stimulated import binge in 1994 created the conditions for a severe economic contraction, a crisis from which the country began a slow recovery in 1996. Mexico's cyclic pattern of sudden contraction and slow recovery, price instabilities, extremely high interest and inflation rates, and a currency of questionable stability does not bode well for export led growth and foreign financing, for which macroeconomic stability is a precondition. Yet the issue is not so much that stability is lacking in Mexico, but that NAFTA–since it is 'only' a trade agreement–lacks provisions that would allow country members to intervene in order to lessen the effects of instability.

Perhaps the absence of such provisions is attributable to Mexico's success in 'selling' itself. The NAFTA negotiators moved ahead in the belief that problems in Mexico's economic history of cyclic instability would not reappear. If instability did reappear, it could potentially affect the volume of trade and services between NAFTA countries but not the underlying rules that governed trade.[2] Nevertheless, as the Clinton administration's rescue package clearly demonstrated, intervention by

[2] For information on trade negotiators' prior discussions of instability-engendering factors in the Mexican economy, such as capital flight, see del Castillo and Vega Cónovas (1996). According to the Trade Related Investment Measures (TRIMS) working group of the Uruguay Round: 'Following an examination of the operation of GATT articles related to the trade restrictive and distorting effects of investment measures, negotiators should elaborate, as appropriate, further provisions that may be necessary to avoid such adverse effects on trade' (quoted in del Castillo and Vega Cónovas 1996, p. 286).

Mexico's trading partners was essential in guaranteeing the economic viability of Mexico and of the NAFTA agreement itself.

Perhaps the unwillingness to face the possibility of economic instability in Mexico within the NAFTA context reflected the negotiators' refusal to contemplate the possibility that North-South transfers might be needed in order to avoid such instability and avert its effects on trade. Further, social funds were likely beyond what was politically feasible in both Canada and the United States as NAFTA would also have to be 'sold' in both countires. What is clear is that foreign investors in Mexico never fulfilled the (perhaps unrealistic) expectations that Mexican technocrats had of them as the source of job-creating investments and technology transfers that would make Mexican manufacturing competitive in global (and especially in North American) markets. Instead, foreign direct investment, small at about one-fifth the total size of portfolio investments, has failed to reduce unemployment and underemployment rates; nor can portfolio investments, which are apt to take flight at the smallest sign of political or economic instability, serve as the basis on which to build a job supply.

NAFTA: THE FIRST THREE YEARS

Despite the enormous challenges posed by Mexico's economic difficulties, NAFTA is functioning. Any attempt to assess its effectiveness at this early date must be regarded as highly preliminary given that NAFTA's main effects will appear not in years, but in decades. The US Congress required that a major review be conducted of NAFTA and its impacts on the US economy as of mid 1997. (see Executive Office of the President 1997). Moreover, so many influences operate on each member country's economic situation and on the trilateral relationship itself that it is difficult to determine with any degree of certainty how much impact each factor exerts on the complex sequence of events. Thus, in this section we will limit our assessment to the progress made in setting up NAFTA institutions, initial impacts on trade and investment flows and other issues which have emerged during this initial period.

NAFTA Institutions and Procedures

The trilateral agreement includes a management tool for continued integration and provides for an organizational structure to administer its mandates. At the top of the structure is the NAFTA Commission, comprised of cabinet-level representatives from each of the three countries. The main activities of the Commission are to supervise the work of NAFTA committees and working groups, as well as to make interpretive rulings on the content of the agreement relating to dispute resolution. The NAFTA Secretariat, located in Mexico City, basically supports NAFTA Commission's work, as well as other bodies related to NAFTA (Appleton, 1994).

As noted in previous chapters, three supplemental accords (side agreements) were appended to the agreement prior to its approval by the legislatures of the three member countries. These side agreements covered labor standards, the environment and 'import surges'. The inclusion of labor and environmental concerns in NAFTA is widely considered to be one of the trade accord's most innovative aspects. The supplemental agreements convey the authority to monitor the enforcement of laws already on the books in the member countries and provide mechanisms for consultation and cooperation on labor and environmental issues.

The labor side agreement (the North American Agreement on Labor Cooperation) established a trinational Commission for Labor Cooperation, which includes, in turn, a Ministerial Council and a Secretariat. The Commission compiles and publishes data on labor-related issues submitted to it, and also plans and coordinates cooperative activities. The Commission may examine disputes and apply compensatory mechanisms (such as fines and/or trade sanctions) in three areas: threats to health and security, the employment of minors and violations of minimum-wage laws. Additional matters, such as labor union activities, may be referred to the Commission but recourse in these areas is limited to consultation with the respective governments (Pérez-López, 1996). There are national Commission offices in each member country, and the full Commission comes together to meet annually. The Secretariat (located in Dallas, Texas) provides technical and administrative support.

The environmental side agreement (the North American Agreement on Environmental Cooperation) created the Commission on Environmental Cooperation, which, like the Labor Commission, consists of a tripartite, cabinet-level council of ministers, assisted by a Secretariat (located in Montreal, Quebec). There is also a Joint Public Advisory Committee, with representatives from each member's National Public Advisory Committee. The Ministerial Council oversees the implementation of the agreement, conducts discussions and cooperative projects, and settles disputes. The Commission has no enforcement power, but it is obliged to monitor the environmental impacts of the expanded trade and investment flows that are expected to result from NAFTA. However, environmental conditions on the US-Canadian and US-Mexican borders are still dealt with primarily within the framework of existing bilateral mechanisms between the United States and Mexico and between the United States and Canada. In the case of the former, bilateral negotiators are primarily concerned with the issues of acid rain and water quality in the Great Lakes (Schwartz, 1994).

In the second (US-Mexico border) case, key environmental issues relate to the rapidly expanding population and booming *maquiladora* industry, both of which have aggravated transborder contamination of air, water and soil. These issues, which have become increasingly contentious in recent years, were not systematically addressed prior to NAFTA. Since NAFTA's implementation, two organizations have been set up to deal with environmental issues: the Border Environmental Cooperation Commission (BECC), which supports research and action projects to clean up the border environment; and the North American Development Bank (NADBank), which provides financial support for large environmental infrastructure projects. The NADBank was established through a separate agreement, and hence, it does not include Canada. Its financing operations are limited to the US-Mexico border region (defined as stretching 100 kilometers north and south of the international boundary). NADBank capital (now equaling US$224 million) has come from the US and Mexican governments; it is expected that these funds will be used to leverage private-sector funding in the future to total US$1.5 billion in lending capital. As of August 1996, after eighteen months in operation, NADBank had yet to extend its first loan. The US General Accounting Office has identified at least three major problems with the NADBank: (1) a requirement that NADBank's loans be made at or above market rates makes alternative sources of financing more attractive; (2) the small communities on both sides of the US-Mexico border which most need NADBank's help do not know how to deal with the many intricacies of governmental bureaucracies; and (3) constitutional prohibitions do prevent border communities in Mexico from borrowing from foreign lenders, making it necessary to channel NADBank's resources through Mexico's Federal Treasury.

Perhaps procedural problems such as those affecting the NADBank reflect the newness of NAFTA. However, they may also reflect a lack of attention on the part of the member countries. In this regard, it may be significant that the first official version of NAFTA, as published by the Office of the US Trade Negotiator, had omitted the North American Agreement on Environmental Cooperation, the North American Agreement on Labor Cooperation and all of the US restrictions on Mexican agricultural exports. In a second published version, the two side agreements were appended as attachments but looked to have been produced hurriedly on a low-end printer. These omissions may be indicative of the slight importance that the US and Mexican governments attached to these issues, despite the fact that they were items of heated interest and debate in the Canadian and US legislatures (Cameron and Grinspun, 1993).

Trade Growth

Obviously one key criterion for evaluating a free trade agreement should be its success in expanding trade. Table 8.1 presents export data for the NAFTA region from 1992 to 1996, covering the two years prior to NAFTA and the four years since its implementation.

When looking at the data in Table 8.1 it is important to remember, first, that the Canadian-US free trade agreement had already been

Table 8.1 NAFTA Export Performance (percentage growth, 1992–96)

	1992	1993	1994	1995	1996
Intra-NAFTA exports	14	11	19	10	10
Total NAFTA exports	8	5	12	15	7
Intra-NAFTA exports as percent of total	43	45	48	46	47.3

Source: Inter-American Development Bank, *Integration and Trade in the Americas: Periodic Notes,* (various issues) and www.iadb.org (web site of the Inter-American Development Bank).

in force since 1989 and intra-NAFTA exports were already expanding rapidly as a consequence of that agreement; and, second, that the Mexican economy entered a severe recession in December 1994, with a dramatic devaluation of its currency and a sharp decline in total output and imports.

From the perspective of growth of all the variables included Table 8.1, 1994 stands out as an exceptional year. Total NAFTA exports grew by 12 percent during 1994, while intra-NAFTA exports (exports among the three countries) grew by a startling 19 percent and intra-NAFTA exports as a percentage of total exports rose to 48 percent. This growth ended with the economic crisis, as the 1995 figures show. Even so, trade between the United States and Canada and between the United States and Mexico continued to grow despite Mexico's economic woes.

Foreign Investment

Given that the promotion of investment flows is a key component of NAFTA, and attracting increased foreign direct investment (FDI) was one of Mexico's primary motivations in seeking to join Canada and the United States in this trilateral trade agreement, this area must also be assessed when evaluating NAFTA's success during these first years of its implementation. Although the data are far from plentiful, and what information exists tends to be blanketed within aggregate data, we can discern some surprising trends in investment flows among NAFTA countries during 1994, the first year of NAFTA's operation.

First, US direct investment in Mexico during 1994 actually registered a drop of 23.5 percent over the preceding year (JETRO online: http://www:jetro.go.jp/[3]). However, this almost surely represents investor unease over the political and economic events in Mexico during that year–including assassinations of high-profile politicians, the appearance of the Zapatista National Liberation Army, and suspicions that an overvalued peso could soon be ratcheted downward–and not a response to NAFTA incentives. Indeed, Mexico's Ministry of Commerce and Industrial Development (SECOFI) has noted that in both 1994 and 1995, foreign direct investment from both the United States and Canada flowed most heavily into the sectors that had been liberalized under NAFTA. This suggests that investors will respond to the incentives created by NAFTA provisions and that the investment flows toward Mexico should increase on par with that country's ability to reassert macroeconomic and political stability.

Despite the drop in US investments, Mexico was still able to increase the total flow of foreign direct investment into the country during 1994, largely in investments from non-NAFTA countries hoping to establish operations in Mexico in order to compete in the North American market under the 'rules of origin' provisions of NAFTA.

A second finding is that FDI flowing from the United States to Canada in 1994 rose by 350 percent (to US$72.8 billion) over the preceding year. This also is surprising in light of the fact that investment flows between these two countries had already enjoyed several years of preferential treatment under the bilateral CUSFTA agreement.

The United States attracted high levels of foreign direct investment during 1994 (US$504.41 billion, an 8.7 percent increase over 1993), but most of this came from non-NAFTA countries, such as the United Kingdom and Japan. Canada, with US$43.2 billion, was the fourth largest source of FDI to the United States in 1994, and this level of investment reflected an increase of 33.9 percent over 1993.

[3]See 'other links' at this site.

NAFTA's EFFECTS ON LABOR AND THE ENVIRONMENT

Most economists agree that it is difficult, if not impossible, to provide accurate, unbiased estimates of the effects of a trade agreement on employment, wages, benefits and working conditions. There are many methodological difficulties involved in making such estimates, the major one being the fact that the implementation of a trade agreement is just one factor influencing the performance of the economy. Business cycles, external shocks to the system such as the 'Asian contagion' of the late 1990s or the Mexican peso crisis of 1994, automation, subcontracting to other areas of the world as well as the effects of other trade agreements on tariff rates must also be taken into consideration in such calculations. Therefore, in assessing the contradictory claims of NAFTA proponents and critics the choice of a methodological approach is key in determining which estimates have more validity.

In this section, we look at the debates on NAFTA's effects on the environment and labor that have been advanced in the US where the debates over free trade have been the most spirited and have paralyzed the President's ability to negotiate any new trade agreements since NAFTA's implementation in 1994. Another reason for looking at the US situation is that the NAFTA Implementation Act in the US required a comprehensive assessment of the operation and effects of the agreement during the fourth year (1997) of the agreement's implementation, which in turn stimulated other organizations to carry out their own studies.

According to the official US report, which is based on studies carried out by US consulting companies and government agencies, 'These estimates suggest that NAFTA has boosted jobs associated with exports to Mexico between roughly 90,000 and 160,000' (Clinton, 1997 p. iii). The report also notes that because of NAFTA's two side agreements on labor and environmental protection that 'oversight and enforcement of labor laws' (p. iv) in all three countries has been enhanced while 'encouraging regional cooperation on broader environmental issues and improved enforcement of Mexican environmental laws' (p. vii).

In direct opposition to the official report are two reports carried out by think tanks associated with labor and consumer groups. The first, 'Nafta's Broken Promises: Failure to Create US Jobs' (Public Citizen, 1997a) is partially based on a survey of US firms that in 1993 had promised to create new jobs if NAFTA were implemented. Of the eighty firms interviewed only seven kept their promises. The report also notes that many of these firms that had promised to create jobs had actually laid off workers because of NAFTA, as certified by the special NAFTA unemployment assistance program of the US Department of Labor. Finally, the report places its estimate of total job loss due to NAFTA (by the end of 1996) at over 600,000.

The second report, 'The Failed Experiment: NAFTA at Three Years' (Economic Policy Institute, 1997b) argues that while NAFTA has been 'good for some North Americans, the costs–to many more North Americans–have been much heavier' (p. 1). The report then argues that: NAFTA has contributed to a downward pressure on US wages due to increased imports from low-wage trading partners. US firms have used the threat of moving to Mexico in negotiating over wages and working conditions and many firms have actually closed down US operations to fight union organizing drives when forced – through binding arbitration–to bargain with a union. Total job losses due to the increased trade deficits with both Mexico and Canada under NAFTA are estimated at approximately 420,000 (at the end of 1996). That is, while US exports increased between 1993 and 1996, US imports increased even more. The North American Agreements on Labor and Environmental Cooperation have both been ineffectual and should be revised to include enforceable labor and environmental standards. So, what are we to conclude? Are labor and environmental conditions better or worse as a result of NAFTA? With respect to US job loss and labor conditions, as noted above, evaluations here depend on the methodological approach of the researchers. This point is made in a study that appeared in late 1996 (Hinojosa Ojeda et al., 1996) which suggests an alternative system for tracking trade and investment flows in the North American context which in turn will yield new estimates of the impacts of those flows. Using this alternative system these researchers acknowledge that there has been both job loss and gain and that the net employment effect of NAFTA has been 'slightly positive'. The report, however, does not comment on the effect of NAFTA on wages and job conditions.

With respect to environmental conditions, it is clear that the major problems exist on the US-Mexican border where conditions are visibly deplorable and have not markedly improved since NAFTA's implementation. However, it is important to note that environmental management on both sides of the US-Mexican border is a process increasingly subject to international agreements and evolving patterns of transborder cooperation. In modern times such agreements go back to 1944, when the International Boundary and Water Commission (IBWC) was created in its present form to deal with what its title implies, international boundary and water issues on the US-Mexican border. Subsequently the 1983 La Paz Agreement on 'Cooperation for the Protection and Improvement of the Environment in the Border Area' provided a framework for addressing a wider range of border environmental issues. Then in 1991 an 'integrated Environmental Plan for the Mexican-US Border Area, First Stage (1992–94)' (IBEP) built on the La Paz Agreement and took joint cooperation on border environmental issues to a higher stage. Finally, 'Border XXI' was presented in 1996 in order to broaden the scope of collaborative issues and increase coordination among all levels of government and border communities.

At this point a myriad of governmental agencies and non-governmental organizations are involved in defining and managing US-Mexican border environmental issues. Nevertheless, the general objective of this new constellation of organizations is that bringing together technical monitoring, academic analysis and grass-roots participation with governmental processes and financial leverage can result in a politically acceptable and environmentally sound set of policies.

As the process is relatively new it is still too early to assess its effectiveness. Still, the concept represents a great deal of progress over the traditional 'top-down' processes dictated by the two nations' capitals that prevailed for so many years. Thus, while NAFTA's implementation has not directly resulted in an improvement in border environmental conditions in the short term, a new framework is now being implemented that, in the long term, could reverse the environmental deterioration that has marked this region for the last three decades.

CONTEMPORARY MEXICO IN NAFTA

How has Mexico fared under NAFTA? There are at least two ways to determine this. The first is to evaluate NAFTA's impact simply as a trade and investment agreement. The second would include the social aspects which today concern many Mexicans, which perhaps are not directly associated with the signing of the North American Trade Agreement itself.

As a trade and investment agreement, NAFTA has bolstered both of these dimensions throughout North America, and this success has served as an incentive for the rest of Latin America to engage in the trade liberalization process and encouraging other free trade agreements. As mentioned earlier in this book, extensive trade relations already existed in North America, so NAFTA further facilitates and cements this reality. It also constructed mechanisms for trade dispute settlement so that traders and investors could be guaranteed a process which could be followed in case trade disagreements arose.

Any evaluation of NAFTA and its consequent trade and investment flows must take into account the very particular circumstances of an economic arrangement between two advanced industrial economies and a developing country such as Mexico. This asymmetry is significant when Mexico is struck by recurrent macroeconomic problems when both trade and investment patterns are disrupted.[4] In general terms, what must be clear is that as long as Mexico's economy is stable, trade

[4]The cycles of instability that occur in Mexico are not difficult to describe, although complex economic models have been developed to explain these patterns. Pressures usually build up on the peso as government revenues fall, either because there are reductions in income from oil sales, of capital flight or a fall in the Mexican stock exchange. To contain the flight of capital (mainly short-term speculative funds) or the exchange of pesos for hard currency, interest rates are increased. These measures cause a devaluation of the peso adding to the inflation caused by the rise of interest rates. These cycles of crisis and recovery take approximately two to three years to overcome and regain macroeconomic stability.

Table 8.2 Mexico's Exports to NAFTA (billions of US dollars)

Country	1994	1995	1996	1997
US	106.4	120.1	148.1	178.1
Canada	3.1	3.3	3.9	4.1

Source: www.naftaworks.org.

Table 8.3 Mexico's Balance of Payments (billions of US dollars)

	1994	1995	1996	1997
FDI	10.9	9.7	7.5	12.1
Reserves	6.1	17.5	28.0	8.6

Source: www.naftaworks.org.

and investment flowing south will also be stable. This atmosphere of stability encourages entrepreneurs and governments to go on with the process of trade liberalization. Thus if we focus on the post 1994 peso crisis era, we can observe that Mexican trade with its two North American partners has increased substantially as shown in Table 8.2.

In the same context, foreign direct investment (FDI) has also experienced a resurgence after the dramatic decrease in 1995. For 1997, Mexico reported a 60.1 percent increase in FDI over 1996, reaching somewhat over US$10 billion. This figure incorporates numbers which integrate *maquiladora* investments, reinvestments of profits and intrafirm transactions. Of the US$6.8 billion registered before the Registro Nacional de Inversiones Extranjeras (RNIE) we must add US$1.1 billion of new investment by *maquilados* plus US$2.15 billion in reinvestment of profits. These positive numbers follow the economic recovery after the 1994 crisis. In that year, FDI stood at US$10 billion, falling to US$9.7 billion in 1995 and to US$7.5 billion in 1996.

There is one point which should be emphasized involving the relationship between trade and investment in Mexico. As the cyclical crises described earlier evolve, Mexican exports always increase, with Mexican goods gaining a comparative advantage because of the devaluation of the peso accompanying the crisis. At the same time, because foreign goods become more expensive there is an increase in foreign reserves. These patterns are shown in Table 8.3.

As Mexico's exports increase there is increased pressure from both

Table 8.4 Mexico's Balance of Trade (billions of US dollars)

Country	1994	1995	1996	1997
US	–3.1	12.4	13.0	12.1
Canada	–9.13	0.51	0.42	0.18

Source: www.naftaworks.org.

Mexican and other North American entrepreneurs to have a more stable and predictable trading regime. There is also increased presssure to accelerate trade if possible. Under these conditions NAFTA has become the right instrument present at the right time to carry on the job of increasing trade and investment. As these two elements intensify, however, there is also the possibility for increased conflict. NAFTA also provides the tools to try and resolve such conflicts. These conflicts arise from different interpretations of NAFTA and because of political pressures designed to obtain some form of protection for specific industries. The gains from trade so widely advertised in the United States have been hard to sell domestically, especially when macroeconomic conditions in Mexico create economic contractions limiting US exports. Table 8.4 shows the Mexican trade balance with Canada and the United States. Remember that a positive number for Mexico means an 'unfavorable' balance for the US and Canada.

In other words, when Mexico experiences economic difficulties as described above, it experiences a trade surplus and this becomes problematic for US politicians who see this as a loss for US industries. In the nebulous rhetoric of Washington, what in reality demonstrates Mexican economic health (during the years 1995–97) is reinterpreted as a problem for the United States. Many members of the US Congress (and their varied constituencies) see a Mexican trade surplus being the result of 'unfair trade practices' by Mexico which need correction.

With the Mexican economic recovery after the 1994 crisis, pressure accelerated to liberalize trade further and more rapidly than the original four-phased schedule which appeared in the 1994 NAFTA. The liberalization which has taken place at a rapid rate corresponds to those products where there already has been increased trade; in other words, and with respect to this dimension only, trade does not occur because of liberalization but the other way around, increased liberalization is taking place because there is already significant trade. In this respect, the NAFTA Commission agreed during April 1998 to liberalize or reduce tariffs on approximately 500 products with a trade value of almost US$1 billion. This acceleration of tariff reductions affects the three NAFTA members differently with the US contributing US$500 million in tariff reductions while the Canadian value amounts to US$62 million In contrast, Mexico liberalizes US$380 million on American products and US$9 million on Canadian goods.

The types of goods being 'liberalizated' fall within the sectors of textiles (such as synthetic threads), cotton and woolen cloth and semi-finished clothes. This sector comprises approximately 97 percent of all liberalized goods. Other products include chemical-pharmeceutical goods, watches and hats. Observers within the trade ministry in Mexico (SECOFI) argue that this liberalization was possible because of the close cooperation which exists between the private sectors of the three NAFTA countries; such cooperation has led to an ongoing process of consultation which then allowed the participants to invoke Article 302.3 which permits negotiations to increase the rate of tariff reductions.

As was mentioned above, liberalization has occurred when trade is already significant. Yet, this round of tariff reductions has another dimension and represents a significant shift in world trade. The liberalization of the textile industry which occurred within NAFTA was in response to the trade-diversion effects of NAFTA. In other words, because there has been a shift for US producers to source textiles from Mexico rather than Asia, Mexican textiles and apparel exports to the US have grown more each year than from any other country. Since 1995 such exports have doubled. In 1997, US apparel imports from Asia amounted to 36 percent of the total, while Mexican and Caribbean imports accounted for 39 percent.

From a Mexican perspective, this liberalization of trade within the context of NAFTA is not an isolated incident. At the same time that negotiations for further liberalization within NAFTA has taken place, Mexico began discussions and negotiations with the European Union, with the European Commission announcing in March 1998 that it would follow a fast-track approach to conclude a free trade agreement with Mexico. In addition, a free trade pact between Mexico and Nicaragua took effect on July 7, expanding ties between Mexico and Latin America. As mentioned above, in parallel developments, Canada signed a free trade agreement with Chile in 1996.

This enthusiasm for freer trade by Mexico does not come without some costs, even in the context of NAFTA. Some would say that these costs are present because of NAFTA, and because of the asymmetry existing between NAFTA partners. The conflicts which have arisen among NAFTA countries arise very often because of the dominance of the US. The conflict resolution panels designed to deal with trade conflicts have had some success; but the experience of the trilateral panels of NAFTA, in comparison to the previous experience of CUSFA, seems to indicate that there are at least two trends. First, the panels appear to be taking very long to be constituted, because countries have objected to individual panelists in a consistent fashion thereby delaying the beginning of the resolution process. Second, once the process has begun, the constant trilateral consultations appear to take more time than specified in NAFTA. Under NAFTA, the maximum time allowed to hold consultations, for a panel to be formed and for it to present a resolution, was stipulated to be in the neighborhood of 165 days. An example is the case of Canadian rolled steel on which Mexico imposed countervailing duties of 30.8 percent and which later were increased to 108 percent. Canadian exporters asked the NAFTA Commission to consider these as punitive measures, seemingly inconsistent with NAFTA. As a matter of record, the NAFTA panel partially favored the Mexican position but it is noteworthy that this process took from January 1996 to August 1998 to provide a final decision. This period of time certainly surpasses anything provided for in NAFTA. Equally lengthy was the case of Mexican straw brooms where the US imposed various safeguard measures (new tariffs) to protect its domestic industry from Mexican producers. This case began in March 1996 and ended in February 1998 with a bilateral panel deciding against the American position. Another important case has been the outright refusal by the US, in December 1995, to permit Mexican trucks to engage in transborder operations as had been agreed under NAFTA. This unilateral ignoring of NAFTA by the US administration has led to two steps of the conflict resolution process to take place; there were a series of consultations over the nature of the problem and then the second stage began with the meeting of the NAFTA Commission in August 1998. The final stage–the empowering of a panel has yet to take place at the time of writing, but as it is, this process will certainly last at least three years. The decision to restrict transborder traffic by the US was not the result of any of the relevant trade-responsible institutions in the US, but by political pressure on the White House by US trucking interests (that is, the Teamsters Union heavy support for the Democratic party) seeking protection for their members. Under the WTO and NAFTA agreements, countries can choose to have WTO dispute panels hear cases instead of NAFTA panels. Canada has chosen the WTO option in a number of recent disputes. This further calls the efficacy of the NAFTA disputes system into question.

At the time of NAFTA's ratification many Democratic members of Congress had been ambivalent or opposed to NAFTA. In 1997 they joined Republicans to oppose any fast-track extension preventing President Clinton from negotiating further trade agreements, especially the Free Trade Area of the Americas (as had been proposed at the Economic Summit of the Americas in December 1994) or extending NAFTA to incorporate Chile. The lack of fast-track authority by the Clinton administration means that very little can be done in the near future. Just as the US Congress defeated the wishes of the Clinton administration, the administration was hampered by the lack of support for any widening of the NAFTA agenda by the US business community. The surprising lack of support by the US business community for the Free Trade Area of the Americas and the necessary fast-track procedures contrasts with the efforts by the US private sector through its many lobbying entities in support of fast-track during NAFTA negotiations in the spring of 1991. One possible explanation for the lack of presence by US business in the efforts to liberalize trade with the Americas is that here is a case where the political process was ahead of economic realities. That is, we can view NAFTA as an experimental agreement formally integrating two advanced economies with a developing area, however, the business community was still uncertain as to how this relationship would finally develop. A clear picture of business dealings and government practices was needed through NAFTA (a case where most of 1995 and half of 1996 had to be written off because of the macroeconomic instability in Mexico), before such practices could be extended to the rest of Latin America. In this context, and from a business perspective, NAFTA is still an experiment which needs the test of time before it can be widened to encompass all the many other markets and institutions of Latin America.

NAFTA AND ECONOMIC INTEGRATION

NAFTA's Impact on Infrastructure

NAFTA is just one more step toward making North America a region without economic borders. While the barriers to most labor mobility remain in place, the obstacles to trade and investment will largely disappear over the next fifteen years and firms from the member countries will become relatively free to export to, import from, and locate their operations anywhere in the region.

Economic integration generally increases trade flows between member countries.[5] Expanding trade flows, usually expressed in terms of their total monetary value, result in increasing flows of tangible goods (freight flows). This, in turn, heightens the pressures on all existing transportation infrastructure, including highways and railroads, as well as airport and seaport facilities. If the transportation infrastructure is already operating at or near capacity, this could delay the delivery of inputs and/or finished products, offsetting some of the competitive advantages (such as lower tariffs and reduced transaction costs) that economic integration is supposed to guarantee.

Resolving transportation bottlenecks as they appear will require

[5]Trade flows consist of traditional exports and imports as well as informal border transactions between neighboring communities on international borders. The latter may or may not increase, depending on many other factors, including exchange rates and limits on merchandise that consumers can bring directly into the country.

close collaboration between private firms and government agencies in NAFTA countries. Transportation planning must be done internationally in order to ensure fast and dependable access to the tri-national market. For trade to flow easily, inspection facilities at international borders must be expanded and improved; although NAFTA cuts tariffs and nontrade barriers, border inspections are still needed to enforce rules of origin and sanitary and phytosanitary restrictions and to interdict smuggled drugs and undocumented border crossers. New inspection technology is being introduced at expanded border inspection stations on both the US-Canada and US-Mexico borders, but the expanded volume of freight stimulated by NAFTA still threatens to overwhelm existing capabilities.

Harmonizing Trade Laws and Commercial Documents

NAFTA is regarded by many observers as a monumental accomplishment, opening North America to new opportunities for market access and cross-border investment. However, important issues are still to be resolved, including the standardization of trade and investment documents and the harmonization of trade and investment laws among the three countries. While there are many institutions involved in this task, one serves as the hub of such efforts: the National Law Center for Inter-American Free Trade, located at the University of Arizona in Tucson. The Center works with counterpart organizations in Canada and Mexico. This section draws heavily on materials obtained from the Center.

The US and Canadian legal systems (with the exceptions of Quebec and Louisiana) are based on common law, which relies on judicial precedents, while Mexico's system is based on civil law, which focuses on written, constitutional codes and statutory provisions. Thus, in some areas there are no parallel legal concepts, and new difficulties are introduced when legal vocabularies must be translated from one language to another. Litigation is also carried out differently in the two systems; what may be a civil case in one system may have criminal implications in another. Such a minor detail as assigning liability for merchandise damaged in transit–easily resolved when it occurs within one country–may not have resolution when merchandise moves from one country to another. Ordinary business practices also vary significantly between the three countries. For example, in the United States and Canada, inventories and accounts receivable normally serve as collateral for bank loans to firms. In Mexico, loan collateral has traditionally been land. This difference is linked to the manner in which bankruptcy proceedings are conducted in the two legal systems. Variation in legal documents, including warehouse receipts and bills of lading, can result in lost time and added transaction costs. The absence of uniform accounting standards is another area where differences are especially problematic: investors have difficulty comparing statements of earnings and profits between, say, US and Mexican corporations. Most of the differences between legal structures and business practices have the potential to affect businesses on a practical, day-to-day basis. The differences in powers of attorney, franchise agreements and banking practices, among others, must be standardized or firms must develop expertise in both systems, if NAFTA is to fully succeed in its goals. There are other areas in which a lack of structural symmetry could impact the way that individuals and firms conduct cross-border business. Two areas that are of special importance are educational and professional standards (applying to medical doctors and lawyers, for example) and environmental regulations (including uniform monitoring standards for measuring air and water quality).

The Changing Business Environment

NAFTA is creating an increasingly open economic environment which will determine where and how North America (and the world) does business. In this section we examine the changing business environment and the opportunities and challenges it presents.

The free-trade, market-oriented position of multilateral institutions created to manage the global economy (such as the WTO, IMF and World Bank) have frequently been at odds with countries whose economic strategies stressed a strong role for government–and sometimes outright protectionism. The contradiction that emerges when countries design their own domestic industrial policies but participate in open markets at the international level was historically handled quite differently by Mexico, Canada and the United States. In the post-World War II period Mexico was significantly more protectionist than Canada and the United States,[6] and the Mexican government was much more proactive than the other two. Despite the entry of large US, European and Japanese multinational firms into Mexico after the war, these two differences (along with differences in language, culture and legal system) served to keep small and medium-sized firms from the United States and especially Canada from participating in the Mexican economy. Now, under NAFTA, increasing integration in North America through trade and investment has become a fact of life. The 'domestic market' is becoming synonymous with 'North America', with three national economies grounded in three different political, legal and cultural systems and three main languages, with transactions across national boundaries using three national currencies.

This new 'domestic market' exists within a global economic system with its own dynamics and 'rules of the game'. As firms increasingly venture beyond the confines of their domestic economy into the North American domestic market and discover its advantages, pressures will build to expand this framework to include other, and perhaps most, of the nations of the Western Hemisphere. In order to succeed in these new markets, key actors in North American firms must acquire: (1) working knowledge of the dynamics of the global economic system (its history, institutions and mechanisms), (2) familiarity with the history and socioeconomic structure of each potential trade partner and (3) communication skills, including linguistic and cultural skills appropriate for the region. The need for such knowledge and skills holds important implications for designing business school curricula, foreign language programs and internships (Clement, 1993).

There are, of course, many ways of doing business. A firm can enter a foreign market by buying goods from and/or selling goods to another country. Buying can be done by importing directly, by forming a joint venture with or acquiring an already established firm in

[6] Significant differences remain. In 1994–95 average tariffs were 6.6, 6.7 and 14.2 percent, respectively, for the United States, Canada and Mexico.

another country, or by establishing a subsidiary in that country. Similarly, selling can be done by exporting directly through a distributor in another country or by licensing technology to a firm there, which will then produce the product. Joint ventures with another firm to produce a product in a foreign country is another possibility, as is establishing a subsidiary (Fraser, 1992). Each option produces a different set of benefits and costs (less/more risk, less/more control, the promise of higher/lower long-term profits). The ultimate choice of how to do business is a function of both a firm's capabilities and the 'comfort zone' of its management, employees and board of directors.

The Mexican market, like many other Latin American markets, presents some unique opportunities that are currently not available in the United States or Canada. Mexican firms need technology and capital in order to modernize their operations, which have long stagnated under protectionism and high interest rates. Many Mexican firms are also in need of guidance on how to enter the Canada-US market, already somewhat integrated through CUSFTA.

Firms going into Mexico will also find some attractive attributes there. Mexican labor costs are low in comparison with those in the United States and Canada. Cheap labor, however, is not the whole story. High labor productivity is also essential. Companies that have made sizeable investments in training and equipment have generally found Mexico's labor force to be of high quality. One area in which Mexico remains deficient is transportation infrastructure, where a shortage of modern rail and port facilities can add time (and cost) to doing business.

One important mechanism by which outside firms have taken advantage of the incentives for doing business in Mexico is the border-based *maquiladora* industry. NAFTA will phase out the *maquiladora* program as it currently exists, but Mexico will remain an attractive export-processing platform and low-cost manufacturing site as long as firms are able to use inputs from NAFTA countries. The *maquiladora* functions as an export-processing zone, where Mexican or foreign firms can import inputs into Mexico free of duty and assemble them for export, paying duty only on the value added in Mexico. Recent changes allow some of the products to be sold in Mexico, but only under certain conditions. Most *maquiladora* plants are located along Mexico's northern border, for ease of access to the US market and to circumvent the problems inherent in relying on the inadequate transportation infrastructure in the country's interior. Asian firms, especially electronics producers, began entering the *maquiladora* sector when NAFTA negotiations began in order to gain preferred access to the entire North American market under NAFTA's 'rules of origin' requirements. They have become an important presence in Baja California, now the world's premiere producer of television sets.

NAFTA and the Location of Economic Activity

How will the NAFTA change the economic geography of North America? First, as intraregional trade expands, firms with high transportation costs will likely try to lower these costs by relocating their production and/or distribution facilities closer to the trade corridors that run from north to south through the three countries. Several trade corridors which have appeared in recent years serve as 'gateways' for firms involved in cross-border transactions. Examples are the Red River Trade Corridor (connecting Manitoba, North Dakota and Minnesota) and El Camino Real (running from Taos, New Mexico, across the border at El Paso-Ciudad Juárez, and continuing through Chihuahua to Mexico City). Other changes in the 'location' of many economic activities[7] will reflect firms' efforts to maximize opportunities as they confront changing price structures, both within and outside of the NAFTA area.

In the years since the Canada-US Free Trade Agreement went into effect, the easing of trade and investment barriers have allowed firms in the two countries to make location decisions without regard to borders. Some US and Canadian firms have reorganized their operations, sometimes consolidating two plants, one in each country, into one plant in one or the other country. In other cases, firms expanded their operations into the other country. Their motivation was clearly profit

[7]Under NAFTA, incentives to firms locating in Mexico's border regions will be phased out over time so that there will be a 'level playing field' for firms on both sides of the international boundary.

maximization, mainly based on the economies realized through large-scale production (in the case of consolidation) or 'economies of scope', in the case of expansion into another country.

Another factor that will trigger changes in the spatial location of economic activity is the increased competition that exists in a borderless environment. As inefficient producers in one country are outmatched by more efficient producers elsewhere, some firms, perhaps entire industries, will simply disappear as local markets begin to be supplied totally through imports.

The net effect of these changes is that, over time, economic activity will tend to move from regions that offer less to those that offer more in terms of attractive costs, labor skills, infrastructure, innovativeness and quality of life. Border regions present some special characteristics in this regard. Traditionally border regions have tended to be relegated to the periphery of economic activity, primarily because access to their geographical markets–their natural hinterlands–was constrained by an international boundary. As economic borders recede and eventually disappear due to regional and/or global economic integration, new opportunities present themselves. Local trade and commerce becomes more 'transborder', and firms on opposite sides of the border may find new bases for working together based on complementarities such as now exist on the US-Mexican border (where low-wage Mexican workers are employed manufacturing while high-wage US workers are employed in research and development facilities). Such opportunities may attract new firms and new industries and/or stimulate the expansion of existing ones, potentially driving new forms of economic development in border regions. Of course, these new conditions do not guarantee that economic development will surge in border regions. Economic development in the post-Cold War era may prove extremely elusive precisely because of the new, more competitive environment that now exists. Thus many border regions are likely to remain in the periphery, both geographically and economically.

What differentiates the cities or regions that will prosper in the new economy from those that will stagnate or decay? No single factor provides the complete answer. Clearly, location is important, as is having a diversified economic base, a well-trained work force, links with research institutions, modern telecommunications and transport facilities, a high quality of life and 'the institutional capacity to develop and implement future-oriented development strategies' (Commission of the European Communities 1992, p. 22). However, in the case of border regions, there is one more important factor: a well-developed system of transborder cooperation. In this regard, NAFTA could have a decidedly positive effect. As Paul Ganster (1995, p. 177) noted:

> NAFTA has been a catalyst, for it made border issues a high priority on the bilateral agenda and brought increased federal involvement and funding to border issues, particularly by the US federal government. At the same time, the longstanding inclination of the US government and the decentralization process in Mexican public administration have combined to facilitate greater transborder cooperation at the local level in the border region.

NAFTA's Technical Deficiencies

There are technical details that will plague NAFTA in future years, and they are the same ones that have been thorns in the side of the Uruguay Round of GATT negotiations. Three appear to be most important.

First, NAFTA lacks a common regulatory framework on dumping, subsidies and countervailing duties. These problems have been discussed exhaustively within GATT, and they were a major reason why Canada sought a free trade agreement with the United States. Since early in the Reagan administration, Canada had become a frequent target of US antidumping actions, and it hoped that a free trade agreement would lessen the pressures on Canadian exporters (del Castillo and Vega Cónovas, 1996).

A second deficiency in NAFTA is that it does not allow for 'industrial policies'. This focuses attention on subsidies, technical standards and government procurement policies, which all countries in the region use to foster development through research and development and so on. The Uruguay Round and the new WTO are beginning to address these issues; for example, there is now a classification scheme for subsidies (defined as 'an action by a national or sub-national government that bestows a financial benefit') that specifies how various kinds of subsidized export products should be treated (Morici, 1996). As many Uruguay Round and WTO rules and procedures like the subsidies classification are not incorporated within NAFTA, in late 1995 the Canadian government asked that a working group be set up within NAFTA to resolve subsidies issues, without which the principle of market access would be no more than a sham.

The third deficiency relates to NAFTA's 'newborn' status. As NAFTA is still embryonic, it is vulnerable. Perhaps the most significant danger is that the agreement could become the stepchild of special interest groups exercising pressure in Washington, Ottawa or Mexico City. Pressure tactics often are effective with weak or receptive governments, and the danger is that whenever the interests of a special group are threatened by the process of free trade, that group will take action to prevent the implementation of the offending provision.

Some cases may serve to illustrate this point, including the Clinton administration's failure to implement the transport services provision of NAFTA, which is to allow Mexican and US truckers to handle cargo on a transborder fashion. As suggested above, this provision was not implemented in a timely fashion because of successful lobbying by the Teamsters' union, whose members objected to Mexican competition. The delay was, in effect, a reward for the Teamsters' support in Clinton's reelection campaign. In a similar vein, Southern California avocado growers objected to the import of Mexican avocados; the US Department of Agriculture bowed to the pressure, citing a parasitic threat as its justification for forestalling avocado imports. It was not until early 1997 that Mexican avocado growers finally gained access to limited sections of the US market. In neither of these two cases did Mexico take action under NAFTA conflict resolution panel structure. Interestingly, immediately after implementation of NAFTA, Mexican milk producers in Baja California objected to the importation of milk from the United States. The response from Mexico City was that they should face up to the new world of competition. On the Mexican side,

United Parcel Service (UPS), a US firm has not yet been granted national treatment, to the benefit of small Mexican delivery systems.

The question is, how far will such interest-group-driven actions go? Given the protectionist climate in the United States, there are strong indications that this type of political action can be rewarding, especially if lobbyists use the argument that a 'distant international bureaucracy' is impinging on national sovereignty or that special 'secret' panels are making decisions contrary to the US Congress's intentions. The only protection against this tendency is to 'deepen' the NAFTA agreement–that is, to carry it to higher levels of integration.

BEYOND NAFTA

In the first four years of NAFTA, trade and investment expanded despite Mexico's crisis and the deteriorating Asian economies. Moreover, an institutional structure has been put in operation, overcoming initial delays and funding shortfalls and a dispute resolution mechanism has been established and as noted above has received mixed performance reviews.

Looking toward the future, we see NAFTA evolving in three ways. First, as it matures it could grow into the structure that is envisioned in the originating document; foreshadowings of this are already visible in the areas of dispute resolution and environmental and labor concerns.

Second, NAFTA could be modified to correct the deficiencies present in the initial document. The areas most in need of reform and strengthening are antidumping, subsidies and countervailing duties; industrial policy; capital movements and investment; and dispute settlement. Another area is labor mobility; while the United States is not eager to admit more foreign nationals, a bilateral plan for managing crossborder labor flows might be more efficient than the present unilateral one (del Castillo and Vega Cónovas, 1996). Such reforms would result in a 'deepening' of the trilateral relationship.

Finally, the NAFTA relationship could be 'widened' by the 'accession' (inclusion) of additional individual country members or by somehow merging with one or more regional trade blocs.

Widening and/or deepening is likely to be resisted, at least in the short term, because of the strong anti-free trade sentiment that has developed in the United States. During NAFTA negotiations and approval process, most criticism of the agreement came from labor and environmental groups traditionally associated with the political left. However, in recent years, attributable in part to the instability and recession in Mexico, many conservative groups have joined organized labor and environmentalists in their objections to NAFTA–and to the World Trade Organization as well–claiming that they threaten 'America's sovereignty'. Their opposition kept free trade initiatives off President Clinton's agenda throughout the 1996 election year severely restricting his leadership at the second Summit of the Americas in Santiago, Chile in 1998.

Even so, a number of proposals, both official and unofficial, have been advanced that would expand the integration process. These include:

- Repeated (unofficial) appeals to create a North Atlantic Free Trade Zone between NAFTA and the European Union (Nelson, 1996) as a way of avoiding growing economic and political tensions between the two groups of nations.
- Building stronger free trade ties between the United States (and NAFTA) and the Asian Pacific Economic Cooperation group of seventeen Pacific Rim nations (Stout and Robbins, 1996).
- Negotiating the accession of individual countries into NAFTA; Chile has long been considered the strongest candidate for entry into an expanded NAFTA. Negotiating a hemisphere-wide free trade agreement (a Free Trade Agreement of the Americas, FTAA) by building on the Enterprise of the Americas Initiative originally introduced by President Bush in 1990 and confirmed by President Clinton at the Summit of the Americas meeting in Miami in 1994. Two follow-up meetings in 1995 (Denver) and 1996 (Cartagena) and the ongoing efforts of several working committees have kept this process very much alive but out of US newspaper headlines. This work was all to come together in the

second Summit of the Americas in Santiago, Chile, but because President Clinton lacked 'fast-track' authority significant progress was blocked.

- Extending the Group of Three (G-3) free trade agreement between Mexico, Venezuela and Colombia, signed in June 1994.

Any such negotiations would require President Clinton or his successors to seek congressional approval for fast-track authority, which is not considered likely at this time in light of congressional sentiments.

As outlined above, at the same time that the United States is dragging its feet on trade issues, Canada and Mexico are expanding their free trade ties. Additionally, Latin American countries are eager to open their economies to competition from other countries within the region at roughly the same level of development, and eventually with the United States and other developed countries as well.

In order to facilitate this process, the major Latin American economic and political organizations–including the Economic Commission for Latin America and the Caribbean (ECLAC), the Inter-American Development Bank (IDB) and the Organization of American States (OAS)–have mounted a collaborative effort to analyze the complex web of economic integration agreements in the region. The four main trade blocs in the region are the Central American Common Market, the Caribbean Common Market, the Andean Community and the Southern Cone Common Market (MERCOSUR). However, free trade agreements between individual countries and these common market groups are also growing. For example, MERCOSUR has signed free trade agreements with Chile and Bolivia and is currently negotiating agreements with other Andean countries. Finally, a variety of relationships (such as nonreciprocal preferential agreements and free trade agreements) are being formed between Latin American groups and individual countries, including Mexico and the European Union. Nevertheless, shrinking exports in Asia might stimulate the US Congress to take a more proactive position *vis-à-vis* new trade agreements and grant President Clinton or his successor 'fast-track' authority to negotiate a Free Trade Agreement for the Americas.

PRELIMINARY CONCLUSIONS

There are a number of issues that deserve mention in this final section. First, it would be easy to conclude that the United States could be left out of the global movement toward free trade if it does not act quickly, it is clear that the mere size of its market gives the United States options that few other nations can claim. The US, however, is far too important in world markets to be excluded from making trade policy globally.

Second, any book on North American economic integration would be remiss were it not to mention, however briefly, the important and related topic of North American political integration. There are two broad issues here. The first revolves around the asymmetrical political systems of the three countries of North America. Although all three embrace a federalist form of government, there is great diversity with respect to degrees of centralization and the specific form of federalism utilized (for example, Canada's parliamentary system versus the congressional systems of the United States and Mexico). The main questions here are: Will such political diversity inhibit or facilitate North America's economic integration? If so, how? These questions are of considerable importance in view of Mexico's current political reforms, Canada's constitutional crisis centered on Quebec, and the fiscal strains imposed by the New Federalism in all three countries.

The third issue relates to the future of overall North American integration. If North America goes the way of European integration, we can expect that some sort of 'North American Trilaterism' might someday evolve that would bring the three countries together for increased integration in a variety of areas. Again there are two issues here. First, we might ask if the current NAFTA institutional structure is conducive to the growth of continental-trilateral integration in other areas. If so, how far are these institutions likely to take the three countries down the road of integration, given the economic, cultural and political asymmetries between them? (Randall, 1995).

At this time it is difficult to imagine a 'United States of North America' or something similar. However, just a decade ago few observers foresaw anything like a NAFTA or the European Union. As circumstances change, new challenges and opportunities could arise that are difficult to predict from today's vantage point regarding the future of North American Trilateralism in the twenty-first century.

The fourth and final issue relates to NAFTA in the context of the phenomenon of globalization. Recent developments in the international economic arena have stimulated a great deal of debate as to the benefits and costs of an 'open' international economy that transmits economic trends from one national economy to others virtually instantaneously. Clearly, the dramatic crises in Indonesia and other developing Asian economies, as well as in Russia in 1997–98, coming on the back of several years of stagnation in the world's second largest economy, Japan, have caused a great deal of concern with the phenomenon frequently referred to as 'globalization' (see Chapter 3). Of course, regional trading blocs like NAFTA may or may not lead to more globalization in a technical sense (for example., producing more trade creation than trade diversion). Nevertheless, in recent years events have fueled the perception that open economies invite increasing macroeconomic instability–especially financial instability–and this perception is forcing decision makers, including politicians, of all political persuasions to reassess the world's recent movement toward more open and less regulated markets.

It is in this context that we can say that the future of NAFTA is likely to be determined by the outcome of this debate which has heated up in recent years as a consequence of the global financial instability noted above. On the one hand are the proponents of globalization who argue that 'free and open markets' will lead to increased competition, which will produce:

- An accelerated pace of technological innovation which in turn generates new products and/or higher worker productivity and lower unit labor costs in innovative firms/industries.
- Larger international trade and investment flows resulting in increased efficiencies based on comparative advantage, economies of scale and locational advantages.
- Higher (average) living standards resulting from increased pro-

ductivity and lower prices.

Proponents of this position also argue that while some industries, firms and individuals will suffer as protection is decreased or eliminated the gains to society as a whole will be much larger than the costs. On the other hand, the critics of 'free and open markets' argue that while some of the benefits noted above may occur, there are certain 'unintended consequences' including:

- Decreased national sovereignty as governments lose their ability to employ national industrial policies involving subsidies and protection for certain industries.
- Increased income inequality between rich and poor families and between prosperous and poor regions and countries.
- Increased strains on the environment leading to deterioration of local communities and need for better environmental protection laws and better enforcement of those laws.
- Increased competition between regions for firms to locate some or all phases of their operations forces such communities to create:
  – a more 'business friendly' institutional structure (for example, lower taxes, fewer regulations on the environment and the workforce) and more incentives to attract inward investment
  – dedicate more resources for labor force training and economic infrastructure.

The essence of this debate revolves around the distribution of the costs and the benefits of freer markets not over the existence or their size. The proponents argue that the total benefits outweigh the costs and therefore society is better off letting the (global) market allocate resources. The critics argue that the benefits of freer trade mainly accrue to those corporations and individuals whose position will be improved as protection is dismantled. The costs, however, inordinately accrue to workers who are either displaced or receive lower wages due to the increased competition with workers in low wage countries. Communities can be negatively impacted by jobs moving offshore, by the environmental damage that certain types of production generate and/or the need to provide incentives to highly mobile corporations that simultaneously demand lower taxes, better trained workers and expanded infrastructure, all at the communities' expense.

The implications of this debate for the future of NAFTA is simple and direct. While the tangible benefits of expanded trade and investment flows under NAFTA can easily be documented, the less visible costs of adjusting to the new, more open economic space in North America can only be inferred, based on indirect evidence. Additionally, the average citizen will perceive the benefits of NAFTA not by abstract trade and investment figures but by the economy's ability to provide prosperity, and a high quality of life in a context of relative stability. Thus, in Mexico, where economists used to say, 'When the US economy sneezes, the Mexican catches a cold', now it is clear that when Indonesia (or Russia or China) gets sick, all countries of the global economy suffer as well.

How far globalization will go and what its effects might be are not clear at this time. Institutions such as the IMF, charged with coordinating global monetary relations, are experiencing their own problems as critics charge that they have pushed countries in crisis with inappropriate policies that are out of step with the new, market-oriented and increasingly globalized environment. Here again, some critics advocate more non-market intervention while others advocate less. The fact is that the problems and the new international economic environment are complex and there are no quick-fix solutions in sight.

Clearly, there are benefits and costs to more open trading regimes. It is equally clear that decisions are not made purely on the basis of economic efficiency. Thus, decisions based upon a myriad of non-economic factors influence the formation of economic policies. The future of NAFTA can hinge upon such factors as economic and political events in China, the possible impeachment of a US president and events related to the hemispheric war on drugs. As pointed out above, however, the US is the key player in North America and when that country is mired in domestic matters, the NAFTA process slows down markedly.

Perhaps the most that we can ask for in this context is continued debate, evaluating the evidence in a context of openness and rationality. Nonetheless, the stakes in the free trade game are high and vested interests will do everything possible to influence the public and their elected representatives. North American integration is a road with many turns, many red and amber lights, but few signs indicating the appropriate direction. As yet, it is a road not travelled far.

References

Alarcòn Gónzalez, Diana (1994), *Changes in the Distribution of Income in Mexico and Trade Liberization*, Tijuana, Baja California, Mexico: El Colegio de la Frontera Norte.

Appleton, Barry (1994), *Navigating NAFTA: A Concise User's Guide to the North American Free Trade Agreement*, Toronto: Carswell.

Avramovic, Dragoslav (1994), 'Developing Countries: Export Prices of Commodities and Manufactures, Terms of Borrowing, and Returns on Capital' in Enrique Iglesias (ed.), *The Legacy of Raúl Prebisch*, Washington, DC: Inter-American Development Bank.

Banco de México (1980), *Inversión Extranjera Directa, Cuaderno 1938–1979*, Vol. II, Mexico, DF: Subdirección Económica.

Banco de México y Secretaría de Hacienda (1999), *Principales Indicadoes Economicos: 1999*, Mexico, DF: Banco de México y Secretaría de Hacienda.

Balassa, B. (1975), *European Economic Integration*, Amsterdam: North-Holland.

Barker, T.S. (1977), 'International trade and economic growth: an alternative to the neo-classical approach', *Cambridge Journal of Economics*, **1**(2), 153–72.

Baumol, W.J., S.A. Batey Blackman and E.N. Wolff (1989), *Productivity and American Leadership: The Long View*, Cambridge, MA: The MIT Press.

Borjas, G. (1994), 'The economics of immigration', *Journal of Economic Literature*, **32**(4), 1667–717.

Bowker, M.M. (1988), *On Guard for Thee*, Hull, PQ: Voyageur Publishing.

Bureau of Economic Analysis (Various), *Survey of Current Business*, Washington, DC: Government Printing Office, various issues.

Burtless, G. (1995), 'International trade and the rise in earnings inequality', *The Journal of Economic Literature*, **33**(2), 800–816.

Cadsby, C.B. and K. Woodside (1993), 'The effects of the North American free trade on the Canada-United States trade relationship', *Canadian Public Policy*, **19**(4), 450–562.

Cameron, Maxwell A. and Ricardo Grinspun (eds), (1993), *The Political Economy of North American Free Trade*, Montreal: McGill-Queen's University Press.

Chilcote, Ronald C. and Joel C. Edelstein (1986), *Latin American Capitalist and Socialist Perspectives of Development and Underdevelopment*, Boulder, CO: Westview.

Clement, Norris C. (1993), 'Trilateralizing Business Education in North America: Integrating the Economic, Political and Social Systems', in S. Kerry Cooper and Julian E. Gaspar (eds), *Trilateralizing Business Education*, Houston, Tex.: Center for International Business Education and Research, Texas A&M University, pp. 19–31.

Cline, W.R. (1997), *Trade and Income Distribution*, Washington, DC: Institute for International Economics.

Clinton, William J. (1997), *The Study on the Operation and Effect of the North American Free Trade Agreement (NAFTA) as required by section 512 of the NAFTA Implementation Act*, Washington, DC: Office of the President.

Commission of the European Communities (1992), *Regional Development Studies: urbanization and the Functions of Cities in the European Community*, Brussels: Directorate-General for Regional Policy.

Creighton, D.G. (1965), 'The Economic Objectives of Confederation', in J.J. Deutsch, B.S. Keirstead, K. Levitt, and R.M. Will (eds), *The Canadian Economy: Selected Readings*, Toronto: Macmillan Co., pp. 444–464.

Curtis, Thomas B. and John Robert Vastine, Jr (1971), *The Kennedy Round and the Future of American Trade*, New York: Praeger.

De la Peña, Moisés (1964), *El pueblo y su Tierra, Mito y Realidad de la Reforma Agragia en México*, Mexico, DF: Cuaderuos Americamos (Dice Eduardo que el no conoce esta cita).

Destler, I.M. (1994), *American Trade Politics*, 2nd edn, Washington, DC: Institute for International Economics.

del Castillo V., Gustavo (1993), 'The NAFTA: A Mexican Search for Development' in Richard S. Belous and Jonathan Lemco (eds), *NAFTA as a Model of Development: The Benefits and Costs of Merging High and Low Wage Areas*, Washington, DC: National Planning Association.

del Castillo V., Gustavo (1995), 'Convergent Paths toward Integration: The Unequal Experiences of Canada and Mexico', in Donald Barry (ed.), *Toward a North American Community? Canada, the United States and Mexico*, Boulder, CO: Westview.

del Castillo V., Gustavo (1996), 'NAFTA and the Struggle for Neoliberalism: Mexico's Elusive Quest for First World Status', in Gerardo Otero (ed.), *Neoliberalism Revisited. Economic Restructuring and Mexico's Political Future*, Boulder, CO: Westview.

del Castillo V., Gustavo and Gustavo Vega Cónovas (1996), *The Politics of Free Trade in North America*, Ottawa: Centre for Trade Policy and Law, Carleton University.

Doern, C.B. and Brian W. Tomlin (1991), *The Free Trade Story: Faith and Fear*, Toronto: Stoddart.

Eckstein, Salomòn (1966), *El Ejido Colectivo en México*, Mexico, DF: Forndo de Cultura Económica.

Economic Policy Institute (1997), *The Failed Experiment: NAFTA at Three Years*, Washington, DC: Economic Policy Institute.

Economic Report of the President, 1997 (1997), Washington, DC: Government Printing Office. .

Eichengreen, B. and Peter B. Kenen (1994), 'Managing the World Economy under the Bretton Woods System: An Overview,' in P.B.

Kenen (ed.), *Managing the World Economy: Fifty Years after Bretton Woods*, New York: Institute for International Economics.

Emmanuel, Arghiri (1972), *Unequal Exchange: A Study of the Imperialism of Trade*, New York: Monthly Review Press.

Executive Office of the President (1997), *The North American Free Trade Agreement as by Section 512 of the NAFTA Implementation Act: Report to the Congress*, Washington, DC: Government Printing Office.

Flanders, M.J. (1964), 'Prebisch on Protectionism: an Evaluation', *The Economic Journal*, **71**, 305–26.

Fraser, Dave (1992), 'Down Mexico way', *Business Quarterly* (University of Western Ontario), Autumn, 13–15.

Ganster, Paul (1995), 'United States-Mexico Border Region and Growing Transborder Interdependence', in Stephen J. Randall and Herman W. Conrad (eds), *NAFTA in Transition*, Calgary, AB: University of Calgary Press.

Grunwald, Joseph and Kenneth Flamm (1985), *The Global Factory: Foreign Assembly in International Trade*, Washington, DC: The Brookings Institution.

Hermández L.E. and J. Córdoba (1982), *La Distribución del imgreso en México*, Mexico, DF: Centro de Investigación para la Integración de las Sociedad.

Heston, A. et al. (1994), *Penn World Tables* (Mark 5.6), National Bureau of Economic Research, Boston: Harvard University Press.

Hinojosa Ojeda, R., et al. (1996), *North American Integration Three Years After NAFTA: A Framework for Tracking, Modeling and Internet Accessing the National and Regional Labor Market Impacts*, Los Angeles: University of California, North American Integration and Development Center.

Hufbauer, G.C. and K.A. Elliot (1994), *Measuring the Costs of Protection in the United States*, Washington, DC: Institute for International Economics.

Hurst, J.W. (1981), *Law and Markets in United States History*, Madison, WI: University of Wisconsin Press.

Innes, H.A. (1930), *The Fur Trade in Canada: An Introduction to Canadian Economic History*, Toronto: University of Toronto Press.

Innes, H.A. and W.T. Easterbrook (1950), 'Fundamental and Historical Elements,' in G. Brown (ed.), *Canada*, Berkeley: University of California Press.

Instituto Nacional de Estadistica, Geografia e Informitica (INEGI) (1984–94), *Encuesta Nacional de Ingresos y Gastos de los Hagares*, Mexico, DF: INEGI.

Instituto Nacional de Estadistica, Geografia e Informitica (INEGI) (1994), *Estadistica Históricas de México*, Mexico, DF: INEGI.

Inter-American Development Bank (IADB) (1990), *Economic and Social Progress in Latin America 1990 Report*, Washington, DC: IADB.

Inter-American Development Bank (IADB) (various issues), *Integration and Trade in the Americas: Periodic Notes*, Washington, DC: IADB.

Inter-American Development Bank (IADB) (1992), *Latin America: The New Economic Climate*, Washington, DC: IADB.

International Monetary Fund (IMF) (1998), *Direction of Trade Statistics*, Washington, DC: IMF.

International Monetary Fund (IMF) (1995), *International Financial Statistics Yearbook*, Washington, DC: IMF.

International Monetary Fund (IMF) (1998), *International Financial Statistics*, various issues, Washington, DC: IMF.

International Monetary Fund (1998), *International Financial Statistics Yearbook*, Washington, DC: IMF.

Keesing, D. (1966), 'Labor skills and comparative advantage', *American Economic Review*, **56**(1), 249–67.

Mackintosh, W.A. (1923), 'Economic factors in Canadian history', *The Canadian Historical Review*, **4**(1), 12–25.

Maddison, A. (1989), *The World Economy in the 20th Century*, Paris: Development Center of the Organization for Economic Cooperation and Development.

Maddison, A. (1991), *Dynamic Forces in Capitalist Development: A Long-Run Comparative View*, New York: Oxford University Press.

Maddison, A. (1994), 'Explaining the Economic Performance of Nations', in W. Baumol, R. Nelson and E. Wolff (eds), *Convergence of Productivity: Cross National Studies and Historical Evidence*, New York: Oxford University Press.

Markusen, J.R. (1995), 'The boundaries of multinational enterprises and the theory of international trade', *The Journal of Economic Perspectives*, **9**(2), 169–189.

Morici, Peter (1996), 'Resolving the North American subsidies war', *Canadian American Public Policy*, **27**, 86–94.

Muñhoz, Heraldo (1994), 'A New OAS for the New Times', in A.F. Lowenthal and G.F. Treverton (eds), *Latin America in a New World*, Boulder, CO: Westview.

Nair, C., R. Karim and C. Nyers (1992), 'Health care and health status in Canada-United States: statistical comparison', *Health Reports*, **4**(2) (82–003), Ottawa: Statistics Canada.

Nelson, Mark M. (1996), 'Kissinger, Scowcroft support creation of a North Atlantic free-trade zone', *Wall Street Journal*, September 27.

Norrie, K. and D. Owram (1996), *A History of the Canadian Economy*, 2nd edn. Toronto: Harcourt Brace and Co., Canada.

Ohlin, B. (1933), *Inter-Regional Trade and International Trade*, Cambridge, Mass.: Harvard University Press.

Pedersen, Rick (1995), 'U.S. firms set to invade', *Calgary Herald*, June 27, A1–A2.

Perdikis, N. and W.A. Kerr (1998), *Trade Theories and Empirical Evidence*, Manchester: Manchester University Press.

Pérez-López, Jorge F. (1996), 'Conflict and cooperation in U.S.-Mexican labor relations: The North American agreement on labor cooperation', *Journal of Borderland Studies*, **6**, 72–86

Porter, Michael (1990), *The Comparative Advantage of Nations*, New York: The Free Press.

Posner, M.V. (1961), 'International trade and technical change', *Oxford Economic Papers*, **13**, 323–41.

Public Citizen (1997a), *NAFTA's Broken Promises: Failure to Create U.S. Jobs*, Economic Policy Institute, Washington, DC.

Public Citizen (1997b),'The Failed Experiment: NAFTA at Three Years' Economic Policy Institute, Washington, DC.

Randall, Stephen J. (1995), 'Managing Trilateralism: The United States, Mexico and Canada in the Post-NAFTA Era', in Stephen J. Randall and Herman W. Conrad (eds), *NAFTA in Transition*, Calgary, AB: Univesity of Calgary Press.

Ricardo, David (1951), 'On the Principles of Political Economy and Taxation', in P. Straffa (ed.), *The Works and Correspondence of David Ricardo*, Cambridge: Cambridge University Press.

Rostow, Walt W. (1960), *The Stages of Economic Development: A Non-Communist Manifesto*, Cambridge: Cambridge University Press.

Sargent, T. C. (1995), 'An Index of the Generosity of Unemployment Insurance', unpublished paper presented at the Canadian Economics Association Annual Meetings, June, Montreal.

Sau, Ranjit (1978), *Unequal Exchange, Imperialism and Underdevelopment: An Essay on the Political Economy of World Capitalism*, Calcutta: Oxford University Press.

Schott, Jeffrey J. (ed.) (1990), *Completing the Uruguay Round: A Results-Oriented Approach to the GATT Trade Negotiations*, Washington, DC: Institute for International Economics.

Schott, Jeffrey J. (1994), *The Uruguay Round. An Assessment*, Washington, DC: Institute for International Economics.

Schwanen, Daniel (1993), 'A growing success: Canada's performance under free trade', *C.D. Howe Commentary*, no. 52, Toronto: C.D. Howe Institute, September.

Schwartz, Alan M. (1994), 'Canada-U.S. environmental relations: a look at the 1990s', *American Review of Canadian Studies*, **24**(4), 489–508.

Secretariá de Comercio y Formento Industrial (SECOFI) (1995), *Inversón extranjera en México 1989–1994*, Mexico, DF: SECOFI.

Smith, Adam (1961), *An Inquiry into the Nature and Causes of the Wealth of Nations*, Edwin Cannan (ed.), 6th edn, London: Metheun.

Statistics Canada (1991), *Adult Literacy in Canada: Results of a National Study*, (89–525E), Ottawa: Statistics Canada.

Statistics Canada (1993), *Education in Canada: 1992–93*, (81–229), Ottawa: Statistics Canada.

Statistics Canada (1994), *Universities: Enrollment and Degrees: 1991*, (81–204), Ottawa: Statistics Canada.

Statistics Canada, (various issues), *Canadian Economic Observer*, published monthly, various issues, (11–010), Ottawa: Statistics Canada.

Statistics Canada (1998), *Canadian Economic Observer, Historical Statistical Supplement: 1997/1998*, (11–210), Ottawa: Statistics Canada.

Stewart, Terence P. (ed.) 1993, *The GATT Uruguay Round: A Negotiating History (1986–1992)*, Deventer, The Netherlands: Kluwer Law and Taxation Publishers.

Stout, Hillary and Carla Anne Robbins (1996), 'Clinton to revive free-trade issue during Asia trip', *Wall Street Journal*, November 14.

Sunkel, Osvaldo (1993), *Development from Within: Toward a Neostructuralist Approach for Latin America,* Boulder, CO: Lynne Rienner.

Unger, Kurt and Luz Consuelo Saldaña (1989), 'Las economías de escala y de alcance en las exportaciones mexicanas más dinámicas', *El Trimestre Económico*, **56**(2), 471–95 (April-June).

United Nations Development Programme (1997), *Human Development Report*, Oxford: Oxford University Press.

Vernon, Raymond (1974), *El Dilema del Desarrollo Económico de México*, Mexico, DF: Editorial Diana.

Vernon, Raymond (1966b), 'International investment and international trade in the product cycle', *Quarterly Journal of Economics* **80**, 190–207.

Waite, P. (1987), 'Between Three Oceans: Challenges to a Continental Destiny', in Craig Brown (ed.), *The Illustrated History of Canada*, Toronto: Lester & Orpen Dennys, Ltd.

Watkins, M.H. (1963), 'A staple theory of economic growth', *Canadian Journal of Economics and Political Science*, **29**(2), 141–58.

Winham, Gilbert R. (1986), *International Trade and the Tokyo Round Negotiation*, Princeton, NJ: Princeton University Press.

World Bank (1991), *World Development Report 1991: The Challenge of Development*, Oxford: Oxford University Press.

World Bank (1992), *World Development Report 1992: Development and the Environment*, Oxford: Oxford University Press.

World Bank (1997a), *World Development Report 1997: Latin America in the Post Importation Era*, Oxford: Oxford University Press.

World Bank (1997b) *World Development Report, 1997*, New York: Oxford University Press.

Glossary

Absolute advantage: the production situation where one country is more resource efficient in the production of a good than another country. It underlies a theory for why countries will engage in international trade. Trade based on absolute advantage is a situation where one country has an absolute advantage in production of one good and the other country has an absolute advantage in the production of another good. Each country specializes in the production of the good it is more efficient at producing and exports that good, while at the same time importing its requirements of the good it would produce inefficiently.

Accepted retaliation: a GATT principle whereby a country accepts that if it violates its GATT commitments in a way that injures trading partners, those partners have the right to impose trade penalties on the offending country up to the value of the damage suffered without the fear of retaliation from the original offending country. In short, if injured by a GATT violation, a country can impose trade sanctions without fear of re-retaliation, thus preventing trade wars.

Ad valorem: a term usually applied to taxes (particularly tariffs) which are calculated as a percentage of the value of a good.

Aggregate demand: the sum of the demands of all individuals participating in a market.

Anti-dumping duties: tariffs imposed on the goods of a foreign firm deemed to be trading unfairly by selling below the full cost of production–it is dumping.

Autarky: the situation where a country does not engage in international trade.

Balance of payments: an accounting of a country's trade and financial transactions with the rest of the world over a specified period, commonly one year.

Balance of trade: an accounting of a country's trade in goods with the rest of the world over a specified period, commonly one year.

Bank of Canada: the Canadian central bank.

Bank rate: the Canadian benchmark interest rate established by the Bank of Canada.

Border measures: tariffs and other restrictions imposed on goods if they enter a country's customs territory.

Capital flight: the rapid movement of relatively liquid investment capital out of a country which has lost the confidence of the investment community.

Common market: an international trade relationship between two or more countries where: (1) all tariffs are removed between the member countries; (2) the member countries agree to a common external trade regime; and (3) there is unfettered movement of labour and capital among the countries.

Comparative advantage: an explanation for international trade in which one country is more resource efficient in its production of all goods–has an absolute advantage in all goods–relative to another country. Trade will still be mutually advantageous if the more efficient country produces and exports the good which it is comparatively better at producing and the less efficient country produces and exports the good it is comparatively least worst at producing.

Consumer durables: consumer goods which are consumed over relatively long periods of time; for example, houses, cars, refrigerators, and so on.

Consumer price index: an index of changes in the prices of goods and services purchased by a typical consumer. The index value can be compared to the cost of the same basket of goods and services in a base period.

Countervailing duties: duties imposed on the goods of a country whose producers have received a subsidy which is deemed unfair and trade distorting. The size of the countervailing duty should be set at a rate which offsets the damage suffered by the injured country's firms.

Current account balance: a statement of a country's trade in goods and services with the rest of the world over a specific period of time.

Current account deficit: when imports of goods and services exceed exports of goods and services over a specific period.

Debt servicing cost: the cost of meeting the interest payments on a loan as well as any contractual arrangements to repay the principal.

Deficit financing: when government expenditure exceeds taxes collected and the shortfall is made up by borrowing.

Dependency theory: a theory of international economic relations where the economic performance and development of a country is determined by its more developed trading partner(s) and/or source(s) for investment funds.

Dollarization: when the economic accounting and transactions of a country (or major international market) are (at least in peoples' minds) denominated in US dollars rather than the local currency.

Economic bloc: regional economic groupings of countries into free trade areas, customs unions, common markets and so on and where these countries are perceived to act in unison when dealing with other countries or economic groupings of countries.

Economic integration: arises when there is any economic interaction among states. It represents a very wide spectrum of international activities and the degree of integration can range from near autarky to there being no discernible policy induced difference between the economies of different countries.

Economic rent: a payment made for the use of a productive input, such as land, that is in fixed supply in the short run–and often in the long run. As these inputs cannot be moved to other uses, their earnings in alternative uses will be zero and any payments made for their use represent economic rent.

Economies of scale: the long-run decline in unit costs that occur as a firm's size increases. It is assumed that no factors of production are fixed in the long run.

Environmental dumping: when goods exported by a country do not reflect their full cost of production because the environmental costs associated with their production have not been fully accounted for. Usually applied to the goods of developing countries with lax environmental regulations or enforcement.

Escape clause relief: a temporary tariff allowed in response to a sudden surge of imports which is injurious to a domestic industry in an importing country.

Export-oriented industrialization: a strategy whereby a country's exports are expected to provide the major impetus for economic development.

Export processing zones: areas within a country which are allowed special tax dispensations for activities which lead to exports. Often inputs which are specifically imported to be components of products which will be exported can be exempt from tariffs in such zones.

Fixed exchange rate: a method of regulating the exchange of currencies whereby a currency is assigned a fixed value which is to be used when it is exchanged with other currencies–a separate value for each individual foreign currency. The government is pledged to maintain that exchange rate through buying and selling its currency in international currency exchange markets.

Flat rate tariff: a tariff charged at a fixed monetary amount (for example, $500 per car) on each unit of a good entering a country no matter what the value of the good.

Flexible exchange rate: a method for determining exchange rates between currencies by the interplay of market forces. See also: floating exchange rate.

Floating exchange rate: a method for determining exchange rates between currencies by the interplay of market forces. See also:

flexible exchange rate.

Free trade area: a classification of regional trade associations having the characteristics that the countries involved have agreed to eliminate (substantially all) tariffs and non-tariff barriers among themselves but retain the right to maintain separate trade regimes for their international dealings with other countries. As a result of differing levels of protection against non-members, rules of origin provisions are required to prevent goods entering a member with low external tariffs and then being shipped tariff-free to a high-tariff member country. Reduction of further barriers to economic integration such as the free movement of labor and capital among member countries or harmonization of social policies are not generally associated with free trade areas.

Full economic union: a classification of regional trade associations characterized by the removal of all tariffs and non-tariff barriers, a common external trade policy, no barriers to the free movement of factors of production, harmonization of social and tax policy and a single macroeconomic policy. Hence, while separate political systems continue to exist they can exert little independent influence on the functioning of the economy.

GDP per capita: the value of all the goods and services provided in a country over a set period–usually a year–divided by the population. It is a rough measure of individual well-being often used to compare the economies of different countries or the performance of an economy over time.

Gini coefficient: a measure of the degree of inequality in a distribution. Typically it is used to measure the distribution of income and can be used to compare countries or changes in a country over time.

Glasnost: a Russian word meaning openness in government process through public scrutiny and open debate. It was the official policy of the Soviet Union after 1985 up until its dissolution.

Global production sharing: the phenomenon whereby (usually labor intensive) manufacturing of components has shifted to low labor cost developing countries in the last thirty years of the twentieth century in response to a more open trading environment and rising technical capability in developing countries. The components are then sold to developed countries for final assembly and/or distribution.

Globalization: the closer economic integration of the international economy in the last fifteen years of the twentieth century fostered by the revolution in electronic communication which reduced the costs associated with the movement of information, technological improvements in transportation and reduced barriers to international trade and commerce.

Hacienda: Spanish word meaning an estate in a rural area with a dwelling house on it. Economic activities could include farming, livestock raising, mining or manufacturing.

Hedgemonic: a country which has clear dominance in international economic relationships and/or international politics.

Heterodox: doctrines, opinions or policies which are not in accordance with the established or generally accepted view.

Import quota: a quantitative (for example, 50,000 units) limit on imports of a product over a stated time period–usually one year.

Import-substitution industrialization: a strategy for economic development whereby manufacturing is encouraged through high tariffs or non-tariff barriers. Behind high trade barriers, domestic producers will produce substitutes for products which were formerly imported. Once a country became industrialized and had reaped the benefits of economies of scale and learning by doing they were expected to become internationally competitive and the trade barriers could be removed. A number of countries, particularly in Latin America, followed this strategy in the 1950s and 1960s. The empirical evidence suggests that international competitiveness was seldom achieved and most countries subsequently abandoned it as a development strategy.

Infant industry: a newly established industry. It is sometimes argued that infant industries need protection from imports to allow time for them to become fully established.

Injury test: used in dumping and countervail cases to determine if the industry in the importing country has been harmed by the unfair trade practices of foreign firms or governments. In other words, it is not sufficient simply to find evidence of dumping or unacceptable subsidization to impose an anti-dumping duty or countervailing duty, it is also necessary to show that the domestic industry has been harmed.

Intra-firm: a transfer of goods or services between different divisions (which may be in different countries) of the same firm.

Just in time: a strategy for minimizing inventories which concentrates on well organized ordering and supply systems to reduce the probability of disruptions to input supplies and, hence, the need to hold inventories.

Liquidity crisis: a situation where there are insufficient funds available to meet current debt service obligations.

Managed trade: where governments intervene in international trade as opposed to free trade where trade flows should arise as a result of the interplay of market forces.

Maquiladora: a Spanish word used to denote those firms which process (assemble and/or transform in some way) components imported into Mexico which are then re-exported.

Mercantilism: a set of ideas and policies first developed/implemented in the seventeenth century. The underlying premise was that national wealth (and, hence, military power and prestige) were dependent upon a positive balance of trade (exports greater than imports). The positive balance of trade would allow reserves of gold to be accumulated. To ensure a positive balance of trade, mercantilists advocated restrictions on imports and the promotion of exports. This early theory of political economy was criticized by classical economists.

Military-industrial complex: military officers and weapons manufacturers in the US, the USSR and many other countries in both the capitalist and socialist world during the Cold War. They were accused of being sufficiently powerful to influence the domestic political agenda in ways which increased the allocation of resources to defense.

Monetary targeting: when the size of the money supply becomes the key policy objective of monetary policy.

Net investment: new investment less depreciation of existing capital.

Non-border measures: economic policies aimed at assisting the ability of firms to compete with imports which do not involve taxes or restrictions on goods when they enter a country's customs territory. Examples include subsidies, tax holidays and preferred access to government contracts or public facilities such as transportation.

Nondiscrimination: a basic WTO principle whereby all other WTO members are to be treated equally in a member country's trade policy.

Nondurable consumer goods: goods which are consumed over a short time such as coffee, pork chops and matches.

Offshore sourcing: the purchase of inputs from outside the country of manufacture.

Openness in trade relations: exports plus imports divided by GDP.

Overvalued currency: when an economy's exchange rate is set at a rate where a country's currency can be exchanged for more foreign currency than the underlying economic forces can sustain.

Pegged exchange rate: when the exchange rate of a national currency is set at a fixed (pegged) level relative to other currencies.

Perestroika: a Russian word denoting economic restructuring which is primarily associated with the economic reformes introduced by the Gorbachev regime in the last years of the Soviet Union.

Prebisch-ECLA thesis: named for its proposer–Argentine economist Raùl Prebisch–and those that developed and refined it at the

United Nations Economic Commision for Latin America (ECLA) which Prebisch headed. The central argument of the theses is that the traditional international division of labor–based on trade between developed industrial center countries and underdeveloped, raw material-producing periphery countries–tends to result in an unequal exchange.

Primary export model: a model of economic development based on developing countries exploiting their natural resources and trading them for manufactures from developed countries.

Product life cycle: this theory maintains that certain countries (with advanced research and development capabilities) tend to specialize in the development of new products while others specialize in the production of older or mature products. Thus each product moves through a life cycle from new to old while the location of production also changes.

Protectionism: a deliberate policy on the part of governments to protect domestic industries from foreign competition through the imposition of trade barriers.

Purchasing power parity exchange rate: an artificially produced exchange rate that converts one currency into another at a constant level of purchasing power. Thus, this technique converts currencies at a rate that keeps their purchasing power constant. This allows a comparison of economic performance in two countries free from the influence of short run currency fluctuations.

Real GDP: the current value of gross domestic product corrected for changes in the price level. It simplifies the comparison of economic performance over time.

Reciprocity: a trade liberalization process whereby countries agree on granting market access on equal terms.

Rediscount rate: the US benchmark interest rate established by the Federal Reserve system.

Section 301 retaliation: tariffs or other trade restriction imposed by the US government under section 301 of its domestic trade legislation for unfair trade practices of foreign firms or governments which are not covered under anti-dumping, countervail or escape clause administrative procedures.

Senile industry: an industry which has lost its ability to compete internationally. This argument is often used to justify protection from imports to allow the industry time to regain its competitiveness.

Stagflation: a situation of depressed levels of real output (and high unemployment) combined with inflation.

Stagnation: a situation where an economy fails to grow.

Staples theory: a theory of economic development first applied to Canada whereby in a small open economy external demand for natural resource products (staples) drives economic growth. The precise way in which growth occurs depends on the economic linkages associated with a particular staple product. Linkages may be backwards, drawing inputs into the economy, or forwards, involving the further processing of the staple.

Strategic goods and services: industries which are considered vital to a country's independent existence.

Structural funds: government expenditures targeted at eliminating specific barriers to growth or development.

Supply side economics: a branch of economic analysis which is concerned with the productive capability of an economy and with policies designed to improve the flexibility of factor markets and thus ensure the highest possible output given the level of aggregate demand. It contrasts with Keynesian economics which concentrates on the management of demand.

Tariff: a tax imposed on goods entering the customs territory of a country.

Tariff-rate quota: certain quantities of imports where a specific rate of tariff applies, other quantities of imports will have different tariff rates.

Tariffication: a core principle of GATT whereby all non-tariff barriers to trade are to be converted into tariffs giving an equivalent degree of protection.

Terms of trade: a price index constructed by dividing an index of a country's export price divided by an index of its import prices. An improvement in a country's terms of trade arises if its export prices rise faster than its import prices.

Total quality management: a managerial strategy aimed at improving a firm's overall performance through a focus on quality at all levels combined with improvement targets and extensive ongoing monitoring.

Trade creation: an increase in international trade and economic welfare that results from the reduction or elimination of trade barriers.

Trade diversion: a redirection of international trade as a result of the formation of a regional trade association. The removal of barriers among members leads to increased trade among members, part of which comes at the expense of non-members who no longer have equal access to the markets of the regional trade association's members.

Trade in services: international transactions involving services (as opposed to goods). Trade in services is regulated by the WTO's General Agreement on Trade in Services (GATS).

Trade related investment measures (TRIMs): an agreement negotiated at the Uruguay round to regulate aspects of international investment. The adoption of TRIMs commitments is left to individual countries.

Trade surplus: when the value of exports exceed the value of imports over a given period.

Transparency: a basic principle of GATT whereby the members agree that all trade arrangements with other countries will be disclosed to member countries–that is, that there are no secret trade deals.

Undervalued currency: an exchange value of a currency which is fixed at a level whereby less of the currency can be exchanged for foreign currencies than the underlying economic forces can sustain. Countries may undervalue their currency to encourage exports and discourage imports.

Variable levy: a tax on goods entering a customs territory of a country which is not fixed (bound) like a tariff. Variable levies can be adjusted at the discretion of the importer. Under current WTO/GATT rules they are no longer allowed and existing levies must be converted to tariffs.

Welfare state: a country that provides comprehensive social benefits such as government-sponsored pensions, unemployment and sickness payments and health care.

Xenophobia: a deep antipathy to foreigners.

Index